Goethe's Cyclical Narratives

UNC | COLLEGE OF ARTS AND SCIENCES
Germanic and Slavic Languages and Literatures

From 1949 to 2004, UNC Press and the UNC Department of Germanic & Slavic Languages and Literatures published the UNC Studies in the Germanic Languages and Literatures series. Monographs, anthologies, and critical editions in the series covered an array of topics including medieval and modern literature, theater, linguistics, philology, onomastics, and the history of ideas. Through the generous support of the National Endowment for the Humanities and the Andrew W. Mellon Foundation, books in the series have been reissued in new paperback and open access digital editions. For a complete list of books visit www.uncpress.org.

Goethe's Cyclical Narratives
Die Unterhaltungen deutscher Ausgewanderten and
Wilhelm Meisters Wanderjahre

JANE K. BROWN

WITH A NEW FOREWORD BY THE AUTHOR

UNC Studies in the Germanic Languages and Literatures
Number 82

Copyright © 1975
New foreword copyright © 2020

This work is licensed under a Creative Commons CC BY-NC-ND license. To view a copy of the license, visit http://creativecommons.org/licenses.

Suggested citation: Brown, Jane K. *Goethe's Cyclical Narratives: Die Unterhaltungen deutscher Ausgewanderten and Wilhelm Meisters Wanderjahre*. Chapel Hill: University of North Carolina Press, 1975. DOI: https://doi.org/10.5149/9781469657189_Brown

Library of Congress Cataloging-in-Publication Data
Names: Brown, Jane K.
Title: Goethe's cyclical narratives : Die Unterhaltungen deutscher Ausgewanderten and Wilhelm Meisters Wanderjahre / by Jane K. Brown.
Other titles: University of North Carolina Studies in the Germanic Languages and Literatures ; no. 82.
Description: Chapel Hill : University of North Carolina Press, [1975] Series: University of North Carolina Studies in the Germanic Languages and Literatures. | Includes bibliographical references.
Identifiers: LCCN 74-26932 | ISBN 978-1-4696-5717-2 (pbk: alk. paper) | ISBN 978-1-4696-5718-9 (ebook)
Subjects: Goethe, Johann Wolfgang von, 1749-1832 — Unterhaltungen deutscher Ausgewanderten. | Goethe, Johann Wolfgang von, 1749-1832 — Wilhelm Meisters Wanderjahre.
Classification: LCC PT1971 .U6B7 1975 | DCC 833/ .6

ACKNOWLEDGMENTS

I would like to express my gratitude to Cyrus Hamlin, who supervised the preparation of this study as a dissertation for the Yale Graduate School. His careful reading of my work has been constantly stimulating. I would also like to thank Stuart Atkins, who first directed me to the sources of the *Wanderjahre*, Franz Mautner for his helpful criticisms of the manuscript, and Barbara Eger for her attentive editorial assistance. The Nationale Forschungs- und Gedenkstätten der klassischen deutschen Literatur in Weimar kindly made available the French source for "Die pilgernde Törin." I am grateful to Mount Holyoke College for a generous grant towards the publication of this book. And finally I would like to thank my husband, who listened to, read and criticized all of this material many times over.

CONTENTS

ACKNOWLEDGMENTS	v
FOREWORD	ix
INTRODUCTION	1

I. *UNTERHALTUNGEN DEUTSCHER AUSGEWANDERTEN*
  1. Backgrounds — 5
  2. The Frame — 9
  3. The First Evening — 13
  4. The "Prokurator" and "Ferdinand" — 16
  5. The "Märchen" — 20

II. *WILHELM MEISTERS WANDERJAHRE* I: PERSPECTIVE, PERCEPTION AND RENUNCIATION
  1. "St. Joseph der Zweite" — 33
  2. "Wer ist der Verräter?" — 44
  3. "Die pilgernde Törin" — 53
  4. "Der Mann von funfzig Jahren" — 59
  5. Makarie and the Imagery of Mediation — 69
  6. Aphorisms — 75

III. *WILHELM MEISTERS WANDERJAHRE* II: PARODY
  1. The *Unterhaltungen* and the *Lehrjahre* in the *Wanderjahre* — 79
  2. Basedow and Campe: The Pedagogic Province — 87
  3. Prior and Percy: "Das nußbraune Mädchen" — 97
  4. Kotzebue: "Der Mann von funfzig Jahren" and "Die gefährliche Wette" — 101
  5. Musäus: Book III, Chapter 1; "Die neue Melusine"; "Die gefährliche Wette" — 106
  6. Sterne and Goldsmith: Book II, Chapter 11 — 115
  7. The *Wanderjahre* and the Eighteenth Century — 124

EPILOGUE	130
SELECT BIBLIOGRAPHY	135

FOREWORD

This book is an edited version of my doctoral dissertation of 1971. It was to be a contribution to the rising interest in the late Goethe and in Goethe the scientist entitled "Goethe's Science in *Wilhelm Meisters Wanderjahre*." The approach eschewed specific ideologies and methodologies; it was simply to be a close reading with strong interest in the organization of long, difficult texts and strong faith in the unity of such texts, at least if they were by Goethe.

As is the case with many dissertations, especially with such a vaguely defined prospectus, the topic grew and developed. It remained centered on arguing for the unity of the text, in formal terms in chapter one, in thematic terms in chapter two, and in stylistic terms in chapter three. Because the first novellas for the *Wanderjahre* originated as a planned continuation of Goethe's *Unterhaltungen deutscher Ausgewanderten*, it became clear that the form of the novel could be best understood as originating in the tradition of novella cycles. Reading against a comparison text became my most essential reading strategy as I realized that Goethe not only drew constantly on previously existing texts but, in fact, was also always engaged in conversation with them in a way that enriched our understanding not only of Goethe's text but also of his and our place in a larger tradition. Thus, the argument presented not only a large-scale formal reading of cyclical texts but also a historical reading of the texts against their places in the Europe of Goethe's day—the French Revolution, the advent of industrialization—and against their places in the larger history of European literature and art. This, I take it, is what Goethe in *West-östlicher Divan* meant with "Wer nicht von dreitausend Jahren / Sich weiß Rechenschaft zu geben, / Bleib' im Dunkeln unerfahren, / Mag von Tag zu Tage leben" (WA I, 6, 110).

Science fell out of the title, but that was a mistake. While I did not examine discussions of science in the *Wanderjahre* in any detail, chapter two develops a general understanding of Goethe's epistemology on the basis of the formal analysis of the importance of perspective. Stated briefly: truth is ineffable and can only be approached by observing the phenomenon repeatedly from many different perspectives. I now regret that I did not conclude chapter two with a discussion of Jarno's insistence on one-sidedness in relation to Goethe's methodological essays of the 1790s, such as "Der Versuch als Vermittler zwischen Subjekt und Objekt," and the *Farbenlehre*. Jarno's insistence on specialization is not wrong, but, in contrast to the world of the *Lehrjahre*, it requires a modern scientific community that develops understanding by assembling the contributions of individuals in communication with one another, that is, the communal ideology of modern science.

The most important development of my understanding appeared in the two terms "irony" and "parody." Ehrhard Bahr was very kind to me when I was using the UCLA library in the summer of 1969 and supportive of my interest in irony. When his trailblazing *Die Ironie im Spätwerk Goethes: ". . . diese sehr ernsten Scherze . . ." Studien zum West-östlichen Divan, zu den Wanderjahren und zu Faust II* appeared in 1972, the year after I submitted the dissertation, I understood why. My work was less mature than his and gave the inaccurate impression that I was talking more about humor than about complexity of vision, despite several passing assertions that I did not deny Goethe's seriousness. I have always chuckled as I read Goethe and am glad that this more relaxed approach to reading him has become widespread. I intended the term parody, like irony, to refer to the same range from comic to deeply respectful homage. At this distance I regret not having laid sufficient emphasis on the serious aspects of the Pedagogic Province, particularly the doctrine of reverence and the Heiligtum des Schmerzes, and on my assertions that parody, narratorial ambiguity, and narratorial ambivalence are the stylistic equivalent of renunciation and the multiperspectivism essential to Goethe's epistemology. Irony, and especially parody, enrich vision rather than undercutting it.

The passage I would most like to rewrite in this book, however, is the acknowledgments, which strike me now as perfunctory rather than just terse. Ted Bahr not only encouraged me but made a special effort to share the books on the *Wanderjahre* that he was using for his important book with a graduate student from across the country who happened to be at his university for the summer. I did not properly acknowledge Christoph Schweizer for his cordial support of the manuscript or the helpful interlibrary loan staff at Yale's Sterling Library for procuring the source for "Die pilgernde Törin" from Weimar, a daunting task in 1969. Above all I did not properly acknowledge, and still probably cannot, the critical support and mentoring I received from both Cyrus Hamlin and from my husband Marshall Brown. The value of reading within generic and topical traditions was the essence of what I had learned from Cyrus. Furthermore, he believed in the quality of my work even before I did, helped me through innumerable difficulties of my own making, and set me an unreachable model of patience and listening. Marshall not only put up with me, as if that would not have been enough, but read and edited drafts tirelessly, and deserves all the credit for whatever merit the writing in this book has. At the time I was too timid about publishing even to ask the kind people at UNC Press to include a dedication, so my last addition to this foreword: This book was always for Marshall.

Jane Brown, January 2020

INTRODUCTION

This study began as an attempt to understand the seemingly chaotic nature of *Wilhelm Meisters Wanderjahre*. It was called "Roman" in the first version of 1821, but the label was dropped from the considerably expanded final version of 1829. At first, then, the tension between novel and cycle of novellas appeared to determine the problem. However, it rapidly became clear that a definition of the form was needed less than an understanding of the implications of the form. These implications are very broad indeed. On the one hand, they lead to important conclusions about how to read Goethe's cyclical works. On the other hand they ultimately force us to consider as well Goethe's relationship to his times and the literary tradition in which he worked.

I started from the assumption that the *Wanderjahre* may be read as a cycle of novellas: the interpretation was to begin by discussing relationships among the novellas or between the novellas and the frame, rather than by considering the linear development of Wilhelm's "education." This assumption seems to be at least historically accurate, since there is good evidence that the novellas which eventually were written for the *Wanderjahre* were originally intended for a continuation of the *Unterhaltungen deutscher Ausgewanderten*. Goethe is frequently assumed to have abandoned the *Unterhaltungen* after six installments because of its poor reception.[1] However, on 26 December 1795 he mentions a probable continuation in a letter to Schiller, and again on 3 February 1798 he writes: "Übrigens habe ich etwa ein halb Dutzend Märchen und Geschichten im Sinne, die ich, als den zweiten Teil der Unterhaltungen meiner Ausgewanderten bearbeiten werde."[2] Interspersed are the first references to the stories which eventually became the *Wanderjahre*. On 4 February 1797 he writes to Schiller about two fairy-tales he will, he hopes, soon write down: one is clearly "Die neue Melusine," which later found its place in the *Wanderjahre*. By May 1799 he had begun to think about "Sankt Joseph der Zweite," later the first novella of the *Wanderjahre*, as a letter to J. H. Meyer of 10 May shows. The intention to continue the *Unterhaltungen* passes imperceptibly into the intention to continue the *Lehrjahre*, but the material to be treated remains the same group of stories. Less than a month

---

[1] See, for example, K. Mommsen, *Goethe und 1001 Nacht* (Berlin, 1960), p. 61.

[2] Goethe, *Briefwechsel mit Friedrich Schiller*, Gedenk-Ausgabe, ed. Karl Schmid (Zurich and Stuttgart, 1964), p. 516. Further references to the correspondence are to this edition, which is abbreviated GSB. The following abbreviations are used to refer to the various editions of Goethe's works: HA—Hamburger Ausgabe; JA—Jubiläums-Ausgabe; PA—Propyläen-Ausgabe; WA—Weimarer Ausgabe.

before Goethe began to dictate the first novellas for the *Wanderjahre* in May 1807, he reread the *Unterhaltungen* in preparing the collected edition of his works.[3]

I begin, therefore, with the *Unterhaltungen*, to establish both the characteristics and the significance of the cycle for Goethe. This detour is all the more desirable because the *Unterhaltungen* has until recently been inexcusably ignored. The readers of the *Horen* did not like it, nor have Goethe's more recent readers been especially enthusiastic. Its final story, the "Märchen," has received considerable attention, while only scattered critics have treated the cycle. But both the cycle and the "Märchen" gain in significance when read together as they were intended.[4]

Three different points of considerable importance for reading the *Wanderjahre* may be distinguished in the *Unterhaltungen*. The first of these is the recognition that the *Unterhaltungen* is a very serious response to the social threat of the French Revolution. The talk about the revolution at the beginning of the cycle is not simply a device to motivate a retreat into story-telling; on the contrary, the real subject matter of the cycle is the problem of establishing and maintaining a harmonious society, and the role the poet can play in that process. Social problems, not literary problems, are the basis of the work. This tendency is shared with the *Wanderjahre*, which, even more than the *Lehrjahre*, deals at length with broad historical problems. In the *Wanderjahre* the issue is not just the revolution, but the very possibility of society in post-revolutionary Europe.[5]

The second important point is the complex relationship between the novellas and the frame. The discussion of the novellas in the frame of the *Unterhaltungen* is by no means straightforward; more often than not, it is deliberately contradictory in an effort to force the reader to think for himself. In particular the commentary on the "Märchen," and that story's relationship to the frame, are playful and subtle. It turns out, then, that Goethe's cycles have their own unity, and their parts cannot be understood separately. This interdependence is even more highly developed in the *Wanderjahre*, where the reader must not only draw comparisons

---

[3] 20 and 21 April. H. G. Gräf, *Goethe über seine Dichtungen*, I (Frankfurt am Main, 1901), 352 f.

[4] Two good essays on the *Unterhaltungen* have appeared since this material was written in 1969. The first is J. Müller, "Zur Entstehung der deutschen Novelle: Die Rahmenhandlung in Goethes *Unterhaltungen deutscher Ausgewanderten* und die Thematik der französischen Revolution," *Gestaltungsgeschichte und Gesellschaftsgeschichte: Literatur-, Kunst- und Musikwissenschaftliche Studien: Fritz Martini zum 60. Geburtstag*, ed. H. Kreuzer and K. Hamburger (Stuttgart, 1969), pp. 152–75, which examines the social background and significance of the cycle. The second, H. Popper, "Goethe's *Unterhaltungen deutscher Ausgewanderten*," *Affinities: Essays in German and English Literature*, ed. R. W. Last (London, 1971), pp. 206–42, interprets the *Unterhaltungen* and the "Märchen" as a unity, as an example of Goethe's dynamic morphology.

[5] Anne-Liese Klingenberg, in *Goethes Roman "Wilhelm Meisters Wanderjahre oder die Entsagenden": Quellen und Kompositionen* (Berlin, 1972), documents the historical background for the sections of the novel that deal with Wilhelm. Since she confines herself to only a part of the novel and treats it as a historical document rather than as a sophisticated literary work, she comes to radically different conclusions from mine about the social statement of the *Wanderjahre*.

among the novellas and between novellas and the frame, but where the narrator himself continually shifts his attitudes toward his stories and characters. The line between fiction (novellas) and reality (frame) is still fairly clear in the *Unterhaltungen*, but in the *Wanderjahre* apparently fictional characters suddenly appear in the frame—characters from the novellas themselves, as well as characters from other literary works. This continually shifting, but always ironic, interrelationship of the parts of the novel, which I will discuss in the second chapter, represents Goethe's ultimate development of the techniques first employed in the *Unterhaltungen*. Indeed, the technique does not remain a question of form, but, through repeated images and discussions, becomes an important theme of the novel— the nature of perception, and its corollary problem of the possibility of didactic poetry.

The relationship of the work to the European tradition is the last point. Here the progress from the *Unterhaltungen* to the *Wanderjahre* is even more pronounced. Goethe self-consciously plays at certain points with the relationship of the *Unterhaltungen* to Boccaccio's *Decameron*. This expresses itself obliquely through a kind of friendly parody. The *Wanderjahre* presents extraordinarily complex and varied examples of similar parody. Scholarship on the novel has already recognized allusions not only to the *Lehrjahre*, but also to works by Musäus, Kotzebue, Prior and Sterne; I will in addition consider sources from the works of Basedow, Campe, Goldsmith and the painter Jakob Ruysdael. Furthermore, it is necessary to clarify the relationship of the *Wanderjahre* to the *Unterhaltungen* as it is expressed in the novel. The parodistic nature of these allusions establishes Goethe's relationship to these various authors and to his own earlier work. This topic has not been considered at all by critics of the novel, yet it is not only fascinating in itself, but also crucial for understanding the overall conduct of the novel. It leads in particular to an understanding of why the novel did not remain a cycle of stories.

A word on the use of the terms "irony" and "parody" here might be helpful. It became clear to me quite early in this study that even more frequently than in his other works Goethe says things or has characters say things in his cycles that he himself does not believe and does not want the reader to think. Thus the reader faces constant discrepancies between disparate points of view, either between characters, between a character and the narrator, or between positions the narrator takes at different times. I use "irony" as a convenient label for these discrepancies, which more often than not also involve humor.

"Parody" appears here in an equally general sense, corresponding to Goethe's own use of the term in the essay "Über die Parodie bei den Alten." There Goethe talks about the relationship between a Greek tragedy and the satyr-play that followed it as a "parallelism in contrast" (JA XXXVII, 292): both are equally sublime treatments of high and low subjects respectively; the satyr-play is not to be considered a travesty. The juxtaposition of the two, he suggests, is remarkable and stimulating, not destructive. Such a juxtaposition of parallel yet contrasting materials is basic for the *Wanderjahre*, which presents many contrasting perspectives on a small group of themes. I do not use "parody" in quite this general a sense, but I do use it to refer to imitation of, or even broad reference to another work or set of ideas. These imitations rarely make fun of their model, and only occasionally criticize it; the references are, however, often playful and made with considerable ironic distance. Their most important aspect is just what Goethe describes in the essay on the Greeks—it is to juxtapose parallel yet contrasting materials. Thus the "parodies" in the *Wanderjahre* do not destroy their objects; instead they draw the works they imitate into the circle of the novel.[6]

Unlike many of Goethe's long recognized imitations—in *Faust II*, the *Divan* and *Hermann und Dorothea*, for example—the *Wanderjahre* uses material from almost contemporary popular figures rather than from undisputed geniuses. More than the other works, the *Wanderjahre* deals with a particular historical period. The parodies thus are important for an understanding of the treatment of social problems in the novel. Most important of all, since Goethe uses works of his own, especially the *Lehrjahre*, as well as works of his contemporaries, this whole aspect of the *Wanderjahre* reflects Goethe's evaluation of himself in relation to his age.

While it has not been unusual to read the *Wanderjahre* as a cycle of novellas, earlier studies have not read it in conjunction with the *Unterhaltungen*. The relatively scanty *Wanderjahre* scholarship has devoted itself almost exclusively to the content of the novel, in particular to the concept of renunciation. Since Max Wundt discusses the *Wanderjahre* together with the *Lehrjahre* and the *Theatralische Sendung* in his classic and thorough study, *Goethes Wilhelm Meister und die Entwicklung des modernen Lebensideals* (1913), I devote little space to the *Lehrjahre*, except as an object of parody. Although my approach is entirely different, I reach conclusions similar to Wundt's concerning the social statement of the *Wanderjahre*. The novelty of this study lies in a different area: in presenting techniques which make it possible to appreciate the interplay of the contradictory tendencies and elusive parody in Goethe's work.

---

[6] A contemporary parody of the *Lehrjahre*, Pustkuchen's *Wilhelm Meisters Wanderjahre* (Quedlinburg and Leipzig, 1821–1828) offers an instructive contrast to the use of parody here. Pustkuchen uses all of Goethe's techniques, but much more tendentiously. He aims solely at displaying Goethe's aesthetic and moral turpitude. Goethe's parody in this novel, on the other hand, is not polemical. Value judgments are made subtly and gently, if at all, and never in personal terms.

I
UNTERHALTUNGEN DEUTSCHER AUSGEWANDERTEN

1. BACKGROUNDS

Zu einer Zeit, wo das nahe Geräusch des Kriegs das Vaterland ängstiget, wo der Kampf politischer Meinungen und Interessen diesen Krieg beinahe in jedem Zirkel erneuert, und nur allzuoft Musen und Grazien daraus verscheucht, wo weder in den Gesprächen noch in den Schriften des Tages vor diesem allverfolgenden Dämon der Staatskritik Rettung ist, möchte es eben so gewagt als verdienstlich sein, den so sehr zerstreuten Leser zu einer Unterhaltung von ganz entgegengesetzter Art einzuladen. In der Tat scheinen die Zeitumstände einer Schrift wenig Glück zu versprechen, die sich über das Lieblingsthema des Tages ein strenges Stillschweigen auferlegen, und ihren Ruhm darin suchen wird, durch etwas anders zu gefallen, als wodurch jetzt alles gefällt. Aber je mehr das beschränkte Interesse der Gegenwart die Gemüter in Spannung setzt, einengt und unterjocht, desto dringender wird das Bedürfnis, durch ein allgemeines und höheres Interesse an dem, was reinmenschlich und über allen Einfluß der Zeiten erhaben ist, sie wieder in Freiheit zu setzen, und die politisch geteilte Welt unter der Fahne der Wahrheit und Schönheit wieder zu vereinigen.... Sowohl spielend als ernsthaft wird man im Fortgange dieser Schrift dieses einzige Ziel verfolgen ... wahre Humanität zu befördern.[1]

This is Schiller's announcement of the *Horen* in December 1794. The first section of the *Unterhaltungen deutscher Ausgewanderten*[2] appeared on pages 49–78 of the same number; in this section a group of exiles decides to ban discussion of politics in favor of more polite conversation in their circle. Goethe sent Schiller the manuscript for the opening of this cycle of novellas, as it is generally labeled, on 27 November 1794. In a letter of 29 November Schiller thanked Goethe for the manuscript and mentioned something of his intentions for the "Ankündigung" to the *Horen*—"Ich [werde] mich in meiner Annonce an das Publikum auf unsere Keuschheit in politischen Urteilen berufen." Schiller seems to have expected the manuscript at the end of the month, although there is no previous written mention of it. Apparently they had discussed Goethe's plans for the cycle, as well as Schiller's plans for the *Horen*, when they met in November. It is no surprise, then,

---

[1] Friedrich Schiller, "Ankündigung," *Die Horen*, 1 (1795), iii f. (spelling modernized). The "Ankündigung" appeared separately in the *Allgemeine Literatur-Zeitung* on 10 December 1794.

[2] *Hamburger Ausgabe* VI, 125–46, line 11. Further references to the *Unterhaltungen* in this chapter will be to page numbers of this volume in parentheses in the text.

5

that Schiller's "Ankündigung" and the opening of Goethe's *Unterhaltungen* should be so remarkably similar in theme.

The relationship of the Schiller passage to the *Unterhaltungen* shows that Schiller probably understood Goethe's work to be written in the spirit of his periodical, and that he therefore considered the cycle to have a serious cultural—indeed, educative—purpose. The section in the first number includes not only the decision to tell stories for entertainment, but also the discussion about what kinds of stories should be told. The Abbé says he plans to tell stories, "die uns die menschliche Natur und ihre inneren Verborgenheiten auf einen Augenblick eröffnen" (143). This is comparable to Schiller's "was rein menschlich... ist." In letters written before and during the composition of the *Unterhaltungen*, Goethe frequently expressed the same need as his characters to substitute what he considers to be meaningful occupations for constant concern with politics. For example, on 17 July 1794 he wrote to J. H. Meyer:

> Übrigens ist jetzt mit den Menschen, besonders gewissen Freunden, sehr übel leben. Der Coadjutor erzählte: daß die auf dem Petersberge verwahrten Clubbisten unerträglich grob werden sobald es den Franzoßen wohl geht und ich muß gestehen daß einige Freunde sich jetzt auf eine Art betragen die nah an den Wahnsinn gränzt. Dancken Sie Gott daß Sie dem Raphael und andern guten Geistern, welche Gott den Herrn aus reiner Brust loben, gegenüber sitzen und das Spucken des garstigen Gespenstes, das man Genius der Zeit nennt, wie ich wenigstens hoffe, nicht vernehmen. (WA IV, X, 174)

And on 22 May 1795 he wrote to Carl Friedrich von Möser:

> Welche Freude würde ich in früherer ruhiger Zeit bey dem Empfang von Ew. Excellenz Briefe empfunden haben, da man zwar nicht im Überfluß, doch bequem lebte und im Stande war zur Zufriedenheit würdiger deutscher Männer manchmal dasjenige im Kleinen zu thun, was sie von der Nation im Großen hätten erwarten können. Leider traf mich Ew. Excellenz vertrauliches Schreiben in der ganz entgegengesetzten Lage, die drohende allgemeine Noth führte jeden auf einen unnatürlichen Egoismus und die Feder versagte mir mehr als einmal den Dienst, wenn ich antworten und mein Unvermögen bekennen wollte. (WA IV, X, 262 f.)

Thus the *Unterhaltungen* are clearly intended as a serious response to the social disruption caused by the French Revolution, much as the "Ästhetische Briefe" were Schiller's response.[3]

---

[3] Cf. "Ich habe über den politischen Jammer noch nie eine Feder angesetzt, und was ich in [den Ästhetischen Briefen] davon sagte, geschah bloß, um in alle Ewigkeit nichts mehr davon zu sagen; *aber ich glaube, daß das Bekenntnis, das ich darin ablege, nicht ganz überflüssig ist.*" Schiller to Goethe, 20 October 1794. GSB, 33. Emphasis mine.

The *Unterhaltungen* are commonly interpreted today as a series of light romance novellas organized in imitation of Boccaccio. Erich Trunz's commentary on the *Unterhaltungen*, for example, suggests,

> sie geben sich nur als gute Unterhaltungsliteratur . . . [Goethe] verschmäht es keineswegs, einmal Unterhaltungsschriftsteller zu sein—und wer der Meinung ist, ein "Klassiker" dürfe nur der "Bildung" und nie der "Unterhaltung" dienen, erkennt nicht die konkrete Situation, aus der heraus Goethe schrieb, und die Freude am Handwerklichen, die jeden Künstler beseelt. (599)

Such a viewpoint, it seems to me, misunderstands "Unterhaltung" as mere "diversion"; "Unterhaltung" and "Bildung" are not necessarily mutually exclusive. On the contrary, they complement one another, in both the *Horen* and the *Unterhaltungen*.

This chapter will attempt to outline the response to the problem of the revolution in the cycle and at the same time to show what kinds of structures and techniques Goethe developed to make the cycle a suitable vehicle for his educative purposes. Particular attention will be paid to techniques that seem to have found further development and application in the *Wanderjahre*. I shall begin with a general discussion of the structure of the cycle in relation to the *Decameron*, which provided a model for all subsequently-written European novella cycles.

In a letter of 28 October 1794, Schiller reminded Goethe of his intention to adapt the "Prokurator" story from Boccaccio. The story is, of course, not from the *Decameron* at all, but from the *Cent nouvelles nouvelles*, a French collection of stories and anecdotes. It is not clear, however, that this slip was an innocent mistake, for he repeated it on 19 March 1795, when he finally received the story from Goethe. Rather it suggests that Goethe and Schiller had discussed the cycle as an imitation of Boccaccio, even though Goethe knew that the story which got him started came from a different collection. There are certainly very important similarities between the *Unterhaltungen* and the *Decameron* which make Boccaccio's influence undeniable.

The clearest similarity is of course the social background of the two works, since in both the characters flee as a group from social chaos. Boccaccio's description of the plague emphasizes the different behavior patterns evoked as responses to the plague, just as Goethe is concerned with behavior in the face of the revolution. The characters of the *Decameron* also ban discussions of their chaotic environment from their entertainments, and establish a bulwark of order within their group according to the advice of Pampinea, the oldest, most experienced member. The group is always to have a ruler chosen by the preceding ruler for the tenure of one day; there is a strictly observed routine of eating, sleeping, dancing and story-telling at fixed times; religious observances also receive due attention (Fridays and Saturdays are devoted solely to religious observance). The plague is not yet over when the group returns to Florence and disperses, but its members have participated in an affirmation of social order and can return to their disordered city with renewed strength. Thus even more programmatically than in Goethe story-telling is a civilizing device. It may be noted in passing that the great classical model for the cycle of stories, *The Golden Ass* of Lucius Apuleius, also presents stories against a background of social disorder—although the disorder springs rather from decadence than from a specific disruptive event—and that the hero of the frame becomes at the end a lawyer, an agent for social order. In Goethe's cycle the civilizing effect of the stories is only implicit in the improved behavior of the group and in the mythical coda of the "Märchen" (see below).

Goethe and Boccaccio also both use the frame to comment on the stories. There is little direct commentary in Boccaccio, certainly less than in Goethe, but there is considerable indirect commentary. For example, there is some correlation between the personalities of the individuals and the stories they tell. The stories tend to deal with extreme—and often socially disruptive—kinds of behavior, but the sober moderation that pervades the frame (except in the figure of Dioneo, whom the others reprimand) belies the gaiety of the stories, and thus indirectly comments upon them. I will show below that there is more direct ironic interplay between the stories in the *Unterhaltungen* and the figures in the frame. In this respect Goethe seems closer to Apuleius, who gives an ironic twist to the whole cycle by having the narrator and critic of society appear as an ass.

The *Unterhaltungen* is not, however, simply a short German imitation of the *Decameron*. The two display basic differences, and these differences reveal central aspects of Goethe's technique, which are only fully developed in the *Wanderjahre*. In the first place, the structure of the *Decameron* is rigid, almost static. The stories fall into a regular arrangement and certainly carry the weight of the work. While the frame has its significance, the stories are the real center of attention. Even in *The Golden Ass*, where the frame itself is a lively narrative, the stories stand in a symmetrical arrangement around the long central novella "Cupid and Psyche." But in the *Unterhaltungen* the center of attention has really moved to the frame. Although the stories, apart from the "Märchen," may seem to fall into pairs, they are not arranged symmetrically. The frame is not interspersed equally between stories, and the introductory section is longer than any of the stories except the "Märchen." The characters in the frame and their problems are developed at length, the story-telling is introduced as a civilizing device, most of the stories—all of the long ones—are told by the senior member of the group: thus the stories are subordinated as a pedagogical response to the problem posed by the frame.[4]

Another important difference between Goethe's cycle and Boccaccio's is

[4] Theodore Ziolkowski, in "Goethe's 'Unterhaltungen deutscher Ausgewanderten': A Reappraisal," *Monatshefte*, 50 (1958), 57–74, argues that the elaboration of the frame heightens the realistic effect of the work. But such realism was hardly a virtue for Goethe in the nineties, when in all spheres of his activities he was seeking to transform reality in accordance with an aesthetic ideal.

that the *Unterhaltungen* is open-ended. At the end of two weeks Boccaccio's characters disperse, but the problem of the frame is never resolved in Goethe. The characters seem on the way to more civilized social intercourse, but what they finally achieve is never shown, just as their return home (and thus to the level of harmony and stability presumably enjoyed before the cycle begins) is not shown. At the end, the "Märchen" takes over and the frame is dropped, precisely to give this open-ended effect. Goethe wrote to Schiller on 17 August 1795: "Ich würde die Unterhaltungen [mit dem Märchen] schließen, und es würde vielleicht nicht übel sein, wenn sie durch ein Produkt der Einbildungskraft gleichsam ins Unendliche ausliefen" (GSB, 96). This movement into the mythical realm is strongly reminiscent of the end of the *Golden Ass* with its many epiphanies, although in the latter, the frame itself makes this movement. Since Goethe was prepared to end the cycle without returning to the frame, he must have considered the frame and the stories, especially the "Märchen," to have a closer relationship to one another than is generally assumed.[5] Thus the open-endedness of the cycle would suggest a more organic relationship between the frame and the stories than in the *Decameron*.

In summary, the *Unterhaltungen* must be considered a serious work, which, although based to a large extent on Boccaccio, differs from that model in its more fluid structure and more integral relationship between the stories and the frame. Having established these points on a general level, I would now like to show in in detail how the cycle presents and develops its central concern.[6]

2. THE FRAME

Like Boccaccio, Goethe begins with a society in chaos; he focuses on an aristocratic family fleeing the revolution. But unlike Boccaccio's group, these exiles cannot separate themselves from the chaotic conditions around them, for even within their group the ordinary rules which maintain social order— "gemeine Höflichkeit" as the baroness later calls them (137)—eventually break down. In fact, the little group is a microcosm of the society around it. The whole spectrum of political opinion is represented, from Karl, the radical aristocrat

---

[5] The "Märchen" is frequently assumed to have no relationship at all to the rest of the cycle, even for example, by such an otherwise subtle critic of the cycle as Gerhard Fricke, who explicitly excludes it from his discussion of the work in "Zu Sinn und Form von Goethes 'Unterhaltungen deutscher Ausgewanderten,' " *Formenwandel: Festschrift zum 65. Geburtstag von Paul Böckmann*, ed. W. Müller-Seidel (Hamburg, 1964), pp. 273–93. By contrast, however, see Hans Popper's excellent study, "Goethe's *Unterhaltungen*," cited in the introduction.

[6] See also Ilse Jürgens' fine discussion of this in "Die Stufen der sittlichen Entwicklung in Goethes 'Unterhaltungen deutscher Ausgewanderten.' " *Wirkendes Wort*, 6 (1955–1956), 336–40: I think, however, that the social, rather than the individual, moral element must be more strongly emphasized and that a more detailed discussion of literary techniques must be applied to that purpose.

passionately and mindlessly devoted to the democratic position, through the Hofmeister, who agrees with Karl in silence, and the Abbé, who disagrees with Karl in silence, to the Geheimrat von S., who is as passionate and rigid as Karl (though with better reason, as the narrator hastens to explain, p. 130) in defending the opposite point of view. A variety of reactions to social upheaval are also represented, from Luise, who cannot think of anything but her fiancé, all the way to the Abbé, who patiently ignores the rudeness of his companions in his attempts to help them to cope better with their difficulties.

This microcosmic society re-enacts the crises and problems of its times, it is "society in a test tube," to borrow an image from the *Wahlverwandtschaften*. The representatives of the two extreme points of view clash and the Geheimrat von S. leaves in a rage. The group has been unable to maintain the virtues of "Unparteilichkeit" and "Verträglichkeit" (128), whose absence in the world at large they themselves regret. Indeed, the baroness treats this catastrophe as an event of the same order as the revolution itself: "[meine Freundin] die schon so lange auf einer ängstlichen *Flucht* herumgetrieben wird . . . , muß schon wieder *flüchtig* werden" (135, emphasis mine); "Müssen denn eure Gemüter nur so blind und unaufhaltsam wirken und dreinschlagen wie die Weltbegebenheiten, ein Gewitter oder ein ander Naturphänomen?" (135). Thus, like society at large, they are faced with the problem of restoring social harmony on some sort of stable basis. The development of harmony in the group proceeds in well defined steps from the initial disruption.

As the first step the baroness defines the bases of social harmony as self-control and the ability to renounce. She maintains that these two virtues are very scarce indeed in the world of men: "wenn ich doch nur einen einzigen [Mann] in meinem Leben gesehen hätte, der auch nur in der geringsten Sache sich zu beherrschen imstande gewesen wäre! . . . Ich wüßte auch nicht einen, der auch nur der geringsten Entsagung fähig wäre" (136). The disaster came about in the first place because neither Karl nor the Geheimrat von S. was willing either to control himself or to compromise his viewpoint. It would be well to note, incidentally, that the narrator condones the viewpoint of neither. The baroness does not try to justify these principles on any philosophical or ethical basis. She says rather: "Ich fordere euch also nicht im Namen der Tugend, sondern im Namen der gemeinsten Höflichkeit auf, mir und andern in diesen Augenblicken das zu leisten, was ihr von Jugend auf, ich darf fast sagen, gegen einen jeden beobachtet habt, der euch auf der Straße begegnete" (137). No ideal, but simply common courtesy dictates self-control. Thus the baroness establishes her request on a purely pragmatic basis, for common courtesy is just another expression for the simplest rules that enable people to live together peaceably.

The practical manifestation or application of these two "virtues" or principles is the ban on political discussions when the whole company is assembled. This ban is not simply an escape: the language in which it is discussed shows its real social, indeed "political," significance. When the baroness says, "es soll mir keiner von euch ein Vertrauen ablocken, aber fordern will ich künftig von euch, befehlen will ich in meinem Hause!" and Karl answers, "Sie sollen sich über unsern Ungehorsam nicht zu beschweren haben" (136 f.), a well defined hierarchical relationship is insisted upon by both sides. Once this pattern of organization is established, the baroness can mitigate her tone, as she does in the following paragraph, but the political overtones of "Rufen wir eine Amnestie aus!" (138 f.) at the end of her long speech reinforce the social significance of her request. Her suggested substitution also has larger social implications. She encourages each member of the group to bring his or her special interests to the entertainment: thus no one member is to take over for the lack of a common topic of conversation, but each is to contribute his part to the smooth working of the group.

The next step in the development is taken by the Abbé, who is above the turmoil of the rest. He has consistently ignored Karl's unhealthy political attitudes and is not even present at the scene between Karl and the Geheimrat von S. Having returned from his walk right after the baroness's request, he wants to start telling about something he has just seen. The baroness had suggested on the preceding page that people bring back interesting things from their walks to share with the rest (139). By fulfilling this request unawares, the Abbé displays himself already capable of at least the level of civilized social participation that the baroness requires. His patience with Luise, who is consistently uncivil to him, shows him to be indeed far beyond this level. He is capable not only of self-control and renunciation—also implied, of course, by his profession as Catholic clergyman—but is further willing to sacrifice himself for his society, as he says to Luise: "Nun, Sie wissen, daß ich mich glücklich schätze, manchmal ein Opfer für die übrige Gesellschaft zu werden" (140). While "Opfer" is certainly a deliberate overstatement here, it still carries its own weight in this context which, as we have seen, consistently points beyond the small group to larger kinds of social organizations.

Now that the group has taken the first step towards more civilized intercourse, it is appropriate for the Abbé to suggest his stories as entertainment. There was no reason for him to offer them before, because no one would have been interested. Ordinarily, according to the Abbé, people are interested in stories only for their novelty ("Reiz der Neuigkeit"), not for their serious implications; he actually says, "lästiger ist [der Gesellschaft] nichts als wenn man sie zum Nachdenken und zu Betrachtungen auffordert" (142). Luise has in fact just been musing on what will replace the newest gossip in their conversations. But the Abbé has little use for stories told only for the sake of their newness or curious qualities, indeed he condemns them severely;[7] instead, his stories deal with basic human problems, and occupy the mind ("Verstand") in a pleasant manner (144). Thus

[7] This condemnation of idle curiosity also found its way into Schiller's foreword to the Horen: "Man wird sich, soweit kein edlerer Zweck darunter leidet, Mannigfaltigkeit und Neuheit zum Ziele setzen, aber dem frivolen Geschmacke, der das Neue bloß um der Neuheit willen sucht, keineswegs nachgeben"—Horen, I (1795), v.

the group must demonstrate a certain readiness for this kind of entertainment if it is to be successful. Indeed, one function of this long conversation is to arouse in Luise enough good will to listen to these stories; for through most of it, she doesn't even try to understand what kind of stories he wants to tell.

Throughout the remaining part of the conversation the nature of the response remains an issue. According to the Abbé, the stories should be pondered and even discussed by the listeners. But they are not to be interpreted as *romans à clef*, as Luise would like to do when she says: "Sie werden uns doch nicht verwehren, unsre Freunde und Nachbarn wiederzuerkennen und, wenn es uns beliebt, das Rätsel zu entziffern?" (145). Yet the Abbé's answer is surprising, in light of his previous earnestness. On the one hand, he says he will not completely forbid interpretation in Luise's sense, because he will always have proof that the story existed centuries before the supposed "real" situation; but, on the other hand, he suggests that he might tell such a *roman à clef* just when they least expect it. Why does he seemingly deny his own principles here? The secret is that the "Reiz der Neuigkeit" does make a story more interesting and absorbing, even if it is not essential. It does make people want to hear stories, which they may then reflect upon. Two years later Goethe had the pastor in "Hermann und Dorothea" defend curiosity on precisely these grounds. When the apothecary criticizes the frivolous curiosity of his fellow-townsmen, the pastor answers:

> ... Ich tadle nicht gern, was immer dem Menschen
> Für unschädliche Triebe die gute Mutter Natur gab;
> Denn was Verstand und Vernunft nicht immer vermögen, vermag oft
> Solch ein glücklicher Hang, der unwiderstehlich uns leitet.
> Lockte die Neugier nicht den Menschen mit heftigen Reizen,
> Sagt! erführ' er wohl je, wie schön sich die weltlichen Dinge
> Gegeneinander verhalten? Denn erst verlangt er das Neue,
> Suchet das Nützliche dann mit unermüdetem Fleiße;
> Endlich begehrt er das Gute, das ihn erhebet und wert macht.
> (I, 84–93)

Schiller's version of this attitude in the foreword to the *Horen* (quoted above in note 7) presents a succinct statement of this principle: "Mannigfaltigkeit" and "Neuheit" will make the periodical more attractive to its readers, but they will be used only in the service of a higher purpose. The Abbé is not so open as Schiller; after all, his audience does not listen to him voluntarily, but as if according to the articles of a peace treaty. Thus he will appeal to their curiosity in order to make them reflect inadvertently on the important aspects of his stories, i.e., he will educate them unawares.[8] The success of this technique becomes evident immedi-

---

[8] Goethe's own attitude towards the stories was as playful as the Abbé's—cf. Schiller to Goethe on 29 November 1794: "Da Sie im Verlauf der Erzählungen ohnehin mit der Auslegungssucht Ihr Spiel treiben werden..." GSB, 42. This attitude appears clearly in Goethe's repeated efforts to stimulate others to interpret the "Märchen" while stubbornly refusing to say anything himself.

ately. At the Abbé's playful answer Luise finally gives up her stubborn refusal to take the Abbé seriously. She senses the implied compromise, agrees to make peace and to hear a story right away.[9] Her final words in the scene are "Ich bin höchst neugierig . . . " (146), to which the Abbé, having labored through the whole conversation to arouse her interest, now ironically answers, "Das sollten Sie nicht sein, Fräulein; denn gespannte Erwartung wird selten befriedigt" (ibid.). He has maneuvered her into exactly the right state of mind. This statement marks the end of the section that appeared in the first number of the *Horen*. Goethe treats his readers here with the same irony as the Abbé treats Luise: having condemned idle curiosity, he leaves the reader hanging as to what comes next until the next number of the *Horen*.

Luise's objection should be considered more carefully. She accuses the Abbé repeatedly of wanting to tell stories that are "skandalös" or "lüstern." Her preoccupation reflects not a fear of such stories, but a desire for them, as the Abbé has already suggested, when he says that there are certain "reviews" she never fails to read (144). In this respect she expresses precisely the idle curiosity that has made the Abbé remain silent about story-telling until this point. Thus Luise starts at the bottom of the Abbé's scale of education in this respect. Since her attitude and position are developed so carefully here, we can reasonably expect her to act as an indicator of the Abbé's progress in his attempt to educate the family without their realizing it.

3. THE FIRST EVENING

The Abbé receives an opportunity to implement his suggestion that very evening, rather sooner than he had expected. His ambiguous speech has successfully aroused Luise's curiosity, so that she actually requests him politely to tell them one of his stories, after he has distracted the group from the day's politics by his bland statement that each should believe what he likes. Her request is the first polite sentence out of her mouth since the beginning of the *Unterhaltungen*, so the reader can gauge what an improvement the Abbé has already effected with this pupil.[10]

As Fricke shows, the story he tells is a trap. The first half is the kind of story he has praised to Luise and the baroness, the second half is a rambling, repetitious description of a strange event—"eine Neuigkeit." The group is interested only in the possible truth of the latter half, thus corroborating the Abbé's claim that most people do not know how to listen. The narrator does not even consider their

[9] The tone of her statement still implies considerable reservation, but it is a first step.

[10] My discussion of the rest of the first evening will be brief: I have little to add to Gerhard Fricke's excellent discussion cited in note 5. There is another good discussion of it by August Raabe, "Der Begriff des Ungeheuren in den 'Unterhaltungen deutscher Ausgewanderten,' " *Goethe: Viermonatsschrift der Goethe-Gesellschaft*, 4 (1939), 23–39.

13

discussion worth reproducing, although the more appropriate responses to the Abbé's other stories are reproduced in detail. The sly old gentleman, true to his intent of educating indirectly, pretends to agree with the group when he remarks ironically "[die Geschichte] müsse wahr sein, wenn sie interessant sein solle; denn für eine erfundene Geschichte habe sie wenig Verdienst" (156).

Fritz's and Karl's stories are to be seen in the same light: if they do not know how to listen to a good story, how should they be able to tell one? Indeed, from Charlotte von Stein and Körner on,[11] Goethe's critics have been disappointed in these stories, though few have given him credit for being able to distinguish their quality himself. Of the two young men, Karl is the worse offender. Fritz simply loses sight of the essentials for the pleasure of the distracting details; for example, he lights on the least relevant element of Karl's second story, the talisman, and pretends to possess one himself, in order to mystify the company. Karl, on the other hand, is as passionately devoted to facts as he is to the ideals of the French Revolution. He states his devotion categorically: "Überhaupt . . . scheint mir, daß jedes Phänomen so wie jedes Faktum an sich eigentlich das Interessante sei. Wer es erklärt oder mit andern Begebenheiten zusammenhängt, macht sich gewöhnlich eigentlich nur einen Spaß und hat uns zum besten . . ." (161). With such an outlook it is impossible for Karl to appreciate the Abbé's concern with relationships, explanations, and feelings that are difficult to define clearly. But it is not just Karl's quality as "poor listener" that is important here. The same outlook that makes him a poor listener is also what makes him such a disruptive member of the family. It is, after all, his inability to see the effects of his passion for the revolution upon his family that brings about the catastrophic scene with the Geheimrat von S.

It is not surprising then, that the Abbé treats him so sarcastically when they discuss the desk which has split open under the eyes of the company at the same moment that its double burned up on the neighboring estate. When Karl bemoans the lack of a hygrometer to establish all the facts in the case, the Abbé remarks blandly, "Es scheint, daß uns immer die nötigsten Instrumente abgehen, wenn wir Versuche auf Geister anstellen wollen" (160). And Karl deserves no more sympathy than that. His mad idea that any explanation must be a joke has made him heedlessly terrify Luise with his joking explanation of the sound of the desk, "Es wird sich doch kein sterbender Liebhaber hören lassen?" (159). Even if the occasion had not led Karl to be so unkind to Luise, it would still be pointless in the eyes of the Abbé; a desk that cracked in sympathy with its burning double is at best a curious fact, not an event of serious human interest. This section works in two ways, however. Luise is also made to look silly for her irrational preoccupation with her fiancé. It may seem heartless to mock Luise for excessive concern for her fiancé: the issue is really that the problems of the group (social harmony) must override individual concerns (fiancé).

[11] See H. G. Gräf, *Goethe über seine Dichtungen*, I, 328.

The stories told on this first evening are unsatisfactory not only in terms of the Abbé's views about story-telling, but also in terms of the basic social qualities defined by the baroness, namely self-control and the ability to renounce. In the Abbé's story these qualities are rejected by both the young man and the singer; in the other three stories they are simply ignored, not because they are not appropriate, but because Fritz and Karl have not learned to think in terms of them. Thus it is significant that the baroness does not preside over this discussion, indeed that she is not even present. This section is in all respects what Fricke calls a a negative example, the group is but a small step indeed beyond its starting point.

When they assemble the next day the Abbé volunteers a story, assuming they would like to hear one. Since the evening before has been devoted to the sorts of curious stories that are naturally appealing, there is little likelihood that his offer will be declined. Before he can begin, however, the baroness sets a series of conditions upon him. To a large extent, as Fricke has shown, her remarks constitute a critique of the stories of the preceding evening, from which Fricke mistakenly concludes that she speaks for Goethe. Her criticisms of *Arabian Nights* cannot be Goethe's, for the rest of the *Unterhaltungen* utilizes precisely the techniques she condemns. In the *Arabian Nights* she does not like interruptions to arouse suspense and so-called "rhapsodische Rätsel" (166). Yet the Abbé deliberately interrupts the Ferdinand novella, and the "Märchen" is *the* "Rätsel" of German literature. Goethe himself said to Schiller that he intended to make use of the freedom afforded by the technique of the *Arabian Nights:* "überhaupt gedenke ich aber, wie die Erzählerin in der Tausend und einen Nacht zu verfahren" (2 December 1794—GSB, 43). Furthermore he thought it very important that the "Märchen" appear in two parts. In spite of two requests by Schiller to the contrary, he still insisted: "Das Märchen wünscht ich getrennt, weil eben bei so einer Produktion eine Hauptabsicht ist, die Neugierde zu erregen. Es wird zwar immer auch am Ende noch Rätsel genug bleiben" (3 September 1795— GSB, 105). The tone of this statement clearly contradicts the baroness's criticism of stories "wo sich der Erzähler genötigt sieht, die Neugierde, die er auf eine leichtsinnige Weise erregt hat, durch Unterbrechung zu reizen" (166).

The ambiguity of this statement is similar to that of the Abbé's discussion of curiosity with Luise, but functions differently. There the Abbé was deliberately ambiguous for his own purposes; here the baroness is perfectly straightforward. The ambiguity arises because the baroness presents views which form a valid critique of the preceding evening. Since she was not present at that session, the reader assumes (correctly) that she speaks for Goethe; yet Goethe strongly disagrees with part of her statement. In the context of the preceding evening she is perfectly right, but in other possible contexts she is not. That is, the narrator can think of cases—the "Märchen" will turn out to be such a case—in which the negative and positive halves of the baroness's remarks can be reconciled.

It is significant in this context that the Abbé does not fully agree with her and has to substitute another story at the last minute for the one he planned to tell. In his ironic way he says that not all his stories are of the desired type: "Kennte ich Sie nicht besser... so würde ich glauben, Ihre Absicht sei, mein Warenlager, noch eh ich irgend etwas davon ausgekramt habe, durch diese hohen und strengen Forderungen völlig in Mißkredit zu setzen. Wie selten möchte man Ihnen *nach Ihrem Maßstab* Genüge leisten können" (167—emphasis mine). Not only in his collection, but in general, stories of the sort she desires are rare. It is, of course, perfectly conceivable that the Abbé really did intend to tell the "Prokurator"—it certainly turns out to have the effect he intends, and it would be better for his educational aims if his audience thought the story was not planned. Whether he did or not, however, it is clear that the Abbé maintains for himself the freedom to tell other kinds of stories and thus frees the cycle from the sole dictation of the baroness.

4. THE "PROKURATOR" AND "FERDINAND"

Having expressed his reservations, the Abbé proceeds with the "Geschichte vom ehrlichen Prokurator."[12] Once it is understood that the Abbé tells the story to educate the company as well as to entertain it, basic parallels between the novella and the frame immediately appear. The merchant's decision to leave his young wife for a few years in order to pursue his business presents a threat to her virtue and thus to the social order.[13] Through his inability to resist his passion for traveling, he fails to control himself and to fulfill his social responsibilities by protecting his wife. The wife learns from the lawyer to control herself and to renounce. In addition, he shows her the way to constructive activity by asking her to sew for the poor as well as to fast. The Abbé thus goes a step beyond the baroness in telling this story: it is not enough to practice self-control in order to maintain social order; renunciation must lead further to useful activity.

The story displays more than this simple thematic relationship to the frame. The Abbé shows the same sly playfulness here as on previous occasions. The lawyer leads the wife to a realization of her ability to control herself through promises to gratify her passion: this is exactly the technique the Abbé uses in his stories—by offering his listeners distraction he will teach them to reflect. This technique is in fact the real irony of the story: it has all the elements of the "lüsterne

---

[12] A thorough analysis of the "Prokurator" and "Ferdinand" would lead far beyond the bounds of this study. In order to confine myself to the elements relevant here the discussions will necessarily be sketchy.

[13] I read this threat to her virtue as a threat to the *social* order because the merchant has ceded his personal rights by leaving and because religion plays no role until the younger man introduces it as part of his plan. It is thus propriety, a sense of her social role, that prompts the young woman's concern for her chastity.

Geschichte" that Luise secretly longs for, yet it turns out to be the paradigmatic moral story. The Abbé has tricked his curious listeners, just as the lawyer has tricked the young woman.[14]

The ensuing discussion of the story is much closer to the Abbé's wishes than that of the preceding evening. The baroness, by far the most civilized of those present and the only speaking character who has understood the Abbé from the outset, starts the discussion off on the morality of the story, and thus helps to elicit the proper reaction from the other members of the family. It is particularly informative to watch Luise's behavior during this discussion. She jumps in with her usual lack of courtesy: "Es bringt Ihnen nicht viel Ehre, daß Sie in Ihrer Sammlung gerade von der besten Art nur eine einzige haben" (185) and "Sie sollten sich doch endlich diese Paradoxen abgewöhnen, die das Gespräch nur verwirren; erklären Sie sich deutlicher!" (186). This time, however, the Abbé manages to draw her gradually into conversation in a serious way. At first she maintains her challenging tone, but there is little challenge left by the time she says, "So könnte es denn also doch unzählige moralische Geschichten geben?" (ibid.). If her next comment, "Hätten Sie sich eigentlicher ausgedrückt . . ." (ibid.), seems to be a relapse, still the statement after that, "Ich kann doch noch nicht ganz mit Ihnen einig sein . . ." (187) is her friendliest expression of disagreement in the whole cycle. By the end of the conversation she is sufficiently involved to request a particular kind of story, a *Familiengemälde*, which the old gentleman obligingly produces.

Luise's request for stories in a local setting represents the cycle's final declaration of independence from Boccaccio. The rather romantic Mediterranean background must be transformed into more familiar German circumstances to prevent distraction from the essential elements of the story.

When the baroness asks for a second moral story, she justifies it with, "Ich liebe mir sehr Parallelgeschichten. Eine deutet auf die andere hin und erklärt ihren Sinn besser als viele trockene Worte" (187). This statement has often been recognized as an important statement of technique both for the *Unterhaltungen* and the *Wanderjahre*. What is interesting about the statement is not so much its content, which is fairly obvious, but the way Goethe uses the baroness as a mouthpiece to say more than she means. The situation is similar to her inadvertent critique of the evening of stories she did not hear. She intends to comment on particular stories she has heard and is about to hear; Goethe uses the remark to comment on the cycle in general—on the relationship of all the stories to one

---

[14] I cannot agree with Theodore Ziolkowski, "Goethe's 'Unterhaltungen': A Reappraisal," *Monatshefte*, 50 (1958), 57–74, that the story somehow fails because the bawdy *pointe* of its model—that the woman renounces out of sheer physical exhaustion—still shows through. Goethe is a master of the unexpected; the ironic disparity of the reader's expectations (a bawdy story) and the conclusion (a moral story) is precisely what gives this story its piquant charm.

another, not just to one carefully paired with it.[15] In fact, as this interpretation has made clear, Goethe also refers to the relationship between story and frame, which illuminate one another as well.

The Ferdinand story deals with the same issues as the "Prokurator," but at a more intense level and in a more complicated way. Ferdinand's parents present two opposing modes of behavior for Ferdinand—the father lacks self-control and is unable to give up any wish, so that he can barely meet his responsibilities to his family; the mother is able to renounce everything in order to handle the unreasonable strains her husband places on the household. If the father always spends too much to leave sufficient pocket-money for the son, the mother does everything she can to smooth her son's path. In spite of his mother's efforts, however, Ferdinand is finally driven to transgress in order to gratify his passions. His theft is a more disruptive crime than the proposed adultery in the other story, because it is one whose control is ordinarily left entirely up to society; accordingly, the emphasis is laid very strongly on the general social implications of this crime, rather than on the family aspects. Ferdinand's ruminations on his relationship to his father's fortune are described as follows:

> Mit diesen und anderen Sophistereien über Besitz und Recht, über die Frage, ob man ein Gesetz oder eine Einrichtung, zu denen man seine Stimme nicht gegeben, zu befolgen brauche, und inwiefern es dem Menschen erlaubt sei, im stillen von den bürgerlichen Gesetzen abzuweichen, beschäftigte er sich oft . . . (192)

The emphasis on the mistake in Ferdinand's doubts about social order is strongly reminiscent of the description of Karl's attitude towards the revolution:

> er hatte sich vielmehr von der blendenden Schönheit verführen lassen, die unter dem Namen Freiheit sich . . . so viele Anbeter zu verschaffen wußte . . . Wie Liebende gewöhnlich von ihrer Leidenschaft verblendet werden, so erging es auch Vetter Karln . . . alle Verhältnisse scheinen in Nichts zu verschwinden . . . (127)

The resolution is more complicated than in the "Prokurator" because it takes place in two steps instead of one. Ferdinand is helped to the first step—his decision to pay back the stolen money—when Ottilie departs and thus removes the occasion for his crime. His business trip enables him to return the money more quickly than he had hoped and opens prospects for future constructive activity. All the goodwill he brings to the task is not enough, however. Through an

---

[15] It is always understood this way when applied to the *Wanderjahre*. It seems strange that criticism of the *Unterhaltungen* should have remained caught in the idea that the stories were intended to go in pairs, for there is not an even number of stories in the cycle.

oversight of his father, Ferdinand is accused of having taken far more money than he really had. It is only the fortunate discovery of that oversight in the right moment, presented in the story as the grace of God, that averts complete disruption of the family. The second step is the decision to renounce Ottilie, whom he loves passionately, but who would prevent him from pursuing useful activities. He must literally tear himself away from her—no outside circumstances come to his aid, as in the first part—in order to make the final break in writing. The story concludes with the picture of a happy family in which each member is educated to be able to renounce on command—"[Ferdinand] behauptete, daß eigentlich jeder Mensch sowohl sich selbst Enthaltsamkeit als andern Gehorsam geloben sollte" (208). This renunciation is thus conceived as a social virtue: obedience to society involves individual renunciation and self-control, just as the baroness said at the beginning. Indeed, the baroness picks up this very point in her comment at the end of the story about the importance of the executive arm of the state.

The baroness does not, however, take the lead in the discussion of the story. Instead, Luise distinguishes herself by demonstrating an understanding of the story. The Abbé tests his audience by ending the story after the first step in the development outlined above. In the same way, Goethe tests his readers by ending the section that appeared in the seventh number of the *Horen* at the same place where the Abbé temporarily ends (204, line 18). The next continuation did not appear until the ninth number, so Goethe's readers had plenty of time to ponder the story before the discussion of it appeared. Luise passes the test with flying colors: she realizes that the story is not over, since the real problem is Ferdinand's uncontrolled passion for Ottilie, not the money. She also recognizes the particular merits of this story and praises it warmly.

But if Luise is the Abbé's star pupil, Karl remains unregenerate:

> "Ich wünschte," sagte Karl, "daß wir gar nicht nötig hätten, uns etwas zu versagen, sondern daß wir dasjenige gar nicht kennten, was wir nicht besitzen sollen. Leider ist in unsern Zuständen alles zusammengedrängt, alles ist bepflanzt, alle Bäume hängen voller Früchte, und wir sollen nur immer drunter weggehen, uns an dem Schatten begnügen und auf die schönsten Genüsse Verzicht tun." (204)

He is still only able to see renunciation as a limitation to his personal freedom, not as a constructive force for social harmony.

The discussion of "Ferdinand" is interrupted by Friedrich's report on the case of the cracked desk at his aunt's estate. The narrator emphasizes his politeness in talking only about the desk and not describing the accompanying bad news. The topic provides further occasion for cheerful, polite conversation—in sharp contrast to the disruption it caused the evening before. No one is still seriously concerned with it, and Karl shortly changes the subject to propose a new kind of story for the Abbé to tell. The interest of various family members in Friedrich's news does not belie the development asserted here. The baroness has not banned politics from their lives—such a thing would be impossible—but only from their common entertainments. Thus Goethe again indicates that he is not proposing simple escapism from the real world.

Led by the Abbé's poetic efforts the group has made considerable progress toward social harmony through self-control and renunciation, which express themselves on the social level as obedience and cooperation. Two members of the group, Karl and Luise, have been singled out from among this microcosm as particular examples of the process going on: Luise seems to be especially educable, Karl scarcely at all. Thus far considerable ironic byplay between characters, especially the Abbé, Luise and Karl, as well as interplay between the frame and the stories, has been observed. All of these aspects come together in the "Märchen," the climax and crowning achievement of the entire cycle.

5. THE "MÄRCHEN"

The "Märchen" and its introduction are the most interpreted and least understood parts of the *Unterhaltungen*. A large part of the difficulty stems from a tendency to take every theoretical statement in the cycle at face value, regardless of who makes it. This tendency can lead to serious pitfalls. The Abbé is an elusive gentleman who rarely says just what he means, while Karl is a negative figure who can hardly be considered to speak for the narrator. One must bear these reservations in mind when reading their dialogue on the freedom of the imagination. Karl's statement reads as follows:

> Die Einbildungskraft ist ein schönes Vermögen, nur mag ich nicht gern, wenn sie das, was wirklich geschehen ist, verarbeiten will. Die luftigen Gestalten, die sie erschafft, sind uns als Wesen einer eigenen Gattung sehr willkommen; verbunden mit der Wahrheit bringt sie meist nur Ungeheuer hervor und scheint mir alsdann gewöhnlich mit dem Verstand und der Vernunft im Widerspruche zu stehen. Sie muß sich, deucht mich, an keinen Gegenstand hängen, sie muß uns keinen Gegenstand aufdringen wollen, sie soll, wenn sie Kunstwerke hervorbringt, nur wie eine Musik auf uns selbst spielen, uns in uns selbst bewegen, und zwar so, daß wir vergessen, daß etwas außer uns sei, das diese Bewegung hervorbringt. (208 f.)

This statement is really a corollary to his earlier view that facts, and not their relationships to one another, are the only things that are interesting. He is just as uncompromising in wanting nothing but fictions when he is not dealing with reality, as he is in wanting only established, measurable facts when dealing with objective reality, or "Wahrheit," as he calls it. This attitude is exactly the same as his inability to see that his enthusiasm for the French Revolution is inconsistent with his own and his family's lives. Thus his statement actually expresses the same inability to comprehend any relationship between objective reality and the realm of the intellect that he has demonstrated throughout the *Unterhaltungen*, and that has kept him from absorbing the Abbé's indirect lessons.

Karl's statement is not completely invalid. The "Märchen" is certainly a work that insists upon its autonomy. It deals with figures that have a life of their own, a world that operates according to its own unique laws; attempts to connect its figures with reality have been notoriously unsuccessful. Yet it is unavoidable—the Abbé will prove to be too smart for him. Indeed the Abbé has long since maintained that reality and imagination could peacefully coexist when he said to Luise, "Ebenso werden Sie mir erlauben, heimlich zu lächeln, wenn eine Geschichte für ein altes Märchen erklärt wird, die unmittelbar in unserer Nähe vorgegangen ist, ohne daß wir sie eben gerade in dieser Gestalt wiedererkennen" (145). The Abbé is not serious when he makes this statement to Luise, he is clearly teasing her. But is it not when the Abbé is not serious—as when he tells stories to curious listeners—that he is really most serious?

His answer to Karl's statement is just as ambiguous:

"Fahren Sie nicht fort," sagte der Alte, "Ihre Anforderungen an ein Produkt der Einbildungskraft umständlicher auszuführen. Auch das gehört zum Genuß an solchen Werken, daß wir ohne Forderungen genießen; denn sie selbst kann nicht fordern, sie muß erwarten, was ihr geschenkt wird. Sie macht keine Plane, nimmt sich keinen Weg vor, sondern sie wird von ihren eigenen Flügeln getragen und geführt, und indem sie sich hin und her schwingt, bezeichnet sie die wunderlichsten Bahnen, die sich in ihrer Richtung stets verändern und wenden. Lassen Sie auf meinem gewöhnlichen Spaziergang erst die sonderbaren Bilder wieder in meiner Seele lebendig werden, die mich in frühern Jahren oft unterhielten. Diesen Abend verspreche ich Ihnen ein Märchen, durch das Sie an nichts und an alles erinnert werden sollen." (209)

The first interesting point about this speech is that the Abbé disagrees with Karl. Both the baroness and Luise also made demands on the stories that the Abbé was to tell; in both cases the Abbé graciously complied, even if it meant telling a different story from the one he had planned. Karl, however, is silenced and told his demands are invalid. But for what reason? For exactly the same reason that Karl has given for his demands—the autonomy of the imagination! The Abbé turns Karl's own argument upside down: he maintains that the premise of the complete freedom of the imagination prevents him from making any restrictions at all on it, even restrictions which would seem to free it. He can do this, of course, because he does not assume with Karl that the intellect and objective reality are separate realms. Thus he does not assume that facts might hamper the imagination, but sees them rather as a stimulus to it. His collection of stories shows that his imagination finds the ordinary facts of everyday life a treasure house of stimuli.

Is the Abbé then basically in close agreement with Karl that the imagination is completely free? I think not. He certainly does not agree with Karl about the value of the absolute freedom offered by the revolution. Freedom, as he shows it in the stories, is possible only when the individual is in harmony with himself and his environment, only when he can submit with good grace to necessities imposed from without. Thus after she has been shown that she can control herself and remain within the norms imposed by her society, the young wife in the "Prokurator" says, "Sie haben mich mir selbst gegeben . . ." (184). Freedom is self-control, not no control. Freedom of the imagination is only possible for the Abbé when it takes reality into account, not when it ignores it. The first evening was an example of complete freedom of the imagination with reality ignored. This situation was presented as an extremely negative one. It is not without reason that the banal issue of the desk has been reintroduced just before Karl's statement on the freedom of the imagination. The case is brusquely treated and dismissed as uninteresting by the narrator, who says, "man ließ der Einbildungskraft abermals vollkommen freien Lauf" (208). Also, the "Märchen" is the first story in the cycle that is not an impromptu performance. All the other stories were told as soon as they were requested, but for this one, the Abbé allows himself the entire afternoon to prepare.

The Abbé's apparent agreement with Karl is misleading, and his final description of what his "Märchen" will be like, "durch das Sie an nichts und alles erinnert werden sollen" (209), embraces both sides of their disagreement. On the one hand, the "Märchen" will refer to nothing, and Karl's demand for autonomy will apparently be fulfilled. But on the other hand, it will also refer to everything, thus fulfilling the Abbé's insistence upon real significance. These opposing demands provide a helpful framework for discussion of the "Märchen."

The total bewilderment in the criticism demonstrates in itself the autonomy of the "Märchen." Perhaps the most delightful example of this confusion is Meyer von Waldeck's chart compiling various interpretations: the serpent, for example, receives there such disparate labels as "der praktische Verstand," "die Gelehrsamkeit," "die Phantasie," "der besonnene Bürgerstand," "die deutsche Literatur des 18. Jahrhunderts."[16] Goethe apparently reveled in the confusion the "Märchen" created. He solemnly agreed with Prince August von Gotha's (joking) interpretation of it as a new product of the author of *Revelations*, who must still be at large;[17] he delightedly asked Schiller to provide Charlotte von Kalb with counter-interpretations to her interpretation of the story, and even suggested a few himself.[18] As late as 1816 he made up a table of three parallel

---

[16] Friedrich Meyer von Waldeck, *Goethes Märchendichtungen* (Heidelberg, 1879). The chart is a fold-out at the end of the book.

[17] WA Briefe, X, 351 f. Prince August's letter is to be found in "Auslegungen des Märchens," ed. Julius Wahle, *Goethe Jahrbuch*, 25 (1904), 40 ff.

[18] 23 December 1795. GSB, 142.

interpretations for the further confusion of his readers.[19] The great pleasure he took in the bewilderment of his readers would suggest that he had deliberately written this confusion into the piece in order to prevent direct connections to the real world.

Scholars have demonstrated the broad variety of sources involved for any given symbol in the story.[20] In their concern for the sources, however, they have bypassed the real issue, which is not the sources of the symbols, but their intended significance; not where they come from, but what they point to, for it is not clear at all that the meaning or significance (referent) of a symbol is necessarily the same thing as its source. This confusion has, I think, been one of the major difficulties in dealing with the figures of the "Märchen." The tendency has been to look for similarities between certain characteristics of the figures and the real world, to say that the real thing inspired its correspondent in the "Märchen," and that therefore the figure in the "Märchen" means the real thing. (The middle step is frequently left out.)

A more realistic and more rewarding way to consider the symbols is not that they happen to be conglomerations of various sources, but that they were deliberately conceived to point in various directions at once. The symbols do not correspond to "reality" on a one-to-one basis because there are deliberate conflicts or at least discontinuities in their iconography. Consider for example, the three kings. The old man identifies them in the investiture scene as "Weisheit," "Schein" and "Gewalt." In accordance with this statement they are frequently taken to stand for the three supporting pillars of the masonic temple wisdom, beauty and strength. Their characteristics are appropriate to this suggestion. The golden king is small but well-formed, and wears a wreath of oak, sacred to Jupiter in Roman times; the silver king is a medieval figure, elaborately decorated with jewels and somewhat vain; the bronze king is a mighty figure with a club and wears the myrtle of the Olympic victor. Their ceremonial speech always suggests a deeper meaning lurking behind it for the initiated, and thus is strongly reminiscent of masonic ceremony. The indication of points of the compass as directions of departure from the otherwise totally unoriented cave also suggests masonic ritual, where the meeting place is always conceived of as the temple of Solomon and oriented to the points of the compass.[21] At the end the kings invest the prince with their qualities, thereby becoming indeed the pillars of the state.

This interpretation immediately runs into difficulty, however, with the second king, who is really identified as "Schein," not "Schönheit." Since the second king clearly has something to do with beauty, "Schein" might be interpreted as Schillerian "schöner Schein" in order to maintain the familiar trio. But what place has Schiller's term in this clearly masonic setting? Must we look for

[19] Wahle, "Auslegungen," 37 ff.
[20] The best and most comprehensive study of the symbols in the "Märchen" is C. Lucerna, *Das Märchen: Goethes Naturphilosophie als Kunstwerk* (Leipzig, 1910).
[21] There is a good development of this interpretation in Lucerna, *Das Märchen*, pp. 123 f.

Schillerian meanings for the other two kings—e.g., "Form" for the golden king and "Stoff" for the bronze one? These are perhaps not totally inappropriate associations, but they have completely removed us from the masonic realm, as well as from the stated meanings of the kings. One must say rather that "Schein" is a deliberate attempt to confuse the easy association of the kings with their apparent meanings of wisdom, beauty and strength.

In the investiture scene the second king presents even more serious difficulties. The statements of the first and third kings are readily reconciled to their stated meanings—"Erkenne das Höchste!" clearly is appropriate in the mouth of wisdom, as is "Das Schwert an der Linken, die Rechte frei!" to strength. But what has "Weide die Schafe!" to do with "Schönheit" or with "Schein"? And why does the silver king hand the prince a scepter? The masonic interpretation simply does not suffice here. This statement is in fact strange in the mouth of a king at all; it is rather to be expected from the clergy, which traditionally terms its congregation "sheep." I would suggest that the silver king, the second king, represents the clergy, the second estate of France. The label "Schein" is entirely in keeping with Goethe's skepticism towards the established church and delightfully ironic in the mouth of the Abbé. Similarly the golden king, the first king—the eldest of the three and the first to speak—represents the aristocracy, the first estate. "Erkenne das Höchste" takes on then a different, but entirely appropriate meaning when the golden king stands for the highest estate. The bronze king is then the third estate, somewhat rude, perhaps, but the massive strength of the land. This interpretation explains why the old man adjures him to ally himself with his two brothers—the common people must work in harmony and good faith with their rulers. The interpretation of the fourth king as Louis XVI of France, best defended by Hans Mayer,[22] is consistent with this interpretation, for in his case the three estates did not work in harmony with one another. Then again, the interpretation is inconsistent in that Louis XVI was not betrayed by the aristocracy, as the image of the gold being removed from the fourth king would suggest. The prince would represent the new king, in whose government the three groups would cooperate, yet the ceremony undeniably also invests him with spiritual qualities, not merely with the loyalty of each king. Thus two interpretations of the kings exist side by side; neither explains everything about the kings, and the two do not have much to do with one another. At times only one of the two explains something, at times both do. Thus the kings cannot be labeled one or the other, or even both all of the time: their meaning is at times fixable, but never fixed.

The other figures can be approached the same way. Lilie points in all directions—innocent, but surrounded by monuments to those she has killed; the

---

[22] In "Das 'Märchen': Goethe und Gerhart Hauptmann," *Gestaltung Umgestaltung: Festschrift zum 75. Geburtstag von Hermann August Korff*, ed. J. Müller (Leipzig, 1957), p. 102.

fleur de lis of France, related perhaps to the kings in their capacity as the three estates; an alchemical allegory for the female half of the philosopher's stone whose marriage has mystical implications of total union with the cosmos; the force of love, as she is labeled at the end; Goethe's enchantress Lili of "Lilis Park," who also makes princes prisoners of her love ("Die armen Prinzen allzumal/ In nie gelöschter Liebesqual!"—l. 7 f.); the enchanted Lila in the play of that name, whose enchantment makes her entire circle unhappy. None of these aspects can be entirely discounted, yet each cannot necessarily be reconciled with every other—e.g. France and the spirit of love, or modest innocence and the mocking enchantress of "Lilis Park."

The serpent is clearly the genius of the landscape, an agathodaimon (commonly portrayed in Greek mythology as a snake). It is difficult to recognize it as such, however, because it brings no luck or particular blessings by its presence; only when it sacrifices itself does it bring benefit to the area. It is indeed a helpful spirit, but in the same way as the other members of the group perform their functions; the giant and the ferryman can also transport people across the river, the man with the lamp can also preserve things from decay: only the self-sacrifice of the snake is a unique contribution to the well-being of the group. The serpent's interest in gold and curious subordination to the will-o'-the-wisps also masks its role as an agathodaimon. Its green color, signifying hope, harmonizes with, but has no organic relationship to its other qualities. The serpent also presents itself as two aspects of time—eternity, when it preserves the prince by forming the traditional symbol of eternity, and the moment of opportunity, καιρός, when it forms a bridge that can be crossed only at the right moment of noon or midnight. These various suggestions give the serpent a series of shifting "meanings," rather than one fixed one.

As a last example, consider the old ferryman. With transformed steering oar in hand he stands next to the new king at the conclusion as steersman of the ship of state. But why is the steersman absent when the temple moves, *like a ship*, from one side of the river to the other? The reason is that Goethe has been very playful with this figure. The steering oar is not only the rudder of the ship of state, it is also the attribute of Τυχή—Fortuna or chance.[23] His toll of vegetables accords with the latter interpretation, since the cornucopia is another very common attribute of Τυχή. The law that the ferryman can only cross the river in one direction is not a necessary one, it has no basis, but an arbitrary one, dictated by "chance." Τυχή is ordinarily portrayed as a woman, so that in respect to sex the ferryman would seem to be rather the minister of state. Thus the figure incorporates both elements. It is, finally, playful irony that makes the helmsman of the new state the "trusty" old ferryman, Chance.

---

[23] See the iconography of Fortuna in B. Hederich, *Gründliches Lexicon Mythologicum* (Leipzig, 1741), p. 912.

Thus the symbols in the "Märchen" are elusive indeed. The Abbé has seen to it that no figure can be unambiguously related to "reality," and has thereby fulfilled Karl's condition "Sie muß sich... an keinen Gegenstand hängen" (209). The story indeed refers to nothing at all, as the Abbé says. But how, then, does it also refer to everything, how does the Abbé prove Karl wrong and relate the "Märchen" to the real world? Let us look at it again from this point of view.

The conditions of the land in the "Märchen" are generally unhappy at the beginning of the story. The princess Lilie suffers from an enchantment under which love cannot fulfill its proper functions, but works in reverse. Living things, which love Lilie and are loved by her (the canary, the prince), die at her touch, but dead things, which have no feeling, are brought to life by it. Even the presence of too many living things around her causes her pain, and visitors can only approach her singly. Just as love cannot perform *its* functions, so the prince's unrequited (and unrequitable) love for Lilie has made him unable to fulfill his functions as ruler. The landscape is divided by a rushing river which imposes all sorts of arbitrary conditions on the inhabitants. Crossing this river is problematic: the ferry goes only in one direction; the snake-bridge is available only at noon and midnight; the giant's shadow, which people prefer to avoid if possible, appears only at dusk. The giant is, in addition, not very dependable, for the only time he is requested to transport someone across the river he refuses. In fact, this giant is another of the problems; although he is hardly malicious, he is a mindless creature whose powerful shadow can be very disruptive. The more hopeful elements in this community are ineffective. The three kings sit in darkness beneath the earth; the hideous fourth king, whose parts are not melted into a harmonious whole, stands alone. The magic lamp which the kings eagerly await cannot come to them, because if it comes alone it will destroy them.

Into this unhappy world come the two will-o'-the-wisps, superficial, but very social, friendly characters. Their sole characteristics are elaborate empty politeness and sociability, but their arrival begins a chain of events. They stimulate the serpent, who eats the gold they scatter. She begins to shine as the gold melts, unlike the fourth king, in whom the gold never properly melts. With her new light she hastens to the underground temple. Once she is there, the old man with the lamp can come and the enchantment will soon end. The old man is, be it noted, by no means a hero,[24] nor can he and his lamp save the community by themselves; it is only when the serpent tells him the fourth secret that he can proclaim "Es ist an der Zeit!" (216). The old man then sends his wife to Lilie to encourage her with the hope of approaching redemption. At the same time she is to pay the will-o'-the-wisps' debt to the ferryman, according to the instructions of the old man,

---

[24] He is "von mittlerer Größe" (215), a phrase which must have been synonymous with "non-hero" for Goethe's contemporaries. In *Götter, Helden und Wieland* Goethe criticized Wieland's *Alceste* by having Wieland say "Als wohlgestalteter Mann, mittlerer Größe tritt mein Herkules auf" (HA IV, 212).

"denn sie werden uns gelegentlich auch wieder dienen" (218). The prince accompanies the old woman to Lilie, and, in desperation at the affection she displays for the ugly little dog the old woman has brought her, kills himself by rushing into her arms. Thus his desperate circumstances bring him to sacrifice his life, and with it all his hopes. The serpent, over whom they have all come to Lilie in the first place, stretches herself around the corpse to preserve it until the man with the lamp can come. The latter duly arrives in his own miraculous way, but cannot immediately solve the problem; instead, he says, "Ob ich helfen kann, weiß ich nicht; ein einzelner hilft nicht, sondern wer sich mit vielen zur rechten Stunde vereinigt" (230). He states exactly what the action has demonstrated thus far: no one figure can carry the burden, but each one does his own part to enable the whole process to come to completion. At midnight he calls them together, saying, "Wir sind zur glücklichen Stunde beisammen, jeder verrichte sein Amt, jeder tue seine Pflicht, und ein allgemeines Glück wird die einzelnen Schmerzen in sich auflösen . . ." (231). Each one then takes his place in the procession to the other side of the river.

This solemn procession turns out to be a sacrificial procession, though of a most unusual sort; for when they have arrived across the river, the serpent announces that she is prepared to sacrifice herself voluntarily for the rest. Through Lilie as mediator the serpent's life passes to the prince, the head of the new community, and thus to the good of the whole community. Her physical remains are given to the river, which, in return, allows free passage of the temple and provides a permanent bridge. When this ceremony of sacrifice is concluded, the group proceeds to the temple, where the will-o'-the-wisps open the doors—the service the old man had predicted. They are now ready to accompany the kings into the world.

The conclusion of the "Märchen" shows the transformation of the world. The temple, risen to the light, has gone from a seed-like state of potentiality to full-blown existence. The prince is invested with the qualities of the three kings, which are joined within him by the force of Lilie's love. He thus replaces the collapsed fourth king, in whom the elements of the other three were never properly joined. The new millenium is distinguished from the previous one by the spirit of love, which is already expressed in the exuberant good will of the will-o'-the-wisps and the sacrifice of the serpent. This spirit also informs the rejuvenation of the old woman and her husband. Even the disruptive giant is confined and forced to become an agent for order (what could be more ordering than telling time?). The story ends with an image of the bridge joining the two sides of the river and the temple visited by people living together in harmony in a new age.

The Abbé's *Märchen*, then, describes the salvation and rejuvenation of a disrupted society through the combined efforts of its members; the process is directed by the man with the lamp, begun and carried through by the spirit of love. The Abbé lays special emphasis on the self-sacrifice or renunciation of the serpent consummated in a solemn ceremony at the climax of the story. This process is exactly what has been attempted in the frame, but on a more general level. The frame, too, shows a community disrupted, where only the efforts of each member to contribute civilized entertainment to the circle can restore social harmony. The baroness decrees politeness the order of the day (cf. the will-o'-the-wisps); each member of the group must renounce his desire to discuss politics or whatever interests him most (like Luise's fiancé) if it disturbs the group. This kind of self-control is clearly parallel to the self-sacrifice that stands at the heart of the "Märchen." Note the recurrence of the baroness' ship-of-state metaphor (128) in the comparison of the temple to a ship when it crosses the river. The frame, of course, shows only the beginning of the process described in the "Märchen"—the group begins to listen to the Abbé's stories more intelligently, the foundations for civilized social behavior have been laid, but by no means fully realized.

The Abbé teases his audience in another way by introducing into the "Märchen" characters drawn from the world "unmittelbar in unserer Nähe" (145), namely himself, Luise and Karl. He himself, regularly referred to as "der Alte" in the frame, portrays himself as the old man with the lamp, "der Alte." This identification is, of course, intended for the readers of the cycle, not for the Abbé's listeners, but those listeners with sharp ears could not miss the significance of Lilie addressing the man with the lamp at the critical moment as "Heiliger Vater" (235). Like the man with the lamp the Abbé directs the action—the development of social harmony—but cannot achieve his purpose without the cooperation of all concerned. He also displays the same qualities of patience, good will, and superior knowledge as his counterpart in the "Märchen" (the old man knows the three secrets and knows of the existence of the three kings). He treats Luise with the same good-humored patience mixed with a little teasing that the old man uses with his wife.

This old woman is indeed Luise's counterpart in other ways as well. Both are argumentative, interested in gossip, somewhat vain but basically good-hearted people. The old woman's preoccupation with her disappearing hand is strongly reminiscent of Luise's exaggerated concern for her fiancé. Still, the old woman contributes her part to the salvation of the group in spite of her hand, just as Luise manages to control her concern sufficiently to participate intelligently in the discussions. While this rather unflattering portrayal of Luise would seem to be one of the arrows the Abbé threatened to use against her (144), the ending—the rejuvenation and remarriage—show his ultimate reconciliation and satisfaction at her progress.

Luise's opposite in the frame—the figure who seems least affected by the Abbé's pedagogy, namely Karl—also finds his place in the "Märchen": the Abbé presents him, somewhat maliciously, as the giant. Both are disruptive without really intending to cause damage. Karl no more realizes the pain his ideas cause the rest of his family than the giant realizes the damage his shadow does as he awakens and stretches his arms; Karl's ideas are as unreal or insubstantial and just as dangerous as the giant's shadow. The device of the shadow is evidently inspired by Karl's regretful comment, "wir sollen . . . uns an dem Schatten begnügen" (204, see above p. 19): the Abbé has tricked Karl by showing the shadow to be more important than the substance—the intellectual realm of relationships and implications more important than the crude reality of unorganized facts. The figure of the giant also is an ironic play on Karl's statement that truth and imagination joined bring forth mostly "Ungeheuer" (209). The Abbé has presented the most delightful combination of truth and imagination, in which the only monster is—Karl. In the transformation of the giant into a sundial we recognize Karl's love of measurement and exactitude. The giant's transformation represents a veiled threat to Karl: those who do not willingly give of themselves to bring about social renewal will be transformed perforce.

With these three figures, then, the Abbé has summarized the basic elements in the occurrences of the frame by showing the teacher with the best and worst pupils set in the context of the rejuvenation of society. The "Märchen" is not, however, simply a repetition of the frame in more fanciful terms. It extends the implications of the *Unterhaltungen* from a reaction to the French Revolution to the most basic questions governing social relationships—the question is no longer how to cope with the disruption presented by the French, but how to establish and maintain social harmony in general. The development of the plot with its eschatological implications also extends far beyond the frame, which shows only the beginnings of harmony in the group of exiles. Whether Goethe really believed in the millenium is unimportant—the important thing is the affirmation of human society and harmony in the face of chaos. It carries the *Unterhaltungen* to a triumphant conclusion; it points on "ins Unendliche."[25]

Such affirmations of society appear repeatedly in Goethe's works of the period, and the patterns of affirmation are remarkably similar to the *Unterhaltungen*. The earliest of these works is *Lila*, a *Singspiel* which Goethe worked on intermittently between 1776 and 1788 and finally published in 1790. Its dedication to the duchess warns the reader to seek a significant statement beneath the magical exterior, just as he must do in the "Märchen"—". . . Du fühlst, daß bei dem Unvermögen/ Und unter der Zaubermummerei/ Doch guter Wille und Wahrheit sei."[26]

Everyone is in despair at the beginning of the play because Lila has gone mad and withdrawn from society (her family). She believes her husband to be in the clutches of a wicked demon and refuses to recognize him. The doctor Verazio cures her by having the family enact a play within the play. He approaches her in

---

[25] To Schiller, 17 August 1795. GSB, 96.
[26] Gräf, *Goethe über seine Dichtungen*, V, 313.

the guise of a magician who encourages her to free her husband and other relatives whom the demon has also captured. Finally she faces the demon, who puts her, too, in chains. Once she has accepted this commitment to her relatives and sacrificed herself by allowing herself to be captured, her chains are magically removed and her husband restored to her. Believing that she has freed him herself, Lila recognizes him as her husband. The play within the play and the play itself end simultaneously with Lila in her husband's arms and the chorus singing in a meter similar to that later used in the final chorus of *Faust II*:

> Weg mit den zitternden,
> Alles verbitternden
> Zweifeln von hier!
> Nur die verbündete,
> Ewig begründete
> Wonne sei dir!
> Kommt ihr entronnenen,
> Wiedergewonnenen
> Freuden heran!
> Lebet, ihr Seligen,
> So die unzähligen
> Tage fortan![27]

Thus Lila is separated from her "society" by the madness that has befallen her, just as her counterpart Lilie suffers under her enchantment. She is restored to her husband and her marriage is renewed through the efforts of all her friends and family, directed by the old *Magus*, just as Lilie is freed by the entire circle of characters directed by the man with the magic lamp. In both cases the central issue is a sacrifice of self, here by Lila, there by the serpent. The language of the final chorus quoted here suggests a similar epoch-making change to the one described at the end of the "Märchen": a society is restored ("wiedergewonnene Freuden") and the foundation is laid for a long happy future ("ewig begründete Wonne," "die unzähligen Tage fortan") based on trust and love.

Although *Lila* was written before the actual outbreak of the French Revolution, the handwriting had long been on the wall. The basic structure was thus prepared for Goethe's direct responses to the revolution, *Die Aufgeregten* and *Der Bürgergeneral*, both written in 1793, and eventually the "Märchen" in 1795. Goethe related the *Unterhaltungen* to these two plays on several occasions,[28] so that they must be considered here.

Goethe never finished *Die Aufgeregten*, nor did he publish the fragment until 1817, but it is still a good example of his efforts to deal with the revolution. The former count of the principality in which the play takes place had signed an agree-

[27] *Jubiläums-Ausgabe*, VIII, 37 f.
[28] See Gräf, *Goethe über seine Dichtungen*, I, 23, 26, 31.

ment with his peasants absolving them from their obligations to maintain the roads in return for certain lands. Although the government now holds the lands, the original of the agreement has mysteriously disappeared and the government is demanding road-service of the peasants. The latter have filed suit with the *Reichskammergericht*, but their case will not come up for another century or two. The comic rabble-rouser Breme von Bremenfeld persuades them to start a revolution like in France; at the same time, the countess decides that the only just course of action is to free them from road-service, since she knows that the document once existed. At the last minute the document is produced after all—the bailiff had stolen it, in order to sell it for his own profit—and all are reconciled. The play shows that the aristocracy can only end social disruption by fulfilling its governmental responsibilities with honesty and good will. The aristocracy cannot pursue its own selfish desires and expect to maintain social harmony; personal wishes must be sacrificed to the unity of the political whole. As in the *Unterhaltungen* the foundations of social order are seen in good will and self-control.

Der Bürgergeneral, a one-act farce, treats the same question of peasant revolution from the point of view of the peasants. The play shows a happily married, hard-working young peasant couple who have grown up with the young nobleman and are still close to him. The wife's foolish father is taken in by the local charlatan Schnapps, who claims to have been chosen by the Jacobins to organize the revolution in their village: to this end he has been made a citizen-general. As he explains the revolutionary ideology to the old man, it becomes clear that he really just wants a good meal: to demonstrate how they will break open the treasure vaults of the nobles, he breaks open the food cupboard; to show how the rich who have made society sour will be punished, he skims the sour cream off the milk and prepares himself breakfast with it. Eventually the loyal peasant returns and drives Schnapps away. The uproar arouses the entire village, and the judge wants to throw them all in jail as dangerous radicals. At the last minute the nobleman enters and sets everything right. At the end the "revolutionaries" look very foolish indeed and the young couple affirm their trust in the local aristocracy. The motif of marriage as an affirmation of society is already familiar from the "Märchen" and forms the heart of "Hermann und Dorothea," Goethe's most widely read response to the revolution. There the marriage of the title characters is presented as the most constructive possible response to the disruption of the revolution, just as the marriage of Hermann's parents was the right response to the fire that disrupted *their* lives a generation earlier.

Goethe treated the same topic once more—allegorically—in 1800 in the playlet *Paläophron und Neoterpe*. Goethe dictated it directly to the actors who were to play it in the course of a few punch breakfasts held for the purpose of writing this play.[29] Such a mode of writing would suggest that he was dealing with

---

[29] See Gräf, *Goethe über seine Dichtungen*, VI, 4.

material long since familiar. Neoterpe, the new age, with her escorts Gelbschnabel and Naseweis, is persecuted by Paläophron, the previous age, and his friends Griesgram and Haberecht. When Paläophron finally catches up with Neoterpe, each realizes that the other might not be so bad after all, if only the objectionable followers were not there. As a gesture of reconciliation, Paläophron sends his two companions away; Neoterpe recognizes the sacrifice and does the same. They then effect a reconciliation through mutual good will, thus initiating, presumably, a new age of harmony.

These parallels to the "reality" of the "Märchen" validate the interpretation in terms of the process rather than the symbols, and justify the Abbé's claim that it refers to everything as well as to nothing. The "Märchen" is, as Goethe wrote to Wilhelm von Humboldt, "zugleich bedeutend und deutungslos."[30] In this way Karl's dry approach is negated. He had said earlier, "Wer [ein Faktum] erklärt oder mit andern Begebenheiten zusammenhängt, macht sich gewöhnlich eigentlich nur einen Spaß und hat uns zum besten, wie zum Beispiel der Naturforscher und Historienschreiber" (161). But the "Märchen" does not work this way. Each fact or figure taken by itself is confusing, it is only the entire context that gives each part its meaning. Of course, the Abbé does have his little joke with the "Märchen." The joke is that Karl and many other readers misunderstand it because they think that each part has meaning and do not see that only the whole—the joke—is the serious part. On 21 November 1795 Goethe commented on his work to Schiller as follows:

> Das sechste Buch meines Romans [Wilhelm Meister] hat auch viel guten Effekt gemacht; freilich weiß der arme Leser bei solchen Produktionen niemals, wie er dran ist, denn er bedenkt nicht, daß er diese Bücher gar nicht in die Hand nehmen würde, wenn man nicht verstünde, seine Denkkraft, seine Empfindung und seine Wißbegierde zum besten zu haben.
>
> Die Zeugnisse für mein Märchen sind mir sehr viel wert... (GSB, 127)

The implications of this joke are far-reaching indeed. Individual details of the "Märchen" have at best questionable significance alone; similarly individual parts of the *Unterhaltungen* are meaningless or misleading when read alone. Rather, individual pieces can only be understood properly in the context of the whole work. Thus the cycle insists upon a much tighter unity than critics have accorded it. In spite of its many disparate parts it must be read with the same attention to relationships between parts as a four-line poem, for all of the pieces reflect upon and correct one another. Yet despite its cunning, the *Unterhaltungen* is by no means the most sophisticated achievement of this sort. I chose to analyze it here to demonstrate on a simple example the problems and the most useful approaches to *Wilhelm Meisters Wanderjahre*, one of Goethe's most complex "serious jokes."

[30] 27 May 1796.

II
WILHELM MEISTERS WANDERJAHRE I: PERSPECTIVE, PERCEPTION AND RENUNCIATION

1. "SANKT JOSEPH DER ZWEITE"

"Wie Ihr uns gestern angetroffen habt, so kennt uns die ganze Gegend, und wir sind stolz darauf, daß unser Wandel von der Art ist, um jenen heiligen Namen und Gestalten, zu deren Nachahmung wir uns bekennen, keine Schande zu machen" (28).[1] Thus Sankt Joseph der Zweite concludes his life story in the first novella in the *Wanderjahre*, in which he explains to Wilhelm that his whole life — his name, his profession, his relationship to his wife Marie, his appearance — has been structured in imitation of the original St. Joseph. Imitation, with its related aspects of correspondence, analogy and perspective, forms the central issue of the novella and its larger setting, on all levels. It first appears as the theme of the novella, and then is generalized and varied in the opening chapters of the novel.

Imitation of the Holy Family is not simply one aspect in the life of the family in the ruined monastery of St. Joseph; rather their entire life is involved in this relationship. Joseph has received his name from the holy foster-father, because the saint had been particularly generous to his family, which for several generations had held the stewardship of the monastery. From his very earliest years Joseph had a special feeling of belonging to this saint; following his example, Joseph chose the trade of carpentry, and as soon as he learned it, began to restore the chapel of his patron. Yet he views the chapel as a place to live, not as a place of worship; his restoration involves only cleaning out inappropriate objects and repairing the building, not replacing objects necessary to religious observance. Although he refers to it as a "Heiligtum" (21), the chapel is a place of reflection and relaxation for him in his youth and the main room of his dwelling in his maturity. Since he lives immersed in the atmosphere of the saint, it is appropriate, then, that he speaks to Wilhelm of his "Wandel," his whole way of life, as imitation.

The chapel is filled with the spirit of the saint, whose life is portrayed in faded paintings around the walls above the paneling. As a child Joseph's favorite occupation was climbing up on the debris piled in the chapel and looking at the pictures; as a youth he chose to become a carpenter on the basis of the picture of

---

[1] All references to *Wilhelm Meisters Wanderjahre* are to volume eight of the *Hamburger Ausgabe*.

Herod's elaborately carved throne (19). Once the chapel is restored, the pictures seem to gain total power over him, as he himself says:

> Hatten jene Bilder und die Gedanken an das Leben des Heiligen meine Einbildungskraft beschäftigt, so drückte sich das alles nun viel lebhafter bei mir ein, als ich den Raum wieder für ein Heiligtum ansehen, darin, besonders zur Sommerzeit, verweilen und über das, was ich sah oder vermutete, mit Muße nachdenken konnte. Es lag eine unwiderstehliche Neigung in mir, diesem Heiligen nachzufolgen. (21 f.)

It is the pictures which capture Wilhelm's attention, too, when he first enters the room, for after a brief summary of the contents of the chapel, we are told, "Was aber die Aufmerksamkeit des Wanderers am meisten erregte, waren farbige, auf die Wand gemalte Bilder" (14). The following list of pictures concludes: "Gleich darauf folgt die Flucht nach Ägypten. Sie erregte bei dem beschauenden Wanderer ein Lächeln, indem er die Wiederholung des gestrigen lebendigen Bildes hier an der Wand sah" (15). It is, in other words, the pictures which Joseph's life resembles; they are his model more than the saint himself.

It is significant in a story so concerned with imitation that the pictures should play such an important role in Joseph's life. Art as an imitation of reality seems quite normal, but reality as an imitation of art is distinctly less normal. This shift in perspectives—the painting, a copy of reality, is here copied—calls the reality of Joseph's world into question. Wilhelm and the reader observe the family with growing surprise; when he learns their names, he, along with the reader as well, is overcome with an uncanny feeling that in this isolated valley he has somehow travelled back eighteen hundred years. But if Joseph and his family seem unreal, the pictures gain a new importance. The normal hierarchy, then, of object and imitation is weakened: Joseph and the pictures seem rather two views of the same thing—whatever is represented by the life of the first St. Joseph—neither is more "real" or more valid than the other. The implications of this equivalence are developed fully only later in the novella "Wer ist der Verräter?"

It is not only Joseph who imitates the pictures in the story; Goethe himself consciously imitates—that is re-creates—some of these pictures in constructing his narrative. In other words, the parts of the story he chooses to relate are determined by the traditional series of pictures depicting the life of Joseph (which Goethe had asked Meyer about in 1799) as well as by certain specific paintings, which were sources for the setting. The range of pictures the reader might expect to find re-created in the story is suggested in part by the list of scenes on the wall of the chapel which the narrator presents when Wilhelm studies them on his arrival:

> Hier sah man [Sankt Joseph] mit einer Zimmerarbeit beschäftigt; hier begegnete er Marien, und eine Lilie sproßte zwischen beiden aus dem Boden, indem einige Engel sie lauschend umschwebten. Hier wird er getraut; es folgt der englische

Gruß. Hier sitzt er mißmutig zwischen angefangener Arbeit, läßt die Axt ruhen und sinnt darauf, seine Gattin zu verlassen. Zunächst erscheint ihm aber der Engel im Traum, und seine Lage ändert sich. Mit Andacht betrachtet er das neugeborene Kind im Stalle zu Bethlehem und betet es an . . . Gleich darauf folgt die Flucht nach Ägypten. Sie erregte bei dem beschauenden Wanderer ein Lächeln, indem er die Wiederholung des gestrigen lebendigen Bildes hier an der Wand sah. (14 f.)

The titles and sub-titles of the first two chapters—"Die Flucht nach Ägypten," "Sankt Joseph der Zweite," "Die Heimsuchung," "Der Lilienstengel"—divide the material into scenes and point to specific models.

The first scene, the Flight into Egypt, is the clearest imitation of a painting. All of the standard iconography of the Flight appears here—a dark-haired Joseph leading the ass, Mary riding with the child in her arms, a few angels (including one with a halo of blond hair) carrying palms. Mary wears the familiar blue cloak over a pale red dress, Joseph is clearly identified as a carpenter. Since the path is too steep for the ass to stop and they quickly disappear, even the haste appropriate to a flight appears here. This description may be compared with Goethe's 1818 description of Sebastian Bourdon's etching of the Flight, which Goethe thought was perhaps intended for a chapel dedicated to Joseph:

Drückt eine eilende Wanderschaft vollkommen aus. Sie lassen eine große Bergstadt zur Rechten hinter sich. Knapp am Zaum führt Joseph das Tier einen Pfad hinab, welchen sich die Einbildungskraft um desto steiler denkt, weil wir davon gar nichts, vielmehr gleich unten hinter dem Vordergrunde das Meer sehen. Die Mutter, auf dem Sattel, weiß von keiner Gefahr, ihre Blicke sind völlig in das schlafende Kind versenkt. Sehr geistvoll ist die Eile der Wandernden dadurch angedeutet, daß sie schon das Bild größtenteils durchzogen haben und im Begriff sind, auf der linken Seite zu verschwinden.[2]

There is no direct evidence that Bourdon's etching in particular is the source of the description in the *Wanderjahre*, nor would it be particularly important. What is important is that Goethe describes here the essential elements of a traditional rendering of the scene and that these elements appear in the description in the *Wanderjahre*. And, in fact, Wilhelm immediately recognizes the scene as the re-creation of an artistic topos: "unser Freund [mußte] die Flucht nach Ägypten, die er so oft gemalt gesehen, mit Verwunderung hier vor seinen Augen wirklich finden" (9).

The beginning of the second chapter, entitled "Sankt Joseph der Zweite," presents Joseph in the product of his work, the restored chapel with the carved doors and furniture. Two of the pictures mentioned in the description show the

---

[2] WA I, 49¹, 158–59. This is the third of four etchings Goethe describes in the essay "Antik und Modern." Bourdon was a seventeenth century French artist.

saint among the products of his craft, and Joseph himself mentions the picture of the carved throne as a particular inspiration to his carpenterial activity. One cannot, however, speak of a special scene or event here.

The next sub-title, "Die Heimsuchung," refers the reader to another specific iconographic subject, Mary's visit to Elizabeth shortly after the annunciation to Mary. In the *Wanderjahre* Elisabeth steps out of the doorway to embrace Marie, as in paintings of the visitation, and Joseph says, to emphasize the correspondence, "Frau Elisabeth, Ihr werdet heimgesucht" (24). There is a slight discrepancy here in that Marie is in an advanced state of pregnancy, not Elisabeth; actually another motif has been superimposed on the Visitation, namely that of Joseph and Mary's trip to Bethlehem, where Joseph leads Mary—pregnant, but not with his child—along on his donkey to shelter.

The last section, "Der Lilienstengel," once more superimposes one picture upon another. The first is Joseph's adoration of the child in Bethlehem, when, in Goethe's story, he takes the child from Elisabeth. The second, and more important one, is the lily springing up between Mary and Joseph when they first meet. Both occur in the list of paintings that Wilhelm sees. In Goethe's story the child takes the place of the lily, and Joseph says "Elisabeth hielt ihn gerade zwischen mich und die Mutter, und auf der Stelle fiel mir der Lilienstengel ein, der sich auf dem Bilde zwischen Maria und Joseph als Zeuge eines reinen Verhältnisses aus der Erde hebt" (26). As in the case of the Flight into Egypt, the narrator points clearly to the re-creation of a specific painting.

The ruined monastery with its columns and arches overgrown with plants is a familiar Renaissance motif.[3] There is, however, a specific source for the conception of Joseph's home—"The Monastery" by the seventeenth-century Dutch landscape painter Jakob Ruysdael. Goethe knew the painting from his visits to the Dresden Museum (1768, 1790), and it apparently impressed him, because he described it in some detail in an essay of 1813 entitled, significantly, "Ruysdael als Dichter."[4] His description of the painting shows clearly that he had it in mind when describing the ruined monastery in which Joseph lives. He begins with a statement of the intention of the painting: "im Gegenwärtigen das Vergangene darzustellen" (HA XII, 139); this is, of course, precisely the sense of Joseph's imitation as well. Wilhelm in fact uses nearly the same formulation when

---

[3] One thinks immediately of Dürer. See, for example, *The Complete Woodcuts of Albrecht Dürer*, ed. Willi Kurth (New York, 1963), pp. 185, 188 ("Adoration of the Magi" and "Repose on the Flight into Egypt"). That does not mean, however, that the novella is based on Dürer's "Marienleben," as Karl Viëtor suggests in *Goethe: Dichtung, Wissenschaft, Weltbild* (Bern, 1949), p. 301. Apart from the iconographical motif of the ruins, Goethe's description does not correspond to Dürer's woodcuts. In particular, Dürer's "Flight into Egypt" has a lush southern background, not a mountainous one.

[4] According to Herbert von Einem's commentary in HA XII, 612, Goethe visited the gallery again in the summer of 1813, but after he had written the portion of the essay devoted to the "Monastery."

he says to Joseph, "macht mich mit Eurer Geschichte bekannt, damit ich erfahre, wie es möglich war, daß . . . die Vergangenheit sich wieder in Euch darstellt" (15 f.). Goethe then describes the appearance of the monastery in Ruysdael's painting:

> Zu seiner linken Hand erblickt der Beschauer ein verfallenes, ja verwüstetes Kloster, an welchem man jedoch hinterwärts wohlerhaltene Gebäude sieht, wahrscheinlich den Aufenthalt eines Amtmanns oder Schössers, welcher die ehemals hieherfließenden Zinsen und Gefälle noch fernerhin einnimmt, ohne daß sie von hier aus, wie sonst, ein allgemeines Leben verbreiten. (HA XII, 139)

The building appears in the *Wanderjahre* as "ein großes, halb in Trümmern liegendes, halb wohlerhaltenes Klostergebäude," and Wilhelm is told, "es wohnt ein Schaffner daselbst, der die Wirtschaft besorgt, die Zinsen und Zehnten einnimmt, welche man weit und breit hierher zu zahlen hat" (13 f.). Even the brook, whose picturesque little cascades Goethe dwells upon, appears in the setting of Joseph's home (16), and there is the same background of gentle hills in both (HA XII, 140 and VIII, 13). Goethe ends with a description of the artist who sits in the foreground, back to the viewer, sketching the scene; he represents, Goethe says, all those who will look at the painting as the manifestation of the past in the present. This element, too, finds its way into the *Wanderjahre*, in a form suitable for the shift of medium: the artist is none other than Wilhelm himself. He writes down the experience with his own reflection added for Natalie, as he explains in the letter to her at the beginning of chapter three.

Joseph's imitation, a matter of content, is thus matched by Goethe's, a matter of technique. The result is a curious doubling of perspectives, since both Joseph and Goethe start from the same series of pictorial motifs. This doubling not only contributes further to the tendency to turn Joseph and the pictures into parallel manifestations of the same phenomenon; it also defines a basic stylistic device of the *Wanderjahre*. Much of the material of the *Wanderjahre*, as I will show in Chapter Three, is imitation or parody of literary texts, just as "St. Joseph" is "parody" of paintings. Here it is specifically in service of the theme "im Gegenwärtigen das Vergangene darzustellen"; it is imitation not for the purpose of satire or correction, but for the enrichment of the reader's vision of the present. Even where imitation doesn't enter thematically, the parody continues to bear this significance; and the problem of realizing the past in the present remains the basic concern of the novel.

I would like to move now from the novella to its placement in the frame. A letter from Wilhelm to Natalie stands on each side of Joseph's narrative. The second of these raises two interesting problems: it presents yet another process of imitation or reflection, and it also provides an early example of an important narrative technique in the *Wanderjahre*. The passage begins:

> Soeben schließe ich eine angenehme, halb wunderbare Geschichte, die ich für dich aus dem Munde eines gar wackern Mannes aufgeschrieben habe. Wenn es nicht ganz seine Worte sind, wenn ich hie und da meine Gesinnungen bei Gelegenheit der seinigen ausgedrückt habe, so war es bei der Verwandtschaft, die ich hier mit ihm fühlte, ganz natürlich. Jene Verehrung seines Weibs, gleicht sie nicht derjenigen, die ich für dich empfinde? und hat nicht selbst das Zusammentreffen dieser beiden Liebenden etwas Ähnliches mit dem unsrigen? (28)

Wilhelm maintains that he has written the text of the novella, and that some of the sentiments expressed may not really be Joseph's, but his own. However, since he and Joseph are in some way related, it is indifferent whose words are on the page, for those of the one would reflect those of the other. He furthermore invites Natalie, as well as the reader, to make an extensive comparison of the two pairs, Joseph-Marie and Wilhelm-Natalie. He himself suggests some similarities and the important difference that he and Natalie are separated. Thus the reader is forced to consider the extent to which the two pairs correspond to one another. This correspondence is parallel to the mirroring process of Joseph and the pictures discussed above; the explicit emphasis placed on the similarities between the two pairs widens the perspective of the novella to include Wilhelm and Natalie, and thus raises the number of families in the story to four—the original Holy Family by implication, the pictured Holy Family, Joseph and Marie, Wilhelm and Natalie.

The other problem raised by the passage is the disorienting shift in narrative perspective from a third person narrator to a character in the story. At the beginning of the novel the reader has no particular suspicions about the narrator. Wilhelm's introduction into Joseph's home is presented in the fiction of a dramatic present, so that the reader assumes that he has a fairly accurate and impartial report of what Joseph said to Wilhelm. But the beginning of Wilhelm's letter informs the reader that Wilhelm himself has written the report, indeed probably not very accurately; suddenly the reader must reconsider his judgments of Joseph's story to take into account the impact of Wilhelm's personality and problems upon it. To what extent is it any longer Joseph's story at all? Since some of the material which must be considered to belong to the novella, like the tableau of the Flight into Egypt, involves Wilhelm and is told in the third person, it is not clear where Wilhelm's report leaves off and the narrator's redaction of it begins.

Like the parody, this proliferation of perspectives widens and enriches the reader's perception; but at the same time it has a serious drawback, namely that the perspectives are not all necessarily of equal validity. This problem is first developed in the larger frame of the Joseph novella, which deals three times with the distinction between imitation and reality, through the "Katzengold," the "Holy Family," and Fitz.

Wilhelm's conversation with Felix at the beginning of chapter one centers on means of perception of natural objects—how to recognize deer tracks, how to identify Felix's pine-cone, how to name the stone he has found. A special kind of problem is presented by natural objects which imitate other natural objects—here the "Katzengold" or false gold that Felix mistakes for real gold. This imitation is not, however, the self-conscious imitation of art, or even deliberate in any way; it is rather a chance similarity which the observer mistakenly interprets as identity or imitation. Wilhelm's playful etymology for "Katzengold"—"weil es falsch ist und weil man die Katzen auch für falsch hält" (7)—suggests clearly this mistaken attitude on the part of the observer that deliberate imitation has occurred, by means of the pun on "falsch" as both "not genuine" and "dishonest." Thus the first perspective on the relationship of image to reality is that of irrelevant similarity mistaken for significant correspondence by the observer.

The "Holy Family" represents a completely different aspect of the problem, for their imitation is clearly self-conscious and deliberate. Yet there is nothing deceptive about their imitation; Joseph makes no pretense to be what he is not. He does not wish to raise himself at the expense of his model, but to do honor to his model by confessing himself to be his imitator.

The last aspect is imitation with deliberate attempt to deceive, and is presented through the figure of Fitz. Fitz, as I will show shortly, is a demonic little tempter, who leads Felix and Wilhelm into all sorts of difficulties. As such, he fills out the ironic divine framework presented by the "Holy Family" with their attendant angels. Tempters rarely wish to be recognized as such, and Fitz is no exception. He passes in the valley around the monastery of St. Joseph for a cheerful, lively lad, who is an object of occasional charity and is tolerated among the children who are the attendant angels of the "Holy Family." He deceives the local inhabitants by pretending to be, that is by imitating, what he is not, an angelic child. This imitation with intent to deceive is the third kind of imitation, and thus fills out the series formed by the "Katzengold" and the "Holy Family."

This variety of perspectives functions as a mode of ironic undercutting throughout the book: when presented with proposed correspondences, the reader must ask himself not only what their significance might be, but whether, in fact, they are real correspondences (as in the case of Joseph), or only spurious, due either to inadequate observation (as with the "Katzengold"), or to deliberate deceit (as with Fitz). To the difficulty of distinguishing suddenly shifting narrative perspectives thus comes the further difficulty that certain kinds of statements in the *Wanderjahre* are of questionable validity. This problem does not remain confined to questions of imitation and correspondence, but is extended to more general statements as well, as the discussion of aphorisms in the novel will show (see below pp. 75–78). This is not to say that it will always be possible to decide which of the three types of imitation listed above is in question, but rather, the inability to decide, the ambiguity of perspectives, will increase the ways in which the problem in question will be viewed, just as changes of narrator increase the number of possible perspectives.

The Joseph novella provides an important example of such ambivalence in its treatment of Christianity. On the face of it, the subject matter of the novella would suggest a return in the *Wanderjahre* to revealed religion as the important world-view for Goethe. But in fact, the emphasis on the pictures effectively undercuts the otherworldliness of Joseph's imitation, a movement consonant with the use of the chapel as a place to live rather than a place to worship. Joseph and his family do not really imitate the Holy Family, they imitate an unknown artist's conception of the Holy Family, and therefore not a natural or divine manifestation, but a human creation. It is significant that Joseph does not say in the passage quoted above on page 34 that the desire to imitate the saint came to him or even arose in him, but "Es lag eine unwiderstehliche Neigung in mir." There is only human motivation, no outside motivation. The saint himself plays no real role in the story, the truly miraculous elements of the story are translated into natural equivalents; the child, for example, is not the son of God, but of the first husband. Thus the miraculous Christian framework that Goethe appears to establish for the novel by setting the novella at the beginning is corrected, as the real St. Joseph is displaced by the thoroughly human world of his successor.

The first chapter of the novel provides a parallel example of this naturalization of the miraculous biblical framework. After Wilhelm has experienced the seemingly miraculous appearance of the "Holy Family" and promised to visit them, he climbs back to the lodge on top of the pass. The text reads: "Er stieg aufwärts und verspätete sich dadurch den Sonnenuntergang. Das himmlische Gestirn, das er mehr denn einmal verloren hatte, erleuchtete ihm wieder, als er höher trat, und noch war es Tag, als er an seiner Herberge anlangte" (11). This prolongation of the daylight until a given task is completed is an oblique imitation of the miracle at Gibeon, where the sun stood still (Joshua 10:12–13). Yet everything occurs in a completely natural way here: as Wilhelm climbs higher, his horizon—that is, the mountains limiting his view—becomes lower, so that he can see the sun longer than if he had remained below. As with Joseph and his family, the natural and real perspective substitutes for and thus ironizes the miraculous perspective.

This irony must not, however, be taken for simplistic rationalism; naturalization does not exclude the miraculous. Perhaps more than any other part of the book these opening chapters arouse a sense of uncanniness and wonder. In the two pages on which the family first appears there is an incredible concentration of words expressing amazement—"sonderbare Erscheinung," "Verwunderung," "Erstaunen," "Verwunderung," "seltsame," "sonderbaren," "wunderlichen Bilder," "Verwunderung," "Erstaunen" (8–9). Wilhelm, along with the reader, observes the family with growing surprise, and when he learns their names, he, and once again the reader as well, is overcome with an uncanny feeling that in this isolated valley he has somehow travelled back eighteen hundred years. The word "Wunder" and its many derivatives ("Verwunderung," "wunderbar," "wunderlich," "wundersam") are ubiquitous in the *Wanderjahre*. A sense for the miraculous pervades the novel, but it applies to nature itself. Even the realist Jarno cannot avoid suggesting a certain wonderful element that permeates nature (at the beginning of chapter four): "Man freut sich mit Recht, wenn die leblose Natur ein Gleichnis dessen, was wir lieben und verehren, hervorbringt. Sie erscheint uns in Gestalt einer Sibylle, die ein Zeugnis dessen, was von der Ewigkeit her beschlossen ist und erst in der Zeit wirklich werden soll, zum voraus niederlegt" (35). Nature does not exclude the miracle, it absorbs it. It will later be seen that this ambivalent view of Christianity persists throughout the novel, particularly in the pedagogic province and the plans for the American settlement.

I would like to return once more to the first chapter in order to make some points about the novella's position in the book. The novel begins: "Im Schatten eines mächtigen Felsen saß Wilhelm an grauser, bedeutender Stelle, wo sich der steile Gebirgsweg um eine Ecke herum schnell nach der Tiefe wendete. Die Sonne stand noch hoch . . ." (7); he is on the pass, which, when crossed, will separate him definitively from his homeland, from Natalie, from his whole past life. There is something ominous about the precipitous descent before him, hence his position is described as "graus," "bedeutend." In Wilhelm's letter to Natalie it is shown that he views crossing the pass as a clear commitment to his renunciation of her and to his life as a wanderer. In the section of the letter written the following morning the descent is presented as a symbolic death. There is a certain finality to the lines "Laß mich mein letztes Ach zu dir hinübersenden! laß meinen letzten Blick zu dir sich noch mit einer unwillkürlichen Träne füllen!" (13), and at the end he specifically compares himself to a dying man, when he says: "der Wirt räumt schon wieder auf in meiner Gegenwart, eben als wenn ich hinweg wäre, wie gefühllose, unvorsichtige Erben vor dem Abscheidenden die Anstalten, sich in Besitz zu setzen, nicht verbergen" (13). The use of the sun in this context also suggests death: at the beginning, when Wilhelm sits at the place just before the descent begins, the sun is high in the sky; as he climbs back up to the top of the pass, back towards where he came from and towards Natalie, the sunset is miraculously delayed; now as he is about to make the descent he says "Noch ist die Sonne nicht aufgegangen, die Nebel dampfen aus allen Gründen . . . Wir steigen in die düstere Tiefe hinab" (13). At the moment of death the life-bringing sun is conspicuously absent.

But Wilhelm's descent, his renunciation, is not only an end, it is also a new beginning. The lines just quoted above read in context: "Noch ist die Sonne nicht aufgegangen, die Nebel dampfen aus allen Gründen; *aber der obere Himmel ist heiter*. Wir steigen in die düstere Tiefe hinab, *die sich auch bald über unserm Haupte erhellen wird*" (13, emphasis mine). At the same time that the first half of the letter laments the separation of Wilhelm and Natalie, it also affirms the strength and permanence of the bond joining them, and ends with the expectation of their eventual reunion. Indeed, Wilhelm's descent brings him to the "Holy

Family," which suggests all sorts of new beginnings. Marie, in the story, has lost one husband, and made a new beginning with another. Rebirth through death is of course the essence of the Christian myth, and is beautifully summed up in this story by the description of the picture of the baby asleep on the two pieces of wood that seem to form a cross (15). Here the dying man on the cross has been replaced with the child just beginning life. When he enters the valley, Wilhelm feels himself set eighteen hundred years into the past; his life begins over again with this "Urfamilie" at the beginning of the time-reckoning of European civilization. The "Stirb und werde" motif is quietly sounded: Wilhelm's renunciation, presented through images suggesting death, is transformed into new life. Thus as soon as the major theme of the book, "Entsagung," is introduced, it is immediately shown from a new, rather unexpected perspective—it is not only bitter necessity, but also the way to new possibilities; it is not only tragic, but profoundly positive as well.

With this double perspective of "Entsagung-Stirb und werde" in mind, the position of the Flight into Egypt as the opening tableau may be better understood. The Holy Family's flight into Egypt must first be understood as a kind of wandering, and, indeed, exactly the same kind of wandering that the *Wanderjahre* as a whole deals with. Joseph and his family must flee their homeland (thus renounce) to maintain their integrity and to preserve their future (both embodied in the child) in turbulent times, in fact, at a turning point in human history. Wilhelm and his friends are also trying to maintain their integrity as individuals and to assert their places in a rapidly changing society, for Goethe clearly realized that the social and political upheavals of his own time marked another major turning point in human history. The immediate parallel in the novel is Wilhelm's significant position poised between two worlds in the opening sentences. Thus the motif of the Flight into Egypt suggests a dark undertone of social disruption and of renunciation. Yet the development of the motif through Wilhelm's initial reaction to the group, and through the second Joseph's narrative is not tragic, but idyllic. Joseph and his family are not fleeing. They are returning to a home where they live in peace and contentment, not at all threatened by changing times in the world around them, and they look towards an equally satisfying future. This dual image of wandering is presented in the same way as Wilhelm's symbolic death, which follows right after it—both have their negative and their positive aspects. In its duality the image is an emblem for the whole book, which unfolds and develops the image of wandering both as renunciation and as new beginning.

The opening chapters of the novel present the reader, then, with a dazzling variety of constantly shifting perspectives. The phenomenon of imitation is repeatedly extended—from imitation of the Holy Family, to imitation of pictures (imitations) of the Holy Family, to the story itself which re-creates the pictures its title character imitates, to the analogy between the characters in the story and those in the frame. At the same time various kinds of narrative irony open up further perspectives: the miraculous is natural and miraculous simultaneously, image and object are not clearly distinguished, and thus reflect one another mutually (rather than just the one reflecting the other). The implied multiplicity of narrative perspectives suggests new perspectives on the same object or event, and simultaneously calls the validity of any given perspective into question. The problematic relationship between an imitation or image and its object further places the validity of any given perception in question. The perception of reality is thus very much a problem in these opening chapters. The reader is presented with a complex set of varied and ever-shifting perspectives of the Holy Family, and left to make what sense he can of them.

Wilhelm leaves Joseph's home in the company of the demonic Fitz. This peculiar figure seems to live in the vicinity of the monastery, though no one in the valley has any idea where he comes from or what his background is—a strange phenomenon in such an isolated area as is presented in Joseph's story. Wilhelm takes an immediate dislike to him, as he does to no other character in either the *Lehrjahre* or the *Wanderjahre*: he considers Fitz a hypocrite who knows how to curry favor with the right person at the right time. In his dealings with Jarno about the "Kreuzsteine," Fitz displays himself a cunning and not entirely trustworthy businessman, and he brings the friends into the company of thieves and smugglers at the charcoal-burner's hut. Twice Fitz tries to lead Wilhelm and Felix into traps for no apparent reason. The first time he directs them by a short-cut to the mysterious "Riesenschloß"; their guide saves them from the trap, since he knows that fallen trees have blocked Fitz's path. The second time Fitz leads them by another short-cut to the estate of Hersilie's uncle; this short-cut, however, leads through the surrounding protective walls via the drainage system and right into a trap designed—among others—for Fitz himself. Of course, Fitz escapes, leaving Wilhelm and Felix behind bars in a highly embarrassing situation.

Yet Fitz is more than just a cunning rogue, for there is a supernatural element to his character that makes him such an uncanny figure. At the charcoal-burner's hut he has a long conversation with a figure whom Jarno identifies as a "Schatzgräber"; the reader may be reminded in this context of the Mephistophelean aspect of the hidden treasures buried in the earth in the first act of *Faust II*. Seemingly by intuition Fitz finds Jarno in the pathless wilderness of the high mountains. In the first version of the novel he explains what traces he followed to find him, but Goethe suppresses this explanation in the final version, thus making Fitz more mysterious. Although Fitz does not accompany Wilhelm and Felix to the "Riesenschloß," he seems to have some closer association with it than is articulated. It is not clear in the final version how Felix knows about it or why he is so interested, but in the first version Fitz is responsible for his enthusiasm. Fitz also warns the guide not to let the travelers wander too far into it—a warning clearly intended to arouse Felix's curiosity rather than to keep him outside in safety. Felix, of course, does wander in too far, and Wilhelm follows after, guiding himself by a thread like Theseus in the labyrinth of the Minotaur. The allusion is not expressed in the text (43), but cannot be overlooked; it forms a submerged mythological level of this strange episode.

In the depths of the "Riesenschloß" Felix finds the mysterious "Kästchen," the dangerous power that stands at the center of his uncontrollable and potentially destructive relationship with Hersilie. Felix immediately senses that the "Kästchen" does not properly belong to him and must be kept a secret, above all from Fitz. The object in question does indeed seem to belong to Fitz, for the key to it is found in the pocket of the jacket he was wearing the very day that he sent Wilhelm and Felix to find it. Fitz has "accidentally" sent Felix to the "Kästchen," of course, just as he "accidentally" leads him into the jail cell on Hersilie's uncle's estate (note how this situation foreshadows his relationship to Hersilie). Fitz thus plays the role of a demonic tempter, and Felix's fall duly occurs in a delightful parody in chapter five. The uncle's estate is presented as a modern Garden of Eden — it is surrounded by high protective walls, it is fertile and has a large variety of things growing in it. But, ironically, it is cultivated. At dinner Hersilie hands Felix the apple and he cuts himself while peeling it — the first in a long series of injuries which he inflicts upon himself for her sake.

The rest of Felix's affair with Hersilie is presented in brief snatches throughout the novel; its end is the closing scene of the narrative. Throughout it is told at a level of emotional intensity that appears nowhere else in the frame. It also maintains, as a second perspective, the strong mythological undertone which Fitz as the Biblical tempter brings to it, although the mythological background gradually shifts from the Christian to the Greek world and ends with the image of Wilhelm and Felix embracing as Castor and Pollux. I shall have occasion to revert to Felix and Hersilie several times in the course of this study.[4a] For the moment I would like to pursue the problem of the multiplicity of perspectives as it is manifested in the novellas and their relationships to the frame.

2. "WER IST DER VERRÄTER?"

While Wilhelm visits the estate of Hersilie's uncle, he receives considerable material to read — several family letters and two novellas, "Die pilgernde Törin" and "Wer ist der Verräter?" The letters and the first novella, which is a straightforward translation of a French original, will be discussed later; I will discuss the second, "Wer ist der Verräter?" first because it deals with the problems of correspondence and perspective in a way similar to "Sankt Joseph der Zweite." As in the latter, it is possible to trace the problem here first in the novella itself, then in

---

[4a] See below pages 52, 69, 73 ff., 115, 117, 129, 133 and 134. It is intimately related to Wilhelm's choice of the medical profession, see below pages 73, 118 and 134.

the posture of the narrator and its relationship to the material surrounding it.

We have seen that the ordinary object-image relationship is turned around in the case of Joseph and the pictures he "imitates," and that this reversal leads to a confusion of perspectives, or confusion of priorities of reality. This shift of perspective from object to image is developed as a central theme in "Wer ist der Verräter?" by means of the mirror imagery, which can be traced through the novella, and then beyond it to the end of the novel.

The most significant object in the central building in the landscape of the story is the enormous mirror in the garden house. Its effect is presented as follows:

> Wer zur Haupttüre hereintrat, sah im großen Spiegel die günstigste Aussicht, welche die Gegend nur gewähren mochte, und kehrte sich geschwind wieder um, an der Wirklichkeit von dem unerwarteten Bilde Erholung zu nehmen: denn das Herkommen war künstlich genug eingerichtet und alles klüglich verdeckt, was Überraschung bewirken sollte. Niemand trat herein, ohne daß er von dem Spiegel zur Natur und von der Natur zum Spiegel sich nicht gern hin und wider gewendet hätte. (94)

Thus the mirror not only reflects or imitates the landscape, but it complements it; neither the landscape nor the mirror suffices for the visitor to perceive the hillside fully, but only both together. This relationship becomes critical at the climax of the first half of the story, which takes place in front of the mirror. Lucidor sees a man passionately kissing the hand of a young woman, but cannot recognize them because the reflection of the setting sun in the mirror momentarily blinds him. Unable to perceive the complement of the natural event in the mirror, Lucidor cannot correctly perceive the event itself: he assumes that the couple, who turn out to be the beloved Lucinde and the feared Antoni, have just plighted their troth, whereas they have really agreed to dissolve their supposed engagement. Lucidor's inability to perceive the situation correctly is here symbolized by the absence of the reflection of the event in the mirror. When Lucidor himself finally holds Lucinde in his arms, it is again before the mirror, into which he looks to enjoy his happiness fully. The mirror is mentioned once more in the story—during Julie's and Lucidor's ride, when Julie says "nun gerade hier spiegeln wir uns oben in der großen Glasfläche, man sieht uns dort recht gut, wir aber können uns nicht erkennen" (110). The final clause has a double implication: Julie and Lucidor first of all cannot see their images in the mirror, and, because they cannot see the reflection too—although they sit face to face—they are still unable to understand one another. Through this progression of images, the reflection or correspondence in the mirror has progressed from the complement of reality to a source of perception clearer than reality.

Mirror imagery is used in a similar way throughout the novel. Makarie's "sittlich-magischer Spiegel" (223), which shows the widow in "Der Mann von funfzig Jahren" her true self, is another example of this version of the mirror image, while yet another is the statement in Part Two, chapter seven: "In der schönsten Jahrszeit entging ihnen weder Sonnenaufgang noch -untergang und keine der tausend Schattierungen, mit denen das Himmelslicht sein Firmament und von da See und Erde freigebigst überspendet *und sich im Abglanz erst vollkommen verherrlicht*" (228—emphasis mine). The fourth to the last aphorism in "Aus Makariens Archiv" (No. 79) also deals with this problem: "Nichts wird leicht ganz unparteiisch wieder dargestellt. Man könnte sagen: hievon mache der Spiegel eine Ausnahme, und doch sehen wir unser Angesicht niemals ganz richtig darin; ja der Spiegel kehrt unsre Gestalt um und macht unsre linke Hand zur rechten. Dies mag ein Bild sein für alle Betrachtungen über uns selbst" (486).

This aphorism adds a new and somewhat disturbing aspect. If until now the mirror has been a source of particularly clear perceptions, the reader is also warned that this new perspective may distort the observer's perception if he does not recognize its particular bias. Thus the aphorism modifies what has come before and balance is maintained—neither the image nor the object itself enables complete perception, but only both taken together. And in this balance the clear distinction between an object and its image or correspondent dissolves. Complete perception and understanding becomes a process of considering something from many different perspectives: an object or phenomenon must be considered in all its various manifestations, which include all analogous or corresponding phenomena.

Goethe occupied himself with the problem of reflection in several different ways in the early 1820's ("Wer ist der Verräter?" was written 1819–1820). In 1823 he wrote a brief essay called "Wiederholte Spiegelungen" in response to a description of the first literary pilgrimage to Sesenheim. The essay outlines in numbered steps the several reflections of his relationship with Friederike—his first impression of the experience, his memories of it, his poetic retelling in *Dichtung und Wahrheit*, the impression this account makes on the sensitive reader who makes his pilgrimage, the event as remembered by someone the pilgrim meets in Sesenheim, and finally, the renewed memory in the mind of the poet when he reads the pilgrim's report. He concludes that this process leads to clarification and intensification of his perception of the experience:

> Bedenkt man nun, daß wiederholte sittliche Spiegelungen das Vergangene nicht allein lebendig erhalten, sondern sogar zu einem höhern Leben emporsteigen, so wird man der entoptischen Erscheinungen gedenken, welche gleichfalls von Spiegel zu Spiegel nicht etwa verbleichen, sondern sich erst recht entzünden, und man wird ein Symbol gewinnen dessen, was in der Geschichte der Künste und Wissenschaften, der Kirche, auch wohl der politischen Welt sich mehrmals wiederholt hat und noch täglich wiederholt. (HA XII, 323)

The "entoptische Farben" mentioned above were a striking example for Goethe of a phenomenon that could not be perceived directly, but only by means of repeated reflections. The term refers to the colored stress patterns visible in various materials in polarized light, which Goethe produced by a process of multiple reflection. He wrote a long essay on the subject in 1820, of which the first two thirds is devoted to detailed description of his experiments dealing with the phenomenon itself, and the final one third—typically—to discussion of analogous phenomena, ranging from acoustics and meteorology to astrology and weaving. In the midst of this second part, he defends himself as follows:

> Sollten wir nun vielleicht den Vorwurf hören, daß wir mit Verwandtschaften, Verhältnissen, mit Bezügen, Analogien, Deutungen und Gleichnissen zu weit umher gegriffen, so erwidern wir daß der Geist sich nicht beweglich genug erhalten könne, weil er immer fürchten muß an diesem oder jenem Phänomen zu erstarren; doch wollen wir uns sogleich zur nächsten Umgebung zurückwenden und die Fälle zeigen, wo wir jene allgemeinen kosmischen Phänomene mit eigner Hand technisch hervorbringen und also ihre Natur und Eigenschaft näher einzusehen glauben dürfen. Aber im Grunde sind wir doch nicht wie wir wünschen durchaus gefördert, denn selbst was wir mechanisch leisten, müssen wir nach allgemeinen Naturgesetzen bewirken und die letzten Handgriffe haben immer etwas Geistiges, wodurch alles körperlich Greifbare eigentlich belebt und zum Unbegreiflichen erhoben wird. (WA II, 5^1, 301 f.)

This passage may be seen as a scientific statement of the idea developed in the novella in literary terms. One must always be willing to see things in all their varying aspects and relationships to the rest of the world, or one runs the risk of a sort of spiritual death—"Erstarrung." Lucidor clearly runs this risk, when he despairs of regaining Lucinde without really having seen in the mirror what was happening, that is, without really understanding the true situation. The end of this passage reiterates the need for an element higher than reality, a spiritual element, both incomprehensible and ungraspable (both senses of "unbegreiflich") —thus the element symbolized by the mirror image—in order to do a phenomenon full justice.

In the same way that the novella establishes a philosophical basis for the variety of correspondences and perspectives in the novel, the technique of the chapters around the novella suggests a formal basis for the narrative peculiarities of the opening chapters. "Sankt Joseph der Zweite" is not properly an inserted novella at all, it is rather a character's life history, as might be met elsewhere, for instance in *Tom Jones*, or even in the story of the unfortunate clerk in *Werther*. Its position at the beginning of the novel is unusual, however, and contributes to the general disorienting tendency of the first chapters. But "Wer ist der Verräter?" and "Die pilgernde Törin" are properly self-contained novellas inserted without ceremony into the novel, like the novellas in *Don Quixote*. The device by which they are inserted—arbitrary as it may seem—is still interesting and must be considered here.

After Wilhelm and Felix have been freed from the trap under the walls of the park into which Fitz has led them, they are ushered through the garden into the palace, where they soon meet Hersilie and her sister. Hersilie introduces herself, her sister Juliette, and the two officials—father and son—who are friends of the family. The circle turns out to be a literary one; in fact, each member of it cultivates a different European literature to contribute to the entertainment of the group—the uncle is interested in Italian, Hersilie in French, Juliette in English, the older official in medieval German literature, the son in modern. Neither of the two novellas that follow was written by the person who gives Wilhelm the manuscript (Hersilie, the younger official), but they both seem to have been collected and prepared for presentation in this circle.

This situation is a familiar one. The uncle's enclosed park, on one level the Garden of Eden, is also the *hortus conclusus* of the *Decameron*, or the estate of the baroness in the *Unterhaltungen deutscher Ausgewanderten*. In this park is a group of people determined to entertain one another by telling stories, and there is, as in Boccaccio, a principle determining the kinds of stories told. While there is no outside threat comparable to the plague or the revolution holding this group together, yet the extreme orderliness of the park contrasts strongly with the wild mountainous terrain from which the wanderers come, and it does need to be protected from the incursions of Fitz and his friends by high walls. Thus the necessary paraphernalia of the cycle of novellas in the tradition of Boccaccio are all present; indeed, two novellas are actually presented within this framework.

Yet the device is also problematic. First of all, it is developed in a most perfunctory manner: scarcely two paragraphs are devoted to the literary circle. Second, the device is never really carried out, for no stories are ever read aloud and discussed; instead, Wilhelm receives them in manuscript—one just before going to bed one night, the other on departure. Third, the device disappears entirely after these two novellas. What purpose does this manipulation serve? It is comparable, I think, to the way the expectations of the Abbé's listeners were manipulated in the *Unterhaltungen*, and it is to be seen in the context of the introductions of the other novellas. The introduction of "Sankt Joseph" as a character's life history and of the next two as part of a traditional cycle of novellas are conventional ways of making novellas parts of longer narrative forms, but not the only ones. For the other novellas Goethe plays with other ways—"Das nußbraune Mädchen" is introduced by means of documents, "Die neue Melusine" is a story told in Wilhelm's presence, "Nicht zu weit" is pieced together from a discussion, the story of the drowned boy is an autobiographical fragment. "Der Mann von funfzig Jahren" is simply inserted and justified *ex post facto* by Wilhelm's contact with the characters in it, while "Die gefährliche Wette" is introduced with the brief excuse of the narrator that it might be irrelevant if it came any later. The disappointment of the reader's expectations for a traditional cycle of novellas, and the peculiar position of Joseph's life-history at the beginning of the novel represent the same playful spirit as these last two introductions. The variety suggests a formal parallel to the variety of perspectives that has been developed as a basic philosophical standpoint of the novel.

I would like to turn now to more specific problems of technique in "Wer ist der Verräter?" The story is given Wilhelm to read by the younger official, whose introduction emphasizes the importance of the variety of perspectives offered by the different novellas. He asks, "Wer ist denn so begabt, daß er vielseitig genießen könne?" (85) and suggests himself that Wilhelm is one of these rare flexible people. Then he proceeds to characterize the story by distinguishing it from the "Pilgernde Törin": this story offers not the "Nettigkeit einer vornehm reichen französischen Verirrung" (85), but the "treue Rechtlichkeit deutscher Zustände" (85) and "der deutsche Mittelstand in seinen reinen Häuslichkeiten" (85).

In accordance with such an introduction, Lucidor, the hero of the story, is an upright, promising young man ready to cooperate cheerfully with all his elders' best intentions for him—in short, the ideal son. His heroine Lucinde matches him in more than name, for she is quiet, serious and devoted to the household. Julie, Lucinde's younger sister, and Lucidor's intended fiancée, plays the villain in this context, for she has none of Lucinde's domestic virtues. Instead she prefers the unknown and unusual: the glamorous traveller Antoni, Lucidor's "ewigen Juden," is far more to her taste than the solid, up-and-coming young Lucidor. In order to underscore her role, Goethe has Julie echo Satan's lines to Christ in Matthew 4:8 with "Nur Geduld, ich will Ihnen die Reiche der Welt und ihre Herrlichkeit zeigen" (109).

On careful examination, the reader can see that these characters are not to be judged in accordance with the young official's simplistic, bourgeois evaluation, for the narrator of "Wer ist der Verräter?" (who is not the young official) treats his characters, especially Lucidor, with some irony. For example, on the morning of the third day Lucidor is prepared to explain his perplexing situation (that he wants to marry the wrong sister) to the girls' father, only to discover that the latter has gone off on business. In the course of the day the others, in particular the old friend of the family, strongly encourage him to reveal himself. Still he does not, although the temptation to do so is so great, as the narrator comments, "daß nur ein so rein gebildeter Jüngling nicht herauszubrechen über sich gewinnen konnte" (92). The implication is that he could have spared himself and the others unnecessary pain and embarrassment, had he not been so perfect. That very evening, having just missed the perfect opportunity to do so, he decides to reveal his perplexity to the old family friend—but it is too late. Similarly, his willingness to renounce Lucinde without understanding the true circumstances (99) makes him overreact with an extremely pathetic gesture in circumstances that offer no room for pathos. As in his monologues, he takes himself too seriously for his own good.

Julie, however, to whom Lucidor reacts so negatively, is the narrator's real favorite, as she is the favorite of Lucidor's father. Her character is developed at much greater length than Lucinde's, she plays a far more important role than Lucinde in keeping their little group going. In part her value is established negatively, by lowering the idolized Lucinde to the level of the rest of them through the revelation that she, too, took her turn eavesdropping on her unduly bashful lover. Julie gains significantly in stature in her dialogue with Lucidor when she describes Lucidor's thoughts in this context: "Sie wollen sagen: diese reine, edle Seele, dieses ruhig gefaßte Wesen, die Güte, das Wohlwollen selbst, diese Frau, wie sie sein sollte [i.e. Lucinde], verbindet sich mit einer leichtsinnigen Gesellschaft, mit einer überhinfahrenden Schwester [Julie herself], einem verzogenen Jungen und gewissen geheimnisvollen Personen! das ist unbegreiflich" (112). Her ironic restatement of Lucidor's distress makes it clear to the reader that he has seen Lucinde and Julie largely through Lucidor's eyes up to this point, and that this view needs some revision.

Significantly, the final evaluation (and correction) of Lucidor in the story is placed in Julie's mouth, when she explains why she did not want to marry him:

> wenn Sie mir auch nicht gerade zuwider waren, so blieb doch der Zustand, der mich erwartete, mir keineswegs wünschenswert. Frau Oberamtmännin zu sein, welch schreckliche Lage! Einen tüchtigen, braven Mann zu haben, der den Leuten Recht sprechen soll und vor lauter Recht nicht zur Gerechtigkeit kommen kann! der es weder nach oben noch nach unten recht macht und, was das Schlimmste ist, sich selbst nicht. Ich weiß, was meine Mutter ausgestanden hat von der Unbestechlichkeit, Unerschütterlichkeit meines Vaters. Endlich, leider nach ihrem Tod, ging ihm eine gewisse Mildigkeit auf, er schien sich in die Welt zu finden, an ihr sich auszugleichen, die er sich bisher vergeblich bekämpft hatte. (111)

Julie ostensibly addresses herself here to her father's behavior, but her description applies as well (intentionally, I think) to Lucidor and his tendency to take himself too seriously. And it is perhaps ironically fitting, that Lucidor, who is otherwise so perfectly suited to succeed the *Oberamtmann*, should also be like him in his deficiencies. In reconciling himself to Julie he seems to accept this criticism; thus in the end he renounces not Lucinde, but some of that exaggerated "treue Rechtlichkeit" for which the young official seems to admire him. Like the Abbé in the *Unterhaltungen* the narrator of the story has thus misled at least one member of his audience.

Within the narrative itself there is also a playful irony which insists on the artificiality of the story.[5] The novella seems to plunge *in medias res* with Lucidor's opening monologue, but immediately after the first speech follows a four page

---

[5] Von Monroy has pointed out the dramatic structure of the novella. See E. F. von Monroy, "Zur Form der Novelle in 'Wilhelm Meisters Wanderjahren,' " *Germanisch-romanische Monatsschrift*, 31 (1943), 6.

expository digression introduced by "Dieses kurze, herzlich-leidenschaftliche Selbstgespräch aufzuklären wird es aber viele Worte kosten" (86). This interruption serves two functions: firstly, it tells the reader bluntly how to interpret the opening speech; secondly, it specifically points out that a long digression is to follow. No sooner has this exposition reached the point at which the story begins, than the narrator begins another digression, again explicitly pointing out what he is doing: "So bedrängt, erreichte er den ersten Abend sein Schlafzimmer und ergoß sich in jenem Monolog, mit dem wir begonnen haben. Um aber auch diesen zu erklären, und wie die Heftigkeit einer solchen Redefülle zu demjenigen paßt, was wir schon von ihm wissen, wird eine kurze Mitteilung nötig" (90). Later the narrator emphasizes his mediating presence again when he refers to Lucidor as "our hero" (92), where he suggests that Lucidor is too perfect for his own good. He also makes his presence felt when he follows a long direct quotation of the younger brother with the observation: "Umständlicher und naiver hatte dies der lustige Junker erzählt" (98). When he uses the same technique to spare the reader a boring passage, it verges on humor—"wie gern hätte Lucidor den guten Alten unterbrochen, wenn es sich geschickt hätte, wie es sich uns, den Erzählenden, wohl ziemen mag" (102). By the time he introduces the arrival of Antoni's carriage with the remark, "Anders war's jedoch von den launischen Göttern beschlossen" (108), the reader knows to read "Erzähler" for "Götter."

What is the function of the ironic distancing that emphasizes the fictionality of the narrative, and how is it related to the ironic distancing from the hero discussed above? It is significant in this context, that one of the examples of this distancing, the reference to "unsern Helden" (92) is also one of the places where criticism of the hero as too well-behaved is implied. The criticism of the hero presents an ironic perspective on the mistaken renunciation proposed in the story (Lucidor's renunciation of Lucinde). In the novel itself, however, renunciation is very serious indeed: for Wilhelm it was expressed as a symbolic death; in the case of Joseph it took on religious overtones. The emphasis on the fictionality of the novella tempers its ironic perspective on renunciation: since the story is *just* a story, the ironic attitude toward renunciation is not to be taken as seriously as the more sober perspective of the novel itself. The narrator of "Wer ist der Verräter?" suggests the same thing when he speaks of "echter Märchen, die den Menschen aus sich selbst hinausführen, seinen Wünschen schmeicheln und ihn jede Bedingung vergessen machen, zwischen welche wir, selbst in glücklichsten Momenten, doch immer noch eingeklemmt sind" (96). If we apply this statement to the story, we see Wilhelm, who has had to renounce Natalie, forgetting himself in the story where the hero does not have to renounce his beloved. In the context of the novel, then, the novella is but a fairy-tale, a dream-wish. The other novellas in the *Wanderjahre* that treat renunciation ironically, or where renunciation is not achieved (e.g. "Die pilgernde Törin," "Die neue Melusine") share this characteristic of "Wer ist der Verräter?"; they, too, emphasize their fictionality in ways that will be discussed. Those novellas in which renunciation is a serious problem, however, merge into the plot of the novel proper ("Das nußbraune Mädchen," "Der Mann von funfzig Jahren") or are presented as incidents in the lives of characters in the novel (Wilhelm's story of the drowned boy, "Die gefährliche Wette," "Nicht zu weit"). Thus the ironic narrative distance serves to define the relationship between the novella and the novel.[6]

The more specific relationships between this novella and the part of the novel immediately surrounding it are also interesting. The constellation of characters in "Wer ist der Verräter?" corresponds very closely to the situation on Hersilie's uncle's estate. In both cases there is a motherless family on its estate or park. There is the pair of sisters, one serious (Lucinde, Juliette), one cheerful almost to the point of frivolity (Julie, Hersilie); in both cases the latter sister receives most of the narrator's attention. There is the father or uncle who is the head of the family, and an eccentric, spoiled brother or cousin (Lenardo). Hersilie's circle consists further of the two officials, father and son; the younger official is of course the young man who gives Wilhelm the manuscript of the story and who takes it so seriously himself. Although nothing is said of a possible match, this young official clearly serves as a parallel to Lucidor and his father, then, to Lucidor's father, who is present in spirit throughout the novella, though not in fact until the end. The place of the traveller Antoni is filled by the wanderer Wilhelm, or better, the wanderers Wilhelm and Felix, with whom Hersilie indeed falls in love, although she is not clear at first with which one (as she later comments, "Ich komme mir vor wie eine unschuldige Alkemene, die von zwei Wesen, die einander vorstellen, unablässig heimgesucht wird," 265). Specific motifs of the novella also turn up in the frame. Lucidor's father and Julie study city plans and maps together; the entrance hall of the uncle's palace is decorated with maps and the main hall with prospects of cities. The uncle's collection of portraits and autographs is reminiscent of the elderly friend's historical picture gallery in the novella.

It has been shown that renunciation is seen in an ironic perspective in the novella. This perspective, too, has its corresponding attitude in the novel. It is developed in the conversation on Sunday observances in the uncle's territory that immediately precedes the novella: Juliette concludes her description of the weekly confession with "Sie sehen heraus, daß wir alle Sorgfalt anwenden, um nicht in Ihren Orden, nicht in die Gemeinschaft der Entsagenden aufgenommen zu werden" and Hersilie cockily adds, "Es ist ein sauberes Leben! wenn ich mich alle acht Tage resigniere, so hab' ich es freilich bei dreihundertfünfundsechzigen zugute" (84). Thus renunciation is not a serious problem for this circle, at least not when the novella is introduced.

But as the novel progresses renunciation turns into a serious problem for both

---

[6] Trunz has pointed out that characters who renounce move into the frame (600).

Lenardo and Hersilie; here the perspective of the novel diverges from that of the novella. In the "real" world of the novel renunciation cannot be shrugged off, as Hersilie would like to do; but in the closed fictional world of the novella the happy ending can be achieved relatively painlessly. Like the emphasis on the fictionality of the narrative, the contrasting group of characters in the frame tempers the perspective of the novella, and reiterates that renunciation is superfluous only in the world of fiction.

This theme recurs in Hersilie's speeches and letters, for in her unwillingness to be serious she sees the world around her as works of fiction. She jokes that it is fortunate that Wilhelm cannot make a long visit, because "es müßte ihm verdrießlich sein, unser Personal kennen zu lernen, es ist das ewig in Romanen und Schauspielen wiederholte" (67). As her involvement with Wilhelm becomes less comfortable and she is faced with the imminent necessity of renunciation, she begins to sense the discrepancy between her world and that of fiction, but she still cannot resist the comparison. Describing the strange figure (surely Fitz in another shape) who brings the greeting from Felix, she writes: "Allerdings etwas Geheimnisvolles war in der Figur; dergleichen sind jetzt im Roman nicht zu entbehren, sollten sie uns denn auch im Leben begegnen?" (267). Later she complains at Wilhelm's uncommunicativeness: "Mein Zustand kommt mir vor wie ein Trauerspiel des Alfieri; da die Vertrauten völlig ermangeln, so muß zuletzt alles in Monologen verhandelt werden, und fürwahr, eine Korrespondenz mit Ihnen ist einem Monolog vollkommen gleich" (319). In comparison to her first gay description of her circle as the normal novel's cast of characters, this last simile—of technique, rather than content—is a little farfetched. As Hersilie faces more serious problems, she moves further and further from her view of life as the easy fictional world of novels and plays.

In this section, then, the problems of correspondence and changing perspective have been more clearly defined and developed than in "Sankt Joseph der Zweite," where a bewildering variety of perspectives and corresponding figures was presented with no guide for the reader to evaluate them; indeed, the narrative technique seemed rather intended to prevent the reader from forming a clear idea of how to interpret the material before him. By contrast, "Wer ist der Verräter?" offers first of all a "theoretical" basis for the mirror imagery so important to the theme of correspondence. In addition, it presents the reader with only two perspectives on the situation presented, and also with ways to evaluate them relative to one another.

3. "DIE PILGERNDE TÖRIN"

I would like to go back now to "Die pilgernde Törin." This story actually appears nearer the beginning of Wilhelm's stay at the estate, but since it is an inserted translation with almost no variation from the French original, it is less directly accessible than "Wer ist der Verräter?"⁷ Indeed, one might ask why Goethe included it at all. The answer to this question provides a helpful approach to the novella.

The story is completely appropriate to Hersilie. She gives it to Wilhelm as her translation from the French, with the recommendation "wenn ich jemals närrisch werden möchte, wie mir manchmal die Lust ankommt, so wär' es auf diese Weise" (51). And it clearly displays the romantic, slightly fantastic, elements that appeal to her. The heroine is a mysterious figure who appears at the fountain as if from nowhere; she has neither train nor baggage. Although she has ostensibly travelled a long way on foot, she appears as neat and tidy as if she has just descended from her dressing room, and disappears without a trace after the denouement. One is reminded of the inexplicable appearances and disappearances of the fairy Melusine later in the novel, or of the watersprite in the original chap-book (*Die schöne Melusine*), or of the one in Musäus's "Nymphe des Brunnens," who simply materializes in human form next to the fountain she guards. This faint suggestion that the strange pilgrim is a pixie is heightened by small changes that Goethe made in the opening of the story. The most extensive change of all occurs in the description of the fountain where Revanne first sees the heroine. Goethe describes it very simply as follows:

> Hochstämmige Bäume ragen über junges, dichtes Gebüsch; man ist vor Wind und Sonne geschützt; ein sauber gefaßter Brunnen sendet seine Wasser über Wurzeln, Steine und Rasen. (51)

In the original it is

> ... une espèce de bocage où le voyageur ne peut s'empêcher de s'arrêter, l'hyver même où les arbres dépouillés offrent encore un abri contre les vents, à la fontaine qui coule entre leurs souches, encore des gasons & des eaux qui semblent rechauffer l'hyver, comme elles rafraichissent dans la belle saison. (121 f.)

The French description centers on the observing *voyageur*—the pleasure he would take in the spot, the shelter he would have from the winter wind, the warmth it would afford him in winter and the coolness in summer. Goethe reduces the element of human convenience in the description to the one impersonal statement about shelter; the grove is presented rather as a *natural* spot existing in itself, and thus more open to supernatural incursions than the highly cultivated French

---

[7] The French original appeared in H. A. O. Reichard's *Cahiers de lecture* for 1789 published in Gotha. Goethe owned a handwritten copy of the story, which varied slightly from the printed text; these variants, but not the text, are to be found in WA I, 25^2, 30–32. A microfilm of the published version was made available to me by the Nationale Forschungs- und Gedenkstätten der klassischen Literatur in Weimar. I have cited to page numbers in that version.

arbor. Another such change is that of the confusing description of the girl's face "agréablement animé par la *fatigue*" (122) to "durch *Bewegung* angenehm belebt" (52, emphasis mine). By removing the implication of a long tiring journey, this change makes the pilgrim's appearance seem more sudden and enigmatic. Like the Melusine of the chap-book, the pilgrim remains only so long as those about her keep their promise not to encroach on the secret of her existence. The younger Revanne's final conclusion, "Mademoiselle sei ein Engel, oder vielmehr ein Dämon, herumirrend in der Welt, um alle Herzen zu peinigen" (64) returns once more to this theme. The suggestion is never explicit—Revanne does not intend his statement to be understood literally—but this supernatural structure lurks just below the surface and lends the story much of its strange charm. It also, of course, emphasizes the fictionality of the narrative.

The story is so appropriate in the novel not only because it seems typical of Hersilie, but also because it touches on themes that are important elsewhere in the *Wanderjahre*. The supernatural flavor returns explicitly in "Die neue Melusine"; indeed, it is already prominent in "Sankt Joseph der Zweite" and the sections on Fitz: Revanne's "Engel oder Dämon" alternative has already appeared once in the ambiguous polarity of the angelic children of the Holy Family and Fitz, the cunning nature spirit. The second and third stanzas of the pilgrim's song toy with the theme of the Garden of Eden and the fall, which had just appeared in the penultimate paragraph preceding the novella, so that the references to paradise in the poem actually emphasize the significance of this imagery in the frame. The love of aphorisms, too, behind which the pilgrim hides her history, has already appeared as an important issue in the frame. The possible conflict of father and son in love is also involved in "Der Mann von funfzig Jahren"; indeed, the older Revanne is fifty years old, like the major in the latter story. The narrator's ruminations on the possible appeal of an older man for a young woman (60 f.) prepare the extensive concern with disparities of age that dominates the first part of "Der Mann von funfzig Jahren."

Perhaps more interesting than these thematic correspondences is the startling appropriateness of the narrative technique to Goethe's context. In its relationship to the frame it resembles "Wer ist der Verräter?": both are invented stories told by Hersilie's friends. As an avowed translation from another language it asserts an even greater distance from the frame than "Wer ist der Verräter?" The double narrator—part of the story is told by someone to whom Revanne has told it, part is direct quotation of Revanne—adds to the effect of insulation and distance, as does the stylized, symmetrical arrangement of the story around the central poem. In its perplexing combination of perspectives it is also like the "Sankt Joseph" section—the story is Revanne's description of a past event, retold by someone else, translated into German by Hersilie, read by Wilhelm. This blurring of the perspective, a condensation of the novel's basic technique, is crucial to the thematic ambiguity that comprises the basic interest of the story—namely, whether the girl's behavior is to be considered mad or too virtuous for normal comprehension.

Goethe's treatment of the story in fact intensifies and deepens the ambiguity of the original, while at the same time it shifts the view of the heroine. The French version ends with the following paragraph: "Je sens bien qu'elle n'est pas assez extravagante pour figurer parmi les folles du moment; mais, avec tant de vertus & tant d'amour pour la fidélité, je pense qu'elle peut pourtant paroitre assez folle aujourd'hui" (141). Such a satirical ending resolves the ambiguity of her actions into the typical fool motif: in her foolishness the girl has shown greater wisdom than most ladies today. Goethe eliminates it altogether, and ends with the preceding paragraph in the French, which closes with "die so flüchtig wie die Engel und so liebenswürdig erschienen war" (64). Thus the final effect is rather one of mystery than of satire, and no explicit judgment is taken as to the value of her behavior.

The extensive changes made in the central poem also increase the complexity of the situation. The ballad describes the plight of a young man hurrying almost naked through a wintry landscape. He has lost his clothes while escaping from the wily miller's daughter, who, after a night of love, has summoned her family to try to force him to marry her. It is told by the young man's scandalized fiancée; she has little sympathy for his sad state. Both versions begin with three stanzas describing the unfortunate young man, but Goethe has considerably toned down the coquettish, pointed original. The French poem fastens immediately upon the most humorous aspect of the embarrassing situation with "En manteau, manteau sans chemise" (128). The first stanza explains how he got there, and the first three are all variations on his state of undress. Goethe, by contrast, begins with a direct question: "Woher im Mantel so geschwinde" (55); the young man at first seems to merit the reader's sympathy and the comic elements are developed much less directly in the second and third stanzas. The bad weather and discomfort take precedence over the ridicule. The contrast in the rest of the poem is even greater. In the original there follow three stanzas of impotent rage at the miller's daughter and her witnesses; Goethe expands them to six describing the confrontation and escape. They express disillusionment, rather than anger; the youth appears as a warm-blooded innocent, who, in the midst of his hectic flight, still mourns, "Und ach! sie war noch immer schön" (eighth stanza). His speech is so long and so sympathetic that the reader cannot help but become involved, contrary to the intent of the outraged fiancée. The result is that the abrupt ironic shift of perspective in the last stanza, the singer's pleasure at the young man's discomfiture, grates harshly after the long sympathetic development of the youth's plight. Since the beginning and middle of the French original are much more pointed and sarcastic, there is not the same break in tone. Thus the song betrays the pilgrim in an unexpected way: she has tried to show that the youth has behaved badly, but the young man's voice takes up too much of the poem, so that he shows equally well that he was mistreated. His perspective is not properly subordinated to hers, but takes on equal weight. Both these perspectives, then, must be taken into account, as with the images in the mirror throughout the novel. After Goethe's revision it is hard to accept the girl's simple evaluation of her relationship to this young man, and hence of her strange pilgrimage.

Why does Goethe give the perspective of the faithless friend equal validity to that of the girl who has renounced all the pleasures and comforts of family life to prove the existence of true fidelity (as she implies to Revanne on p. 64)? The answer lies in the mistaken character of her renunciation. She travels about the country testing herself, to prove that under all circumstances she can remain—through sheer force of will—faithful to the friend who was unable to resist the temptations of the miller's daughter. She thus appears at the end as an apostle of fidelity and morality; she criticizes the younger Revanne and equates him to the friend of the ballad, who seeks to further the interests of his passions against the will and intention of his family. The example of the friend has shown, she maintains, that fidelity is a matter of will—"on n'est infidèle que volontairement; c'est ce que je me suis mis en tête de prouver par l'ami du moulin" (140). Here Goethe has made another small, but highly significant change in translating the passage: "Männer und Frauen sind nur mit Willen ungetreu; und das wollt' ich *dem Freunde* von der Mühle beweisen" (64—emphasis mine). She is no longer an apostle, using the friend as an example, but wants to prove a personal point to that friend. Since she acts for strictly private ends, there is no constructive purpose to her renunciation, and the suffering she causes the Revannes is gratuitous. Her friend cannot even know of the sacrifices she brings in the name of fidelity to him whom she has fled. Indeed, her withdrawal from the Revanne family circle can scarcely be called a sacrifice, since she never intended any emotional involvement with them and apparently had been involved in similar situations earlier.

Thus her renunciation is not valid in terms of the pattern established at the beginning of the novel: it is not a real sacrifice that leads to a new beginning, but rather the vanity of her exaggerated faithfulness, as the narrator half realizes toward the end of the story: "hätte sich auch der Geist durch Eitelkeit oder wirklichen Wahnsinn verirrt" (61). Like "Wer ist der Verräter?" "Die pilgernde Törin" presents an example of mistaken renunciation and therefore, it, too, is insulated from the novel as a self-contained, separate story. Furthermore it is yet again appropriate that this story should particularly appeal to Hersilie, who, as we have seen, takes a dim view of renunciation with no real understanding of it.

The rest of Book One consists of "Das nußbraune Mädchen" and Wilhelm's visit to the collector. After he leaves the estate of Hersilie's uncle Wilhelm visits Makarie, who has already been introduced in the correspondence Hersilie gave him to read, and from there he goes on to meet Lenardo in the chapter entitled "Das nußbraune Mädchen." The latter is hardly a story at all of the type presented thus far in the *Wanderjahre*, but rather a subplot, introduced in the frame and continued in letters of Wilhelm and the Abbé, and finally in selections from Lenardo's diary. It is in effect a story narrated from varying perspectives, only this time the differences in perspective are achieved by different modes of narration, rather than by intrusion of the narrator. The narrative participates in the frame's serious approach to renunciation; in his effort to renounce the cottager's daughter Lenardo throws himself into the constructive work of planning for the Turmgesellschaft's settlement in America. I would like to come back to this story—which is unusual in form even considered as a subplot—in more detail in my last chapter.

Wilhelm's last visit in Book One is to Lenardo's old friend the collector, where he deposits the mysterious *Kästchen* Felix found in chapter four. The collector is Lenardo's opposite, with a love for tradition and historical continuity contrasting with the youthful insistence on beginning everything completely from scratch that makes Lenardo so well suited for the New World settlement. This alternative to Lenardo's adventurousness is not, however, to be understood as mindless conservatism, but as an organically continuous view of history. Indeed, he ends the interview with an image of death and rebirth parallel to those at the opening of the book: "Manchmal sieht unser Schicksal aus wie ein Fruchtbaum im Winter. Wer sollte bei dem traurigen Ansehn desselben wohl denken, daß die starren Äste, diese zackigen Zweige im nächsten Frühjahr wieder grünen, blühen, sodann Früchte tragen könnten; doch wir hoffen's, wir wissen's" (148).

This cyclical structure of renunciation-rebirth reasserts itself in the other two books of the novel as well. Each begins with Wilhelm entering a different landscape which will be a new scene of action and learning for him, as the far side of the Alps was in Book One. In Book Two he and Felix enter the "Pädagogische Provinz" with its varied landscape seeking "den Obern"; the book ends (excluding the aphorisms) with Wilhelm's letter communicating his decision to study medicine and make a new beginning as a useful member of society. The beginning of Book Three finds Wilhelm on his way to rejoin his friends in a gentle, fruitful landscape. Like those at the beginnings of the other books, it is symbolic. It represents not a point of radical departure—death and new beginning —like the mountain pass, nor a place to seek instructors to point to a single way amidst all the variety, as in the pedagogic province, but a state of harmony and complete cultivation: "nirgends [war] etwas Steiles, Unfruchtbares und Ungepflügtes zu sehen" (310). Wilhelm, now trained in his chosen profession, is ready to begin a useful life. The book ends with his first public application of his accomplishment, the rescue of his son from the river. The final tableau of death and rebirth represents the ultimate metamorphosis of renunciation, and its absorption into history.

4. "DER MANN VON FUNFZIG JAHREN"

"Der Mann von funfzig Jahren," which is told in chapters three, four, five and seven of Book Two, may be said to occupy the central position in the novel. In fact, it represents a turning point in the novel, since it begins as a real novella, but ends in the frame late in Book Three. More important, it is the last of the inserted stories actually to conclude with a happy ending (although a happy ending is more or less promised, it is not actually consummated in "Das nußbraune Mädchen"). The unique position of this story leads, as will be shown, to seeming narrative inconsistencies and peculiarities which have offended some critics who otherwise—with justice—consider it one of Goethe's great narrative achievements.

The introduction to the story is the first of these problems. Thus far, all the novellas have been motivated in some way, but this one has only the abrupt introduction:

> Der Angewöhnung des werten Publikums zu schmeicheln, welches seit geraumer Zeit Gefallen findet, sich stückweise unterhalten zu lassen, gedachten wir erst, nachstehende Erzählung in mehreren Abteilungen vorzulegen. Der innere Zusammenhang jedoch, nach Gesinnungen, Empfindungen und Ereignissen betrachtet, veranlaßte einen fortlaufenden Vortrag. Möge derselbe seinen Zweck erreichen und zugleich am Ende deutlich werden, wie die Personen dieser abgesondert scheinenden Begebenheit mit denjenigen, die wir schon kennen und lieben, aufs innigste zusammengeflochten worden. (167)

In the context of the novel the tone is shocking for its excessive dryness and formality—especially the pompous sonority of "Möge derselbe seinen Zweck erreichen." Moreover, the statement is actually quite misleading. As it turns out, the story is in fact presented "stückweise." Furthermore, the introduction implies that the mode of relationship to the novel will be surprising and will perhaps need to be explained (suggested by "Möge . . . deutlich werden"); but neither is the case, for the two sets of characters simply have a common friend in Makarie.

That the passage is consciously ironic, and not a botched result of Goethe's hurry to get his miscellaneous papers into print is corroborated by the first version of the novel, where Hersilie sends Wilhelm the story. The introduction there is an elegantly playful letter from Hersilie complaining that Wilhelm has sent no interesting particulars in his letter about the "nut-brown maid," whom he has finally located. In revenge, she tries to do the same to him in her introduction of her two friends, Hilarie and the widow, whom she brings up as follows:

> Damit Sie aber meinen guten Willen gegen Sie recht deutlich erkennen, so vertrau ich Ihnen, daß zwei allerliebste Wesen unterwegs sind; woher sag ich nicht, wohin auch nicht; zu beschreiben sind sie nicht, und ein Lob erreicht sie

nicht . . . Ich wünschte doch wohl Sie drei Tage zwischen die beiden Herrlichkeiten eingeklemmt zu sehen, am Morgen des vierten würde Ihnen Ihr strenges Gelübde [to stay only three days in one place] gar sehr zustatten kommen.

Zu einigem Vorschmack sende eine Geschichte, die sich einigermaßen auf die beiden bezieht. Was daran wahr oder erdichtet ist, suchen Sie selbst von ihnen zu erfahren. (PA XXXIV, 70)

The first third of the novella follows (chapters four and five were not written until 1823), then comes a substantial postscript, beginning "Hier brech ich ab, teils weil ich gegenwärtig nicht weiter schreiben kann, teils aber um Ihnen ein Stachel ins Herz zu senken" (PA XXXIV, 87). There follows a series of tantalizing questions about the gap between the end of the story thus far, where Hilarie and the widow both seem on the verge of happy marriages, and the Lago Maggiore adventure, where the two of them, now clearly "Entsagende," are travelling together in Italy (chapter twelve in the first version, seven in the second). Since the tantalizing tone of the introduction to the novella is already present in the first version, it seems clear that it is intentional in the second.

The real change between the two versions is in the story's relationship to the frame. The first version presents it from the beginning as part of the plot of the novel—the characters are friends of Hersilie whom Wilhelm is to visit—rather than as an inserted novella. The initial disengagement of the novella from the novel in the second version is puzzling at first, but the course of the discussion will show that it is a necessary consequence of the changed conception of the story in the continuation for the second version.

Differences in technique between chapter three, which was written in the summer of 1807, and the following two chapters (summer 1823) might seem at first due simply to this time lag. Yet is is absurd not to accept these differences as deliberate; Goethe clearly could have recast the first part in the style of the second, as he did the introduction, had he so chosen. Therefore my interpretation will be based on the premise that the discrepancies are significant and interpretable.

The novella begins in the precise, concrete style of *Die Wahlverwandtschaften* —Hilarie's love for her uncle, the major's sudden interest in preserving his youth, the son's involvement with the young widow are all developed with a minimum of interference and commentary from the narrator, apart from the general passage on ladies' needlework (184), which was inserted in the second version to motivate the conversation at the beginning of chapter four. In the course of the next two chapters (four and five) the narrator has more and more to say to his readers directly, and his interference takes on several different forms.

In these chapters the action proceeds not so much through precisely described scenes in which the speeches and actions of the characters further the plot, but rather through summarizing narrative and broad analysis of motives and emotional developments. The courtship of Hilarie and Flavio following Flavio's recovery consists largely in a summary of repeated events; the narrator even makes fun of this undramatic treatment when he describes the mission of mercy the two make in the boat:

> wir wollen gern bekennen, in dem Laufe, wie diese Begebenheit uns bekannt geworden, einigermaßen besorgt gewesen zu sein, es möge hier einige Gefahr obschweben, ein Stranden, ein Umschlagen des Kahns, Lebensgefahr der Schönen, kühne Rettung von seiten des Jünglings, um das lose geknüpfte Band noch fester zu ziehen. Aber von allem diesem war nicht die Rede. (211)

Finally he gives up all pretense to a dramatic presentation: "Unsere Leser überzeugen sich wohl, daß von diesem Punkte an wir beim Vortrag unserer Geschichte nicht mehr darstellend, sondern erzählend und betrachtend verfahren müssen, wenn wir in die Gemütszustände, auf welche jetzt alles ankommt, eindringen und sie uns vergegenwärtigen wollen" (215). In accordance with this broader technique, the narrator allows himself brief commentaries on behavior, like "was der Mund *weislich* verschwieg" (213, emphasis mine), and digressions, like the one on the beneficial effects of ice-skating (213). Such digressions may be quite abruptly introduced, like the one on women, which begins, "Wir machen bei dieser Gelegenheit folgende Bemerkung" (193). Transitions between parts of the story also suffer, as evidenced by the many small horizontal lines separating parts of the narrative from one another. The language itself is used more broadly —concrete precision yields for long stretches to ironically inflated circumlocutions, as the supporting quotations in my next paragraph show.

The narrator also loosens the fabric of the novella by pleading lack of space, lack of knowledge or simply severe difficulty of expression. Only one of the major's many Horace translations is offered as a sample (196), a later poem is given quickly in prose paraphrase (218). Similarly only a small sample of the verse exchanged between Hilarie and Flavio is included, with the pious wish, "und vielleicht ist es uns vergönnt, den ganzen Verlauf dieser holden Kur gelegentlich mitzuteilen" (207). People's feelings on the night of Flavio's arrival are not presented because of supposed lack of knowledge: "Wie diese guten, alles Anteils würdigen Personen ihre nächtlichen Stunden zugebracht, ist uns ein Geheimnis geblieben" (204). Over and over the narrator emphasizes the delicacy of treatment the events demand:

> Wer unternähme es wohl, die aus dem Vorhergehenden sich entwickelnden Zustände zu enthüllen, an den Tag zu bringen das innere, aus dieser ersten Zusammenkunft den Frauen erwachsende Unheil? (205)

> Nun aber wünschten wir wohl den nächsten Zeitverlauf von einer zarten Frauenhand umständlich geschildert zu sehen, da wir nach eigener Art und Weise uns nur mit dem Allgemeinsten befassen dürfen. (208)

> Eine Szene, wie dies zugegangen, wagten wir nicht zu schildern, aus Furcht, hier möchte uns die jugendliche Glut ermangeln. (209)

> Auszumalen ist nicht die innere Gestalt der drei nunmehr nächtlich auf der glatten Fläche im Mondschein Verirrten, Verwirrten. (214)

> ... das wir mit Worten auszuführen nicht unternehmen. (220)

The reader is thus continually aware of the narrator both as an editorial presence and as a commentator of limited capability.

Most important of all, an element of gentle irony and humor enters into the treatment of the characters, especially of their various poetic talents. The major appears a little ridiculous in his sensitivity to all the possible implications of the Ovid passage he wants to send as a compliment to the widow, and the narrator clearly enjoys his discomfiture:

> Das Schlimmste jedoch fiel ihm zuletzt ein: jene Ovidischen Verse werden von Arachnen gesagt, einer ebenso geschickten als hübschen und zierlichen Weberin. Wurde nun aber diese durch die neidische Minerva in eine Spinne verwandelt, so war es gefährlich, eine schöne Frau, mit einer Spinne, wenn auch nur von ferne, verglichen, im Mittelpunkte eines ausgebreiteten Netzes schweben zu sehen. Konnte man sich doch unter der geistreichen Gesellschaft, welche unsre Dame umgab, einen Gelehrten denken, welcher diese Nachbildung ausgewittert hätte. Wie sich nun der Freund aus einer solchen Verlegenheit gezogen, ist uns selbst unbekannt geblieben, und wir müssen diesen Fall unter diejenigen rechnen, über welche die Musen auch wohl einen Schleier zu werfen sich die Schalkheit erlauben. (198)

The humor of this passage lies not only in the extreme sensitivity of the major and the narrator's attitude toward it, but also in the accuracy of the inadvertent comparison of the widow to a spider waiting to trap the unwary. The major would like to see poetry as a social mask, but instead poetry shows him more of the truth than he would like to see. Surely there is irony, too, in the decision not to bother with the poetic execution of the major's poem (paraphrased on 218). Flavio, the son, is taken even less seriously as a poet. The reader is informed of his interest in an ironic circumlocution, "der Sohn, der selbst auf den Ehrentitel eines Dichters seine Absichten nicht verbarg" (189 f.), and sees even less of Flavio's poetry than of his father's. As in the case of the major's poem, so, too, when Flavio's and Hilarie's poems are left out, there is the implication that the reader would not find them terribly interesting. The statement, "Ein gewisses Talent konnte man unserm Flavio nicht absprechen . . ." (208), is sufficiently faint praise to suggest its opposite. In "Wer ist der Verräter?" the narrator's emphasis on the fictionality of the narrative led to an ironic interpretation of the novella. Here, too, the presence of the narrator should alert the reader to possible shifts in perspective. The humorous treatment of the poets in the story already suggests one possible shift in attitude toward the characters, while the treatment of the widow, who gains considerably in stature in the last few pages of chapter five, is another.

After chapter five Wilhelm's letters briefly interrupt the narrative. The tense unhappy situation brought about by Hilarie's determined renunciation yields to the satisfaction derived from practical hard work in chapter six. Wilhelm's description of the circumstances in which he finds the "nut-brown maid" moves the reader from the social chaos in Hilarie's family to a hard working family of artisans in harmony with itself and its surroundings. What greater contrast to the confused affairs of the noble family than Wilhelm's description, "Häuslicher Zustand, auf Frömmigkeit gegründet, durch Fleiß und Ordnung belebt und erhalten, nicht zu eng, nicht zu weit, im glücklichsten Verhältnis der Pflichten zu den Fähigkeiten und Kräften" (225)? The chapter continues with a statement of Wilhelm's own intentions to devote himself steadily to one useful activity, and thus heightens the contrast to the major's disrupted plans for improving the family estate.

The next chapter picks up the thread of the novella again, but under completely new circumstances. Wilhelm makes a pilgrimage to Mignon's ancestral home on Lago Maggiore, where he travels with an artist who paints Mignon in the scenes of her youth. The two of them spend several days there with Hilarie and the young widow, who are traveling to recuperate from the emotional crises of chapter five. With these new circumstances, the story moves off in a new direction.

The tone of the narrative is strikingly different from the preceding parts. Both the concise, objective narration and the dry circumlocutions disappear in the evocation of an unreal, romantically detached atmosphere. Narrative and description are rarely concrete. More common are passages like: "Einige Tage wurden so auf diese eigene Weise zwischen Begegnen und Scheiden, zwischen Trennen und Zusammensein hingebracht; im Genuß vergnüglichester Geselligkeit schwebte immer Entfernen und Entbehren vor der bewegten Seele. In Gegenwart der neuen Freunde rief man sich die ältern zurück" (233). The reader receives very little specific information about the setting or rationale for the action—the journey is introduced in chapter six only as a "fromme Wallfahrt" (226), the setting first appears as "die herrliche Talgegend ... wo er, vor Beginn eines neuen Lebensganges, so manches abzuschließen gedachte" (226). The proper name of the area is never used, and the description of it fades rapidly into a description of the paintings; only after two pages is the palace of the marquis mentioned so that the reader can be sure of the object of Wilhelm's pilgrimage.

The detached impression is heightened by the frank admission of a fictional world into the novel. The painter is openly acknowledged as a piece of romantic machinery when he is introduced: "[Wilhelm] findet sich mit einem Maler zusammen, welcher, wie dergleichen viele in der offnen Welt, mehrere noch in Romanen und Dramen umherwandeln und spuken, sich diesmal als ein ausgezeichneter Künstler darstellte" (226). Even more striking is the admission of the *Lehrjahre* not as Wilhelm's history, but as a published novel. One cannot overlook the delightful irony of the situation when Wilhelm fills in details in the figures the painter has portrayed from the novel, although the events of the novel have taken place so recently that the marquis has not yet returned from the visit to Germany reported at the end of the *Lehrjahre*.

Not only is the novel *qua* novel admitted, but precisely the most romantic element of the novel—Mignon—is the focus. Mignon, as a strange being from another world, interests the painter most in the *Lehrjahre;* she is the subject of his paintings, and, in a sense, the center of the chapter. The landscape is presented as Mignon's background. The pictures described portray situations referred to in the *Lehrjahre;* the language of the descriptions is often familiar. The first one, "Unter dem hohen Säulenportale des herrlichen Landhauses stand sie, nachdenklich die Statuen der Vorhalle betrachtend" (227), is a reminiscence of the second stanza of "Kennst du das Land":

> Kennst du das Haus? auf Säulen ruht sein Dach,
> Es glänzt der Saal, es schimmert das Gemach,
> Und Marmorbilder stehn und sehn mich an. (HA VII, 145)

The description of the painter's fourth picture, the wild mountain scene with its waterfalls, gypsy mules and cave, is based on the last stanza of the same poem:

> Kennst du den Berg und seinen Wolkensteg?
> Das Maultier sucht im Nebel seinen Weg,
> In Höhlen wohnt der Drachen alte Brut,
> Es stürzt der Fels und über ihn die Flut. (HA VII, 145)

The conclusion of the description, "Auch ließ der Künstler mit klugdichtendem Wahrheitssinne eine Höhle merklich werden, die man als Naturwerkstatt mächtiger Kristalle oder als Aufenthalt einer fabelhaft-furchtbaren Drachenbrut ansprechen konnte" (228), is not simply a reminiscence of the poem, but a real travesty which ironically emphasizes the distance between Mignon's world and the world of the *Wanderjahre* at the moment they are seemingly joined. Such irony contributes, of course, to the unreality of the chapter.

"Kennst du das Land" is used to continue this feeling throughout the chapter. The first stanza is evoked in a description of the landscape through which Wilhelm and the painter travel.

> Kennst du das Land, wo die Zitronen blühn,
> Im dunkeln Laub, die Goldorangen glühn,
> Ein sanfter Wind vom blauen Himmel weht,
> Die Myrte still, und hoch der Lorbeer steht. (HA VII, 145)

und nun konnten sie sich eines traurigen Lächelns nicht enthalten, wenn sie, unter Zypressen gelagert, den Lorbeer aufsteigen, den Granatapfel sich röten,

Orangen und Zitronen in Blüte sich entfalten und Früchte zugleich aus dem dunklen Laube hervorglühend erblickten. (229)

The outrageous recollection of "glühn" in "hervorglühend" is again a travesty, but the sad smile shows that even Wilhelm and the painter sense the irony of their position, for they have fallen right into the poem. Thus it is no surprise that the poem is finally articulated (the painter begins to sing it) toward the end of the episode (239), and that its articulation precipitates the sentimental climax.[8]

But these references are not the only distancing technique used in this chapter. As it approaches its climax, when the four friends land together on the island, the painter shows his work to the other three. When they praise it, the narrator suddenly interrupts, "Damit wir aber nicht in Verdacht geraten, als wollten wir mit allgemeinen Phrasen dasjenige, was wir nicht vorzeigen können, gläubigen Lesern nur unterschieben, so stehe hier das Urteil eines Kenners, der bei jenen fraglichen sowohl als gleichen und ähnlichen Arbeiten mehrere Jahre nachher bewundernd verweilte" (235). He thus deliberately suggests that the narrative to this point may well have seemed in need of support. There follows then a page and a half of dry repetitive praise of details, concluding with a brief disquisition by the narrator on the term "Wildheuer." Amusingly enough, the "expert" contradicts something the narrator has already said, for he does not find the high mountain scenes as good as the other pictures, while the narrator picks out the high mountain scene as the best (227). This exaggeratedly sober view of the painter serves as a foil to the strange and romantic atmosphere of the rest of the chapter.

The two letters at the end from Lenardo and the Abbé also emphasize the tone of the chapter, for they return to the busy tone of the American project. Together with chapter six they provide a contrasting practical frame to set off the romantic re-evocation of Mignon and her world.

With this new tone, the novella takes quite a different turn. At the end of chapter five the story had reached an impasse, because Hilarie could not bear to transfer her affection so easily from father to son, and because the widow could not commit herself to a new man. Yet in chapter seven they reappear in an atmosphere ironically supercharged with emotion and eroticism. The question of erotic involvement enters as soon as Wilhelm and the painter catch sight of the ladies' boat: "so sahen sie ein wohlverziertes Prachtschiff herangleiten, worauf sie *Jagd machten* und sich nicht enthielten sogleich *leidenschaftlich* zu entern" (230, emphasis mine). This situation is immediately pronounced dangerous (231), and self-control already needs additional support, for the narrator remarks with almost malicious humor: "Hier war nun Wilhelms Gelübde ein schicklicher,

---

[8] Heidi Gidion remarks in passing, but does not discuss, the presence of images from "Kennst du das Land" in this chapter. *Zur Darstellungsweise von Goethes "Wilhelm Meisters Wanderjahren"* (Göttingen, 1969), p. 123. So also O. Seidlin in "Zur Mignon-Ballade," *Von Goethe zu Thomas Mann: Zwölf Versuche* (Göttingen, 1963), p. 34 and note thereto.

aber unbequemer Zeremonienmeister" (231—the friends cannot follow the ladies on shore for the night, since Wilhelm has already spent his three days there). The attraction between the two pairs increases steadily; it is finally interrupted (partly, too, for the sake of suspense) shortly before the climax by the critical essay on the painter. Hilarie recovers her emotional equilibrium by submerging herself in art with the painter—a pattern reminiscent of the *Unterhaltungen*.[9] The recovery is of course slightly compromised since it is not clear how much is due to the painting and how much to the painter.

On their last evening together the narrative reaches a climax. The painter can no longer contain himself and begins to sing "Kennst du das Land." In the one line which he sings, the unarticulated emotion that has pervaded the chapter surfaces, and all are overcome: "Die Frauen warfen sich einander in die Arme, die Männer umhalsten sich, und Luna ward Zeuge der edelsten, keuschesten Tränen. Einige Besinnung kehrte langsam erst zurück, man zog sich auseinander, schweigend, unter seltsamen Gefühlen und Wünschen, denen doch die Hoffnung schon abgeschnitten war" (239 f.). The passage contains all the elements of the familiar passage in *Werther* where Werther and Lotte stand together at the window after the thunderstorm:

> Sie sah gen Himmel und auf mich, ich sah ihr Auge tränenvoll, sie legte ihre Hand auf die meinige und sagte: "Klopstock!"—Ich erinnerte mich sogleich der herrlichen Ode, die ihr in Gedanken lag, und versank in dem Strome von Empfindungen, den sie in dieser Losung über mich ausgoß. Ich ertrug's nicht, neigte mich auf ihre Hand und küßte sie unter den wonnevollsten Tränen. (HA VI, 27)

The use of the Latin form "Luna" and the superlatives in the same clause bring out the ironic undertone, as does the reminiscence of a passage from *Werther* in a chapter already full of references to another earlier work.[10] The disappointment of the two friends on the following day is heavily exaggerated, as the narrator's almost baroque description clearly shows: "Kein *selbstsüchtiger Hypochondrist* würde so scharf und *scheelsüchtig* den *V*erfall der Gebäude, die *V*ernachlässigung der Mauern, das *V*erwittern der Türme, den Grasüberzug der Gänge, das Aussterben der Bäume, das *vermoosende Vermodern* der Kunstgrotten, und was noch alles dergleichen zu bemerken wäre, gerügt und gescholten haben" (240, emphasis mine).

What is actually at issue in this chapter? In terms of the novella, Hilarie overcomes her refusal to enter into another emotional involvement (with Flavio).

---

[9] There the Abbé's novellas calm the group troubled by the revolution. This theme is developed at some length in the *Campagne in Frankreich* (1822) where Goethe concludes his description of the campaign with a long discussion of his artistic endeavors in the following winter.

[10] Max Wundt reads this passage as parody of Jean Paul; *Goethes Wilhelm Meister und die Entwicklung des modernen Lebensideals* (Berlin and Leipzig, 1913), p. 481. Jean Paul would be equally appropriate here.

This refusal was based on her unwillingness to be frivolous and her horror at the ease with which her love could be transferred from one man to another. Her "cure" comes about through the good offices of the artist, but their relationship must end in renunciation, which is easier for Hilarie only because she has previous experience. All of this is seen ironically, and in a heavily erotic, unreal atmosphere, set against the background of the *Lehrjahre*, a novel in which faithlessness is the dominant moral code.[11] Hilarie's dramatic renunciation at the end of chapter five appears in a new light when viewed in the perspective of her relation to Wilhelm and the painter instead of to the major and Flavio. It now appears less the unquestionable dictate of a sensitive heart than adolescent immaturity embracing a dramatic role.

The ultimate dispensation of these characters supports such an interpretation. In the summarizing fourteenth chapter of Book Three they all appear at Makarie's castle in a storybook happy ending: the major has married the widow, Hilarie has married Flavio. Yet the tone—particularly toward Hilarie and Flavio—is cruelly ironic. Flavio, whose poetic talent received gentle irony earlier, appears as the passionate occasional rhymster who, with Makarie's reluctant consent, bores the company with a lengthy rendition of what everyone already knows and feels. The major, by contrast, recommends himself with his didactic poetic talents. The treatment of Hilarie is even more outrageous:

> Hilarie kam mit ihrem Gatten, der nun als Hauptmann und entschieden reicher Gutsbesitzer auftrat. Sie in ihrer großen Anmut und Liebenswürdigkeit gewann sich hier wie überall gar gern Verzeihung einer allzugroßen Leichtigkeit, von Interesse zu Interesse übergehend zu wechseln, deren wir sie im Lauf der Erzählung schuldig gefunden. Besonders die Männer rechneten es ihr nicht hoch an. Einen dergleichen Fehler, wenn es einer ist, finden sie nicht anstößig, weil ein jeder wünschen und hoffen mag, auch an die Reihe zu kommen. (437)

The passage seems intended to tease readers who still adhere to the view of her behavior presented in chapter five. It should not, however, seem shocking, for the ironic treatment in chapter seven anticipates this critical attitude.[12] The accusation of frivolity has been prepared not only by the events of chapter seven, but also

---

[11] This statement is not intended in a negative sense, but simply as a description of the fact that men move from woman to woman in the novel. It is surely no coincidence that the name of the character Wilhelm admires most, Lothario, is, since Nicholas Rowe's *The Fair Penitent* of 1703, a synonym in English for "seducer." The violent reaction of the Victorians to the *Lehrjahre* testifies to the importance of this aspect of the novel. Thackeray considered it "without delicacy" and "mean"; even George Eliot, one of Goethe's staunchest defenders, conceded that English readers might find the novel shocking and immoral. See L. H. C. Thomas, "Germany, German Literature and mid-nineteenth century British novelists," *Affinities: Essays in German and English Literature*, ed. R. W. Last (London, 1971), pp. 34–51.

[12] Staiger, for example, although he recognizes the importance of changing perspectives in the novel, still finds this shift offensive and uses it as the basis for an argument against the artistic unity of the novel (*Goethe*, III, 133 f.).

by the motif of floating and swaying which runs through the story. It is first developed at length in the ice-skating section of chapter five: "man bewegte sich lustig und lustiger, bald zusammen, bald einzeln, bald getrennt, bald vereint. Scheiden und Meiden, was sonst so schwer aufs Herz fällt, ward hier zum kleinen, scherzhaften Frevel, man floh sich, um sich einander augenblicks wieder zu finden" (212). On the following page, as Flavio and Hilarie skate hand in hand, they cannot bring themselves to return to the castle; they repeatedly approach and move away again. At the crisis, just before the widow appears, all the characters are in a similar suspended state, awaiting Hilarie's decision. The major's state of mind is described with the words, "Ein solches Wanken und Schweben bewegte sich vor den Augen seines Geistes" (222), and this state drives the normally active man to desperation. The Lago Maggiore scenes are full of this motif—Wilhelm and the painter float back and forth on the lake visiting the different spots, they sail back and forth watching for the arrival of the ladies, whom they accompany back and forth once more. Their time together is summarized:

> Einige Tage wurden so auf diese eigene Weise zwischen Begegnen und Scheiden, zwischen Trennen und Zusammensein hingebracht; im Genuß vergnüglichster Geselligkeit schwebte immer Entfernen und Entbehren vor der bewegten Seele . . .
> So abwechselnd hin und wieder geschaukelt, angezogen und abgelehnt, genähert, wallten und wogten sie verschiedene Tage. (233)

When they finally all set foot on dry land together, it is only to part definitively. Thus "Schwanken und Schweben" are Hilarie's element, and the accusation of frivolity in love is really only a new side of that element.

All of the material belonging to "Der Mann von funfzig Jahren" taken together confronts the reader with a game of narrative hide-and-seek. In the first section the narrator presents a serious family problem involving renunciation much in the style of *Die Wahlverwandtschaften*. At this point the story enters the mainstream of the novel, in accordance with the principle that has been observed at work in the opposite direction in "Wer ist der Verräter?" and "Die pilgernde Törin," where non-serious views of renunciation kept the stories separate from the frame. Yet at the same time that the story enters the novel, it also appears in a new perspective—one which sees love and change as more normal, less dramatic processes (this point of view is also suggested by the "faithlessness" of the *Lehrjahre*). In this perspective Hilarie's stubborn renunciation looks mistaken and barren; accordingly, the story, although part of the novel proper, is separated out and made to seem unreal. The more the plot becomes involved with the plot of the novel, the heavier the undercutting and the more the characters are playfully forced back into a fictional world. Probably it was in keeping with this decision to keep the story separate from the novel that Goethe changed the introduction from one showing its involvement with the plot to one that anticipated the ambivalent relationship between the two.

This relationship is also reflected in the relationship between Hilarie and Hersilie. Since these two were presented as friends in the first version of the novel, the phonetic similarity in their names cannot be overlooked. Hilarie comes from the Latin *hilaris* meaning cheerful, gay, blithe, merry; Hersilie was the devoted wife of Romulus and shared his apotheosis, becoming the goddess Hora.[13] At first glance the names seem mixed up. Hersilie is the cheerful, merry one, and Hilarie has cast herself in the role of the devoted wife of a noble man. Yet by the end of the story Hilarie has grown into her name, for she has become the charming, delightful lady who is easily forgiven a little frivolity. Hersilie, by contrast, in her confused devotion to Wilhelm and Felix, becomes increasingly aware of the seriousness of human relationships. Late in the novel she writes to Wilhelm:

> wenn Sie eine Art von Herz und Gemüt haben, so denken Sie, wie mir zumute ist, wie viele Leidenschaften sich in mir herumkämpfen, wie ich Sie herwünsche, auch wohl Felix dazu, daß es ein Ende werde, wenigstens daß eine Deutung vorgehe, was damit gemeint sei, mit diesem wunderbaren Finden, Wiederfinden, Trennen und Vereinigen; und sollte ich auch nicht aus aller Verlegenheit gerettet werden, so wünsche ich wenigstens sehnlichst, daß diese sich aufkläre, sich endige, wenn mir auch, wie ich fürchte, etwas Schlimmeres begegnen sollte. (378)

Hersilie finds herself in a familiar state—"Finden, Wiederfinden, Trennen und Vereinigen." It is, of course, that state just seen associated with Hilarie. Significantly, Hersilie, who once would cheerfully take the opposite side in any argument, can no longer bear such a "floating," undecided state, but rejects the position which becomes increasingly identified with Hilarie. Thus in the course of the novel the two cross paths; each moves from the other's name to fulfill the promise of her own name, repeating once more the structural chiasmus of the novella.

The position of the novella in the novel, then, is a more complicated problem than it originally seemed. Its relationship to the frame is chiastic: the first part, although set off as a novella, moves toward the frame by presenting a serious problem involving renunciation; but the second part, now in the frame, moves back into an enclosed fictional world by means of irony and literary parody. In this symmetrical crossing of real and fictional worlds around the problem of renunciation the story is a central turning point and properly occupies the physical center of the novel.

5. MAKARIE AND THE IMAGERY OF MEDIATION

Sudden shifts of perspective which undercut seemingly definitive points of view are by no means confined to the novellas in their relationship to the novel,

---

[13] Ovid, *Metamorphoses*, XIV, ll. 830 ff.

but also occur within the frame. Two such cases are particularly important for understanding the technique of the novel; they are the treatment of Hersilie's aunt Makarie and the scattered discussion of aphorisms.

The "Makarie myth" has been one of the parts of the novel that has attracted the most serious interpretation and perhaps the most agreement. Although it is not my purpose here to disprove the serious or positive interpretations of Makarie and her functions in the novel, I think they are one-sided.[14] Like many interpretations of the *Unterhaltungen* and the "Märchen" they isolate themselves too much from the often contradictory context of the novel. I wish to emphasize here the alternative, ironic view of the figure. While Makarie on the one hand appears to be one of the most sublime examples of Goethe's myth-making,[15] on the other hand it can be shown that this sublimity is repeatedly undercut and corrected. Ultimately Makarie is, I think, not the favored alternative of the many presented in the *Wanderjahre*.

The entry into Makarie's realm where Wilhelm and Felix go from the estate of Hersilie's uncle, reads just like a medieval romance beginning with a mysterious, unexplained landscape pregnant with allegorical significance. When they arrive at the walls of the park, their guide indicates—the word is "bedeutete," rather than "said" or "explained," for nothing is explained in Makarie's world—that no horses are permitted in the park. Horses, representing passion that must be tamed, are naturally excluded from the realm of the wise one. They proceed on foot to the castle surrounded by venerable old trees. There they discover to their surprise that, though seemingly ancient, it is completely unblemished. Doors fly open of themselves as soon as Felix rings, and they are greeted by a singing portress. Upstairs, in the hall decorated with chivalric pictures and massive oak furniture—which, incidentally, place the preceding inexplicable details into their proper literary context for the reader who has not already discovered their romance origin—they are greeted by a sort of Merlin figure, who is both court astronomer and physician, as well as friend and advisor. Also present is Makarie's companion Angela, who, as her name suggests, is a divine messenger delivering Makarie's communications to posterity through her secretarial work in their archive, as well as an angel in the more colloquial use of the word. This medievalizing presents an extravagant contrast to the extreme rationality of the uncle's estate.

Other elements beside the trappings of medieval romance contribute to the underlying playfulness of the chapter. Suddenly, at one end of the room, a green curtain goes up, revealing Makarie in her armchair, which is then pushed forward,

---

[14] E.g. Staiger, *Goethe*, III, 176 f., and Trunz's extensive commentary in HA VIII, 630–44 and 710–15.

[15] Georg-Karl Bauer in "Makarie," GRM 25 (1937), 178–97, compares her to a Platonic myth, for example.

so that the group can breakfast together. This scene is a deliberate reference to the end of Book Seven of the *Lehrjahre*, where Wilhelm is introduced to the tower, and it partakes of the paradoxical quality of that scene. In both scenes a mystifying theatricality undercuts a situation that is supposed to be dealing with the most genuine elements of human existence. Even without the reference to the *Lehrjahre* there is something so extravagant in the gesture of the rising curtain and the revelation of the precious invalid—one is reminded of Anfortas in *Parzival*—that it cannot be taken quite seriously. The romantic element is still further heightened in Wilhelm's vision of Makarie's apotheosis. The motif of the rising curtain once more occurs, followed by a truly baroque vision of the holy virgin rising to heaven on a mass of billowing clouds. Following this, one scarcely knows what to think when Angela informs Wilhelm in great secrecy that, fantastic as it may seem, Makarie is spiritually an integral part of the solar system.

The bubble of the romance is pricked when the group settles down after breakfast to read aloud an abstruse mathematical treatise. Felix has already become bored with the whole situation and has to be taken away. As soon as the astronomer begins to read, the narrator interrupts with the same ironic politeness that characterizes the later parts of "Der Mann von funfzig Jahren":

> Wenn wir uns aber bewogen finden, diesen werten Mann nicht lesen zu lassen, so werden es unsere Gönner wahrscheinlich geneigt aufnehmen, denn was oben gegen das Verweilen Wilhelms bei dieser Unterhaltung gesagt worden, gilt noch mehr in dem Falle, in welchem wir uns befinden, unsere Freunde haben einen Roman in die Hand genommen, und wenn dieser hie und da schon mehr als billig didaktisch geworden, so finden wir doch geraten, die Geduld unserer Wohlwollenden nicht noch weiter auf die Probe zu stellen. Die Papiere, die uns vorliegen, gedenken wir an einem andern Orte abdrucken zu lassen und fahren diesmal im Geschichtlichen ohne weiteres fort, da wir selbst ungeduldig sind, das obwaltende Rätsel endlich aufgeklärt zu sehen. (118)

He thus emphasizes the disparity between the riddling romance and the implied pedantry of Makarie's circle.

Makarie's bad health, or feigned bad health, recalls the "schöne Seele" of the *Lehrjahre*, whose preoccupation with her soul (of which her poor health is a symptom) prevents her from contributing constructively to the lives of those around her. Makarie is indeed the same figure "in geisterhaft phantastisch gesteigerter Form," as Erich Franz states it.[16] Franz also suggests that ill-health is a symptom of unbalance between the earthly and spiritual parts of man's being and that the girl who can divine what is beneath the earth is provided as an opposite pole to Makarie's extreme spirituality. The need for the union of the two is expressed in the growing friendship between the astronomer and Jarno-

---

[16] Erich Franz, *Goethe als religiöser Denker* (Tübingen, 1932), p. 169.

Montan, the two men who mediate between these extreme women and the rest of the world.

When Makarie reappears at the end of Book Three, the irony is much more open. After Hilarie and Flavio appear in all their banality, Makarie's function as sensitive mediator is also flattened into the prosaic. The reformed loose woman of the *Lehrjahre*, Philine, proves an unwelcome embarrassment to Makarie, although she is the sort one might expect Makarie to help. Indeed there is a similarity be- between Philine and the young widow, for both are coquettes. The highly emotional Lydie has a hysterical conversion at Makarie's feet while the old lady helplessly pats her on the shoulder. At just the proper moment Jarno-Montan, who, as the narrator informs us confidentially, has loved her all his life, enters and Lydie throws herself into his arms for another trite happy ending. In the rash of happy endings—reminiscent of the last scene of a comedy—even Angela is married off. Her fiancé's chief accomplishment is an ability to do long sums in his head; he is introduced into Makarie's circle as a business associate of Werner—the epitome of the prosaic business world in the *Lehrjahre*. The narrator emphasizes the disparity in their backgrounds and talents by hastily informing the reader that the young man has shown hints of greater character than appears on the surface. The crowning irony is the narrator's suggestion that Angela would have married long since, if Makarie could have spared her, and that she is hastening to marry the first eligible party now that a successor has been found. This suggestion is, of course, not explicit, but is implied by: "seitdem aber eine Nachfolgerin denkbar, . . . scheint sie, von einem wohlgefälligen Eindruck überrascht, ihm bis zur Leidenschaft nachgegeben zu haben" (446).

Another element in this undercutting of Makarie's circle is the strange figure of the girl who can divine metals. As suggested above, she represents an opposite pole to balance Makarie's spirituality and tendency to fly off into the sky. She does not, however, share the exaggerated veneration accorded Makarie, but is introduced as a servant to Philine and Lydie. Even among the servants she does not take the position of ladies' maid, but joins the field hands—thus becoming the lowest of the low. While she is regarded as a curious figure by the other servants, they like and respect her; indeed, there is a simple dignity to her withdrawn, rustic life (she is never introduced into Makarie's circle), that contrasts strangely with the hocus-pocus surrounding the supposedly modest and withdrawn older woman.

Goethe's introduction to the essay on Makarie's relationship to the solar system (end of chapter fourteen) emphasizes the incredibility of his fiction: "Leider ist dieser Aufsatz erst lange Zeit, nachdem der Inhalt mitgeteilt worden, aus dem Gedächtnis geschrieben und nicht, wie es in einem so merkwürdigen Fall wünschenswert wäre, für ganz authentisch anzusehen" (448 f.). He pretends the case is of scientific interest: "so wird hier schon so viel mitgeteilt, um Nach- denken zu erregen und Aufmerksamkeit zu empfehlen" (449). But then he proceeds to beg the reader's pardon for his "ätherische Dichtung" and turns to his "terrestrischen Märchen" (452). He ends the description of the girl with the same mocking helpfulness as above: "Wir aber wollten, was uns bekannt geworden, auch unvollständig wie es vorliegt, mitgeteilt haben, um forschende Männer auf ähnliche Fälle, die sich vielleicht öfter, als man glaubt, durch irgendeine Andeutung hervortun, freundlich aufmerksam zu machen" (453).

Makarie has, further, one very significant failure. In spite of her image as the one to whom all turn for help in disturbed relationships, she plays no part at all in the most problematic relationship in the novel—namely that between Felix and Hersilie. It is not Makarie who finally saves Felix from destroying himself, but Wilhelm. Furthermore, the relationship between Felix and Hersilie is not flattened into banality, like those in which Makarie mediates; instead it retains all the intensity of emotion and all the dignity of its highest point. The last two chapters display none of the playful or satiric irony that characterizes the preceding three chapters; the language is straightforward and terse. Even Hersilie has finally learned to be serious. In their simplicity they become a myth of death and rebirth. The image of the physician rescuing the passionate youth to a new life reiterates the theme of the opening of the novel and closes the book, not Makarie's spiral.

The relationship of the names *Felix* and *Makarie* sheds further light on Makarie's role. Both mean "happy." *Makarie* is from the Greek μακάριος meaning "fortunate," "blessed," and implies a divine basis for the happy state (German *selig*). *Felix* is the Latin meaning "fruitful," "happy," "prosperous"; it lacks the other-wordly connections of μακάριος and the Latin *beatus*. The suitability of the names to their respective holders is clear: the holy Makarie spirals off into heaven and remains withdrawn from this-worldly passions, while Felix loves the horses that Makarie bans from her realm and is reborn to live again on earth. Indeed, death and rebirth has been implicit throughout the novel in Felix's series of injuries incurred for Hersilie's sake. Makarie is, then, after all, but one pole of a pair that must be reconciled, while Felix, leading this life of ups and downs, represents the uneasy balance between extremes.

If Makarie plays no role in the drama of Felix and Hersilie, how is the mediation brought about? The answer is: through Wilhelm in his capacity of physician.[16a] Wilhelm's medical skill makes it possible for him to save Felix from the effects of his passion by letting blood at the critical moment. The same skill saves Flavio in "Der Mann von funfzig Jahren," and it is the skill Wilhelm so sorely missed at the death of his friend the fisherman's son (Book Two, chapter eleven). Healing is one of the basic themes of the *Wanderjahre*, and it appears with a force equal to rebirth in the examples of bloodletting above. This connection is made explicit in the first mention of medical art in the novel. In "Sankt Joseph

---

[16a] On Wilhelm as physician see also below pages 118 and 134.

der Zweite" Joseph tells Wilhelm that his mother was a midwife, as he describes it, "in der Kunst erfahren, die so manchen gleich beim Eintritt in das Leben zum Leben rettet" (21). "Zum Leben retten" underlies all of the many scenes of healing —both physical and spiritual—in the book. Indeed, it is another aspect of the rebirth that follows renunciation, for healing is used as frequently in a spiritual sense in the novel, as in a physical one. The act of bloodletting in the final chapter symbolizes the explicit relationship between healing and renunciation. When Wilhelm opens the vein in Felix's arm, the blood spurts out and mingles with the river in which the youth almost drowned. Such a sacrifice of a piece of himself to the element that almost swallowed him up is a symbolic acquiescence to the demand nature has placed on him, and thus an analogy of renunciation. This broadening of the significance of healing is consistent with Wilhelm's character, for Wilhelm is a spiritual healer long before he becomes a physician. Even in the *Lehrjahre*, Wilhelm is drawn to unhappy people—Mignon, the harpist, Aurelie— and does as much as possible for them.[17] He continues this activity in his mediation between Lenardo and Susanne in the *Wanderjahre*, so that when he finally appears as a surgeon late in the novel, it is only the concrete realization of a spiritual faculty that he has always possessed.

But why does Goethe place this particular faculty at the center of his novels of education? The answer lies in the broadening of the physician figure to spiritual healer and advisor, and ultimately to the educator and poet. There are many cases in Goethe's work, particularly from the period of the *Lehrjahre* and the beginning of the *Wanderjahre*, of the merging of healing and teaching. The "Bekenntnisse einer schönen Seele," for example, clearly fill these two functions. They have a calming, healing effect on Aurelie, who upon hearing them finally is able to die at peace with herself and the world. For Wilhelm, who does not stand in need of healing, they are a document in his education—in Book Eight he soberly discusses with Natalie what he has learned from them (HA VII, 517 f.). The identity of the two functions is more clearly affirmed in the *Unterhaltungen deutscher Ausgewanderten*. The Abbé's purpose in telling his stories is clearly an educational one (the Abbé is by profession a spiritual advisor), yet it is an educative one undertaken to heal social rifts. The development of Luise illustrates the healing process more specifically, for as she is educated (along with the others) to her place in the group, she also is cured of her own unhappy preoccupation with the absent fiancé. And in the "Märchen" the old man with the lamp— a poet figure—heals the disrupted society through his advice and direction. The connection is playfully made explicit in "Der Sammler und die Seinigen" (1799), where Apollo is invoked as patron of both doctors and artists—"weshalb ich Verzeihung vom Apoll, insofern er sich um Ärzte und Künstler zugleich be-

---

[17] Very early in the *Lehrjahre* he answers Werner, who enjoys exploiting the weaknesses of others, "Ich weiß nicht, ob es nicht ein edleres Vergnügen wäre, die Menschen von ihren Torheiten zu heilen" (HA VII, 37).

kümmert, erwarten darf" (JA XXXIII, 171). As late as 1830 the connection is still important for Goethe: when Faust meets Chiron in the "Klassische Walpurgisnacht," he addresses him first as "der edle Pädogog" (l. 7337), then as "Arzt, der .../ Dem Kranken Heil, dem Wunden Lindrung schafft" (ll. 7344 ff.).

Wilhelm's choice of profession, then, places him in the very center of Goethe's concerns with the role of the poet in society. The poet, the educator, the spiritual advisor all coalesce in the figure of the surgeon rescuing a young life endangered by excess passion; and it is this surgeon who displaces the saintly Makarie from the position of supreme force for human good in the novel. The healer and educator preserve life for the living—the life for the living which is the center of Goethe's work.

6. APHORISMS

The problem of the aphorism, or pithy generalization, is dealt with largely, though not exclusively, in the sections on Jarno-Montan, the pedagogic province, and in the two collections of aphorisms at the end of the last two books. At first they tend to be treated critically, but in the course of the novel modes of understanding them develop. In these modes lies the basis of Goethe's theory of perception.

Aphorisms or maxims appear early in the novel in a somewhat negative light. Jarno says, for example, to Wilhelm in their first conversation, "Jede Art von Tätigkeit möchte das Kind ergreifen, weil alles leicht aussieht, was vortrefflich ausgeübt wird. Aller Anfang ist schwer! Das mag in einem gewissen Sinne wahr sein; allgemeiner aber kann man sagen: aller Anfang ist leicht..." (36). This statement typifies the problem with maxims: a generalization leads the speaker to one maxim—"Aller Anfang ist schwer!"—but somehow the opposite seems just as true, if not more so. This is precisely the criticism that Hersilie makes of the maxims her uncle has printed in gold letters over doorways in his castle: "Die Maximen der Männer hören wir immerfort wiederholen, ja wir müssen sie in goldenen Buchstaben über unsern Häupten sehen, und doch wüßten wir Mädchen im stillen das Umgekehrte zu sagen, das auch gölte, wie es gerade hier der Fall ist" (66, same criticism repeated 68). The heroine of "Die pilgernde Törin" uses maxims not to express general truths, but to hide specific ones. Revanne says about the family's failure to learn the girl's real circumstances: "Bemerkte sie die Absicht, einige Aufklärung von ihr zu gewinnen, so versteckte sie sich hinter allgemeine Sittensprüche, um sich zu rechtfertigen, ohne uns zu belehren" (59).

The reversibility and generality of aphorisms leads first to a recognition of their limited validity. Wilhelm sees a maxim not as a summing up, but as a beginning of a train of thought, when he says "Kurzgefaßte Sprüche jeder Art weiß ich zu ehren, besonders wenn sie mich anregen, das Entgegengesetzte zu überschauen und in Übereinstimmung zu bringen" (70). Similarly, the maxims in Makarie's archive are jumping-off places: "Resultate waren es die, wenn wir nicht ihre Veranlassung wissen, als Paradox erscheinen, uns aber nötigen, vermittelst eines umgekehrten Findens und Erfindens rückwärts zu gehen und uns die Filiation solcher Gedanken von weit her, von unten herauf wo möglich zu vergegenwärtigen" (125). Understood in the proper context, a generalization thus may have its validity, but it cannot be applied willy-nilly. In "Betrachtungen im Sinne der Wanderer"[18] aphorism 31 warns against unthinking use of generalizations: "Allgemeine Begriffe und großer Dünkel sind immer auf dem Wege, entsetzliches Unglück anzurichten" (287). It is not the generalization alone that creates the problem, but the lack of understanding in approaching it.

Context is thus all-important. In BSW 118 Goethe maintains that a recognized truth should only be applied to things closely concerned with it ("Nächstes"); attempts to apply it widely are bound to cause only errors. But, if the limiting conditions are borne in mind, the general can be perceived through the specific: "Das Allgemeine und das Besondere fallen zusammen; das Besondere ist das Allgemeine, unter verschiedenen Bedingungen erscheinend" (BSW 130, p. 302). In this sense, then, he can say, "Jedes Existierende ist ein Analogon alles Existierenden" (BSW 115, p. 300) and "Das Wahre ist gottähnlich; es erscheint nicht unmittelbar, wir müssen es aus seinen Manifestationen erraten" (Aus Makariens Archiv 3, p. 460). But the general does not, as a result, supercede the specific—each of the "manifestations" or details also must be considered to have significance in its own right, as a later aphorism shows: "Ich bin überzeugt, daß die Bibel immer schöner wird, je mehr man sie versteht, d.h. je mehr man einsieht und anschaut, daß jedes Wort, das wir allgemein auffassen und im besondern auf uns anwenden, nach gewissen Umständen, nach Zeit-und Ortsverhältnissen einen eignen, besondern, unmittelbar individuellen Bezug gehabt hat" (AMA 56, p. 469). The implication, then, is a respect for limiting details, for parts in themselves. The acceptance of this limitation in viewing the cosmos is a kind of renunciation—the overall view is given up, truth can only be viewed from one perspective at a time.

The limitation in perspective can be overcome to some extent by the analogy, a form of generalization with a particular advantage, namely: "daß sie nicht abschließt und eigentlich nichts Letztes will" (BSW 93, p. 296). This kind of generalization makes it possible to respect the details of the context without sacrificing generality; it makes possible the statement, "Das Höchste wäre zu begreifen, daß alles Faktische schon Theorie ist . . . Man suche nur nichts hinter den Phänomenen; sie selbst sind die Lehre" (BSW 136, p. 304). The practical illustration of this point is the teaching of anatomy by re-creating the limb, rather than by dissecting it (Book Three, chapter 3). Jarno actually offers the analogy as

---

[18] Henceforth abbreviated BSW. "Aus Makariens Archiv" will be abbreviated AMA.

a means of overcoming limitation in defense of his insistence on specialization: "Sich auf ein Handwerk zu beschränken, ist das Beste. Für den geringsten Kopf wird es immer ein Handwerk, für den bessern eine Kunst, und der beste, wenn er *eins* tut, tut er alles, oder, um weniger paradox zu sein, in dem *einen*, was er recht tut, sieht er das Gleichnis von allem, was recht getan wird" (37). By limiting himself to one occupation, the gifted individual will thus still participate in the entirety of the cosmos. The analogy is like the mirrors in "Wer ist der Verräter?"; it offers many complementary perspectives to broaden an otherwise limited view, but like the image in the mirror, it is not concrete, that is, not fixable or definitive.

The furthest reaches of the universe are brought into connection by the analogy: looking at the heavens from the astronomer's observation tower, Wilhelm recognizes an analogous order to that of the stars inside himself, when he says, "Darfst du dich in der Mitte dieser ewig lebendigen Ordnung auch nur denken, sobald sich nicht gleichfalls in dir ein beharrlich Bewegtes, um einen reinen Mittelpunkt kreisend, hervortut?" (119). The analogy further becomes the way the individual relates himself to history, the way history becomes tradition. Angela makes this point to Wilhelm as she shows him Makarie's archive:

> Ist man treu . . . das Gegenwärtige festzuhalten, so wird man erst Freude an der Überlieferung haben, indem wir den besten Gedanken schon ausgesprochen, das liebenswürdigste Gefühl schon ausgedrückt finden. Hiedurch kommen wir zum Anschauen jener Übereinstimmung, wozu der Mensch berufen ist, wozu er sich oft wider seinen Willen finden muß, da er sich gar zu gern einbildet, die Welt fange mit ihm von vorne an. (123)

Similarly, recurring patterns in history are the basis of the religious doctrine promulgated in the pedagogic province—the mural of the Old Testament is accompanied by friezes of parallel occurrences in the histories of other peoples. It is not surprising then, that the final scene of the book should be a re-enactment of death and rebirth, analogous to so many scenes in the book (just as the book began with an emblem), and that the final statement should be: "Wer lange in bedeutenden Verhältnissen lebt, dem begegnet freilich nicht alles, was dem Menschen begegnen kann; aber doch das Analoge und vielleicht einiges, was ohne Beispiel war" (AMA 183, p. 486).

The implications of such a theory of perception for the novel are obvious: the novel presents a variety of perspectives on the same problem in the collection of stories, in the continually shifting stance of the narrator, and in the loose collections of aphorisms, which are thus seen to be particularly appropriate to both the theme and form of the novel.[19] In a brief essay of 1827, "Über das

---

[19] Their place in the novel has been a controversial issue, because of a typical misunderstanding of Eckermann's that they were only a stop-gap measure to fill out Books Two and Three. In his commentary Trunz solidly justifies including them (682 f.).

Lehrgedicht," Goethe wrote: "Alle Poesie soll belehrend sein, aber unmerklich; sie soll den Menschen aufmerksam machen, wovon sich zu belehren wäre; er muß die Lehre selbst daraus ziehen wie aus dem Leben" (JA XXXVIII, 71). This statement implies that the novelist cannot present a complete interpretation of his material, for his perspective, as an individual one, cannot be comprehensive.[20] The multiplicity of perspectives in the *Wanderjahre* offers an experimental response to this difficulty. But what the novel gains in comprehensiveness, it loses in compactness and "organic unity." It is no longer an interpreted whole, but rather an interpretable whole. This is the technique of the *Unterhaltungen* taken to extremes. There only general patterns could be interpreted, but not specific references. But here, in this web of complex relationships and reflections, it is even more dangerous to interpret any one part separately from the rest of the novel, much less from its immediate context. It is no longer a question of a single character speaking or not speaking for Goethe, nor even a question of a coy narrator. Events are not recounted from a consistent and authoritative moral viewpoint at all; instead, the reader himself must intuit the truths behind the multifarious manifestations, for, like the images in the mirror, they are ineffable.

[20] Compare the much earlier statement in "Über Laokoon" (1798): "Ein echtes Kunstwerk bleibt, wie ein Naturwerk, für unsern Verstand immer unendlich: es wird angeschaut, empfunden, es wirkt; es kann aber nicht eigentlich erkannt, viel weniger sein Wesen, sein Verdienst mit Worten ausgesprochen werden" (JA XXXIII, 124).

III
WILHELM MEISTERS WANDERJAHRE II: PARODY

1. THE *UNTERHALTUNGEN* AND THE *LEHRJAHRE* IN THE *WANDERJAHRE*

While irony is widely acknowledged in Goethe's late works, criticism of the *Wanderjahre* has concentrated on the most serious aspects of the novel. The good-natured, often clownish humor, the evident delight Goethe takes in teasing his reader, just as the Abbé in the *Unterhaltungen* teased his listeners, has been for the most part politely overlooked even by sympathetic readers of the novel. Goethe's enemies, on the other hand, immediately recognized and bitterly resented the ironic tendencies of the novel. Karl Schütz, in his rambling but vituperative discussion of the *Wanderjahre*, says, for example:

> Eine noch niederschlagendere Bemerkung, aber, die sich bei der Ansicht der neuesten—Schriftstellerei Göthe's, jedem Unbefangenen, ihn *sehend* Bewundernden, seiner Verehrer, aufdringen muß, ist *die*: daß er das Publikum jetzt ungefähr eben so behandelt, wie nach dem *vierten* seiner Venetianischen Epigramme, der *Fremde* in *Italien* behandelt zu werden pflegt; und unter der, von den "Göthlichen" seiner eigenen Schüler geliehenen, Nebelkappe der leidigen *Mystik*, seine Zeitgenossen mit dem, *was* er ihnen jetzt noch gibt, (den *wahren* Wert dieser Gaben selbst nur allzuwohl kennend), auch noch zu *mystificiren*, d.h. zum *Besten zu haben*, sucht.[1]

In the course of the preceding chapter I occasionally pointed out elements of humor, particularly in the shifting attitudes toward various characters; in this one

---

[1] Friedrich Karl Julius Schütz, *Göthe und Pustkuchen, oder: über die beiden Wanderjahre Wilhelm Meister's und ihre Verfasser* (Halle, 1823), p. xxvii. Pustkuchen published his own self-righteous *Wilhelm Meisters Wanderjahre* in 1821, apparently unaware that Goethe intended to do the same. He had a good ear, and the beginning, especially, reproduces the sound patterns and rhythms of Goethe's mature prose remarkably well. The novel re-evaluates the characters in the *Lehrjahre* according to orthodox bourgeois morality, dissects Goethe's other works to display their immorality, and eventually rescues Wilhelm from the clutches of his wicked friends to the straight-and-narrow path of the super-moral poet proclaiming virtue. Subsequent volumes, which Pustkuchen published in 1822, 1827 and 1828 take their licks at Goethe's *Wanderjahre* as well as at the *Lehrjahre*. The work was sufficiently popular to warrant a second edition of the first two volumes in 1823.

I would like to approach this playfulness in a more systematic framework by considering the parodistic incorporation of, and reference to, outside material in the *Wanderjahre*. Naturally, in such a discussion the relationship of the novel to its two predecessors in Goethe's own work, the *Unterhaltungen deutscher Ausgewanderten* and the *Lehrjahre*, comes first. I will then consider Goethe's treatment of the sources for various parts of the novel. These sources form a curious group in themselves—Basedow, Campe, Prior, Kotzebue, Musäus, Sterne, Goldsmith—and since Goethe refers to many of them openly in the text, it is justifiable to make a detailed study of them part of an interpretation of the novel.

Historically, the *Wanderjahre* is the continuation of the *Unterhaltungen*. Given the long genesis of the *Wanderjahre*, this external connection would not be very interesting if the novel did not relate in some other way to the *Unterhaltungen*. Many of the techniques Goethe developed for the *Unterhaltungen* find new and sophisticated applications in the *Wanderjahre*. I tried to trace in Chapter Two the subtle interplay between the novellas and the frame, which is reminiscent, on a higher level, of the interrelationships which I discussed in Chapter One. Similarly, the way certain of the stories are isolated as fictions with respect to the frame is a further development of the Abbé's deliberately telling bad stories to draw out his audience. Most important, is that the *Unterhaltungen* presents various views of a single problem—the behavior of the individual in the face of social disruption; the *Wanderjahre* represents Goethe's ultimate development of the technique of multi-perspectivity.

Yet all of these technical relationships do not constitute literary reference, which is the problem here. Indeed, it cannot be argued that there is a specific reference to the *Unterhaltungen* in the *Wanderjahre*, but it can be argued, I think, that there is a covert parodistic rejection of it, just as there is a covert rejection of Boccaccio in the *Unterhaltungen*. I have shown that Goethe plays with various traditional ways of introducing novellas into the narrative, including the traditional cycle form of the *Unterhaltungen* in the circle around Hersilie (above Ch. 2, p. 48). This passage constitutes one such reference to the *Unterhaltungen*. The abrupt abandonment of the form when Wilhelm leaves Hersilie's home reveals the emptiness and arbitrary nature of the convention.

A similar traditional cycle setting occurs again in Book Three. Wilhelm arrives at an inn, which has been appropriated by Lenardo's band of emigrants. Wilhelm, as an apparent outsider, needs special permission to enter and remain on the premises, just as he was unable to enter the estate of Hersilie's uncle until his acceptability was established. While the members of the band are not openly threatened by the outside world, they are there because their way of life is threatened by the approaching technological society, and they have joined together to form their own society based on their own values. The inn shares the important characteristics of the *hortus conclusus*, like the estate of the baroness in the *Unterhaltungen*.

As one might expect in such a setting, the characters sit around in the evening swapping stories. In the first version it is clear that the setting is intended essentially as a frame for a group of stories, for three stories ("Die neue Melusine," "Die pilgernde Törin," and "Wo stickt der Verräter?") are presented in three successive chapters (14–17). The latter two stories are moved to the earlier setting in the final version, and the section in the inn includes a greater variety of material, but the basic form of the novella cycle still underlies its structure. Although the evening gatherings of the group are not restricted to story-telling, they are not devoted to random gossip; there is always some kind of constructive presentation or discussion—"Unterhaltung" in the fullest sense of the word. In this framework are presented Wilhelm's story of the maker of anatomical models (ch. 3), Lenardo's history (ch. 4), selections from Lenardo's diary (ch. 5 and 13—like the stories in Book One, these are not told, but given Wilhelm to read), "Die neue Melusine" (ch. 6), "Die gefährliche Wette" (ch. 8), "Nicht zu weit" (ch. 10), a discussion of morals in the proposed American settlement (ch. 11), and two speeches (ch. 9 and 12).

At first the diversity of material fitted into this form would seem to extend it and save it from becoming irrelevant, as it did in Book One. Yet in fact, the frame turns out to be just as irrelevant. The introductions to the inserted material tend to be perfunctory, there is no clear indication of the passage of time—even the first story, Wilhelm's, is told not on the first evening they are together, but "Eines Abends" (322). The introduction to "Die gefährliche Wette" bursts the convention of the frame by bursting the convention of the novel. The very brief introduction reads as follows:

> Unter den Papieren, die uns zur Redaktion vorliegen, finden wir einen Schwank, den wir ohne weitere Vorbereitung hier einschalten, weil unsere Angelegenheiten immer ernsthafter werden und wir für dergleichen Unregelmäßigkeiten fernerhin keine Stelle finden möchten.
>
> Im ganzen möchte diese Erzählung dem Leser nicht unangenehm sein, wie sie St. Christoph am heitern Abend einem Kreise versammelter lustiger Gesellen vortrug. (378)

The first of these paragraphs disrupts the convention of the novel as narrative by suggesting the totally arbitrary nature of the novella's position, as well as pointing out the lack of introduction. This break is all the more important, since the second version of the novel contains many fewer such discussions of the difficulty of organization than the first version, where they occur frequently. The second paragraph returns to the cycle-convention, but as an arbitrary choice: "Im ganzen möchte diese Erzählung dem Leser nicht unangenehm sein, wie . . ." suggests, with all the circumspection of its double negative, that the narrator had the choice of which version of the story to offer the reader, rather than that he is reporting the one story that was told on the particular occasion his work treats.

Thus the narrator rejects his narrative conventions in the first paragraph in order to place the story where he wants it, then restores them in the second, but only under the condition, so to speak, that they not interfere with his freedom.

The whole concept is demolished once and for all by "Nicht zu weit." Its introduction points out that it is impossible for such a story to be told in the traditional frame. Odoard has presented his plans to Lenardo and his friends; the discussion becomes increasingly involved in the personal bases for the ambitious plans of both parties. The reader is told,

> Bis tief in die Nacht blieb man zusammen und verwickelte sich immer unentwirrbarer in die Labyrinthe menschlicher Gesinnungen und Schicksale. Hier nun fand sich Odoard bewogen, nach und nach von den Angelegenheiten seines Geistes und Herzens fragmentarische Rechenschaft zu geben, deshalb denn auch von diesem Gespräche uns freilich nur unvollständige und unbefriedigende Kenntnis zugekommen. (393)

The vocabulary—"verwickelte," "unentwirrbarer," "Labyrinthe," "fragmentarische"—emphasizes the impossibility of reducing the complexity of human relationships to a single, comprehensive, presentable perspective. And indeed, in spite of Friedrich's organizing mediation, the story does not coalesce into a real novella. The two conflicting strands—Odoard's and Albertine's—never come together to be resolved, but remain apart, leaving the story a terrifying fragment. Even the novella itself has now become an impossibility.

The material that follows "Nicht zu weit" bears out this conclusion: the following chapter offers only conclusions summarizing a conversation that the narrator will not present in its entirety although, as he says, the latter would be far preferable (404). The last section of inserted material is the end of Lenardo's diary (ch. 13); the story of Lenardo's reunion with Nachodine-Susanne (the two names correspond, of course, to two different views of her: the strange, frightened young girl and the steady, mature woman) seems to fall into the novelistic mode, but it, too, remains unresolved. Thus this "novella," which runs all through the book and which tells its story from so many perspectives (Hersilie's and Makarie's letters, Lenardo's narrative, Wilhelm's letters, Lenardo's diaries), is not a closed form. Rather it illustrates the general problem of the book, the impossibility of simplifying reality to one comprehensive viewpoint.

Thus the cycle convention, which began as an apparently suitable vehicle for presenting a variety of perspectives, is destroyed. The frame is in effect satirized as an arbitrary screen between the narrator and his material, and the novella turns out to impose a false and limiting unity on human phenomena. To some extent the re-evocation and rejection of the cycle, particularly in Book One, is playful, but it is, clearly, also very serious, and leads to a new form of the novel.

Having rejected the intention to continue the *Unterhaltungen* quite early, Goethe decided to make his new cycle of novellas a sequel to *Wilhelm Meister* instead. The thought that the *Wanderjahre* is a sequel to the *Lehrjahre* is at first a little shocking, since the novels follow such different principles of form—the cycle of novellas in one case, the *Bildungsroman* in the other. Yet the contrast is not so great as might seem at first. The romantic novel—of which the *Lehrjahre* is the prototype—derives ultimately from the picaresque tradition, a form whose unity rests only on the fact that everything happens to the same central character. Cervantes tightened this form by making the events the result of Don Quixote's own personality, and the eighteenth-century admirers of Cervantes (including Fielding and Wieland) refined this development. Thus while it is possible to speak of a coherent plot determined by Wilhelm's education in the *Lehrjahre*, the structure remains fairly loose and the underlying unity is provided by Wilhelm's continual presence in the novel. The *Wanderjahre* still participates in this tradition, as indeed the title implies, for at bottom the plot purports to deal with Wilhelm wandering out into the world—the basic picaresque situation. But to what extent can it be argued that Wilhelm's actions or personality form a focal point for the plot? Only, I think, in a very unusual way, in that the novel, as a purported redaction of Wilhelm's papers (378), treats material that has all been perceived by Wilhelm. Wilhelm is in fact the only character who hears or reads all of the inserted material; in this respect the form of the novel takes its most definitive departure from the form of the cycle, where the audience is traditionally a group.

Both Wilhelm Meister novels are concerned with education, but Wilhelm's first conversation with Jarno quickly presents differences in the avowed aims of the two novels. Wilhelm has asked Jarno-Montan to teach him enough geology to answer Felix's questions, but Jarno refuses; he thinks that superficial mastery of any discipline is useless and that people should confine themselves to one thing that can be learned thoroughly. The conversation continues:

> Wilhelm, der indessen nachgedacht hatte, sagte zu Montan: "Solltest du wirklich zu der Überzeugung gegriffen haben, daß die sämtlichen Tätigkeiten, wie in der Ausübung, so auch im Unterricht zu sondern seien?"—"Ich weiß mir nichts anderes noch besseres," erwiderte jener. "Was der Mensch leisten soll, muß sich als ein zweites Selbst von ihm ablösen, und wie könnte das möglich sein, wäre sein erstes Selbst nicht ganz davon durchdrungen?"—"Man hat aber doch eine vielseitige Bildung für vorteilhaft und notwendig gehalten."—"Sie kann es auch sein zu ihrer Zeit," versetzte jener; "Vielseitigkeit bereitet eigentlich nur das Element vor, worin der Einseitige wirken kann, dem eben jetzt genug Raum gegeben ist. Ja, es ist jetzo die Zeit der Einseitigkeiten; wohl dem, der es begreift, für sich und andere in diesem Sinne wirkt." (37)

Wilhelm's question about a broad education is, naturally, an attempt to defend the kind of educational course that would justify his meanderings in the *Lehrjahre*, which were already parodied at the end of that novel by the random educations of Friedrich and Philine (HA VII, 558). Jarno firmly rejects the apparent educational ideal of the earlier book; instead, the individual must become fully competent at one thing. Breadth pertains rather to the society, than to the gifted individual, who must subordinate himself to the group by finding his place in it. Later in the novel Wilhelm meets Jarno again in the pedagogic province, an institution which embodies the latter's educational principles: the pupils learn everything by doing, and they practice one trade. Wilhelm, too, eventually succumbs, giving up the aestheticism of his life in the *Lehrjahre* for the humble surgeon's trade.

But Jarno does not speak for Goethe, and in the end the novel is ambivalent about sacrificing the broad development of the individual in favor of specialization and subordination to society. Goethe summarizes and points out this ambivalence in Lenardo's after-dinner speech in Book Three, chapter one, in response to the unhappiness of his group at their rootlessness. He says, "Haben doch lebensmüde, bejahrte Männer den Ihrigen zugerufen: 'Gedenke zu sterben!', so dürfen wir lebenslustige jüngere wohl uns immerfort ermuntern und ermahnen mit den heitern Worten: 'Gedenke zu wandern!' " (318). Lenardo's revision is more complex than it seems here: the real comparison is not to the *memento mori*, but to the earlier revision of it in the *Lehrjahre*—"Gedenke zu leben!"—the motto of the *Saal der Vergangenheit*. Thus while Lenardo thinks he is emphasizing the positive aspect of their existence—their ability to be useful members of a group anywhere—in fact he really emphasizes the rootlessness and lack of fullness that will characterize their existence in this group.

This ambivalent divergence in the educational aims of the two novels also appears on the level of parallels between characters. Hersilie's family in Book One is an exact parallel to Natalie's family in the *Lehrjahre*. Each one consists of an uncle, a pair of nieces—one lively, one serious—a wayward nephew and an elderly aunt, who is one of the religious elect. It is thus with delightful irony on Goethe's part that Hersilie says to Wilhelm when she tells about the family,

> Es ist mir gewissermaßen lieb, daß unser neuer Gast, wie ich höre, nicht lange bei uns verweilen wird: denn es müßte ihm verdrießlich sein, unser Personal kennen zu lernen, es ist das ewig in Romanen und Schauspielen wiederholte: ein wunderlicher Oheim, eine sanfte und eine muntere Nichte, eine kluge Tante, Hausgenossen nach bekannter Art; und käme nun gar der Vetter wieder, so lernte er einen phantastischen Reisenden kennen, der vielleicht einen noch sonderbarern Gesellen mitbrächte, und so wäre das leidige Stück erfunden und in Wirklichkeit gesetzt. (67 f.)

The last mentioned character is, of course, Wilhelm himself, who indeed accompanies Lenardo on the last leg of his journey home (in the *Lehrjahre*, too, he finally comes to the family as Lothario's friend). The "lousy play" with its clichéd cast just envisioned is none other than the *Lehrjahre!*

This distancing of the sequel from the original appears on a more serious level when the parallel figures are compared more closely, for the values of all the figures are reversed. Lenardo and Lothario are clearly very similar figures, yet they are exact opposites in their relationships with women: Lothario has had a whole succession of women in his life—Aurelie, Therese, her mother, Lydie, Margaret the farmer's daughter (Bk. VII, ch. 7), the lady over whom he fights the duel when Wilhelm first meets him—while Lenardo has none, because he cannot forget a moral obligation to a girl whom he scarcely knows. In the *Lehrjahre* it is the quiet, serious sister, Natalie, who is the real heroine of the novel, while in the *Wanderjahre* the serious Juliette is distinctly subordinate to Hersilie. Similarly, Makarie and the "schöne Seele" are clearly parallel treatments of religious questions, yet how different! The "schöne Seele" is turned totally inward on herself, to the exclusion of the outside world; Makarie, on the other hand, although she apparently isolates herself on her estate is turned completely outward, to the point that she sees her role not as that of a human on earth, but as a heavenly body spiralling ever further outward through the solar system. Makarie also runs an institution for the training of young girls—a task quite inconceivable for the "schöne Seele." The same contrast appears in the fact that Makarie maintains an archive of all sorts of useful material, much of it arising out of discussions, while the "schöne Seele" writes confessions, the most personal possible mode of autobiography. One might also want to draw a parallel between the mysterious children of the two novels—Mignon, who attaches herself to Wilhelm, and Fitz, who attaches himself to Felix. Both are demonic figures initially of unknown origins and of quite surprising capabilities; but while Fitz is a tempter, leading Felix on to his dangerous involvement with Hersilie, Mignon always tries to hold Wilhelm back from unworthy involvements, particularly with Philine.

The heads of the two families, the uncles, display this reversal of values at the most abstract level: the uncle of the *Lehrjahre* lives in an aesthetic world—he collects art and builds the *Saal der Vergangenheit*—which aims at developing the fullest capacities of the individual; the uncle of the *Wanderjahre* lives in a thoroughly practical world devoted to bettering the condition of his fellow man. Instead of art he collects autographs and memorabilia, his castle is decorated with mottoes and maps. He is concerned with the physical well-being of his tenants and neighbors: thus, he provides young plants for anyone in the area who needs them and sends fruit to the mountains; for their religious and social needs, his tenants are organized into congregations that have their religious, political and social meetings all in the same building. The uncle of the *Lehrjahre* appears only through the descriptions of his reverent female relatives, the "schöne Seele" and Natalie; in the *Wanderjahre*, however, the uncle appears in person as quite an eccentric character, without the dignity of distance.

The same divergence appears here that was observed in the philosophies of education: the *Lehrjahre* tends toward the individual and personal via the aesthetic, the *Wanderjahre* towards the submergence of self in obligations to a larger group.

The characters of the *Wanderjahre* are much more outward directed than their counterparts in the *Lehrjahre*, yet at the same time live much less freely. While Lothario may seem more sociable than Lenardo, his love affairs are a kind of *self*-fulfillment; Lenardo's relationship to Susanne-Nachodine is less *sociable*, but more *social* in that it stems from a concern for the demands people must place on one another in order for everyone to survive in a complex society. One cannot help feeling that Lothario's lot is a happier one than Lenardo's, just as "Gedenke zu leben!" is more cheerful than "Gedanke zu wandern!"[2]

There are also more explicit references to the *Lehrjahre* that intensify this distancing effect. They play with the awareness of the *Lehrjahre* as a famous novel, much as the second part of *Don Quixote* playfully recognizes the existence of Part One as a novel. This phenomenon appears in its most interesting form in the Mignon episode in Book Two, where Wilhelm, for whom the *Lehrjahre* represents experienced reality, confronts the painter, for whom Wilhelm's earlier history is a novel. It also appears when minor characters from the earlier novel, Friedrich and Philine, return at the end in roles humorously adjusted to fit the new, more realistic environment. Friedrich's ability to remember random facts has been developed to the point where he serves as a human dictaphone; Philine has become a seamstress, but can control her impulse to cut any cloth she sees no better than she could formerly control her sensuality. Indeed, such is her eagerness that she proves to be a nuisance, and Makarie's friends look forward to getting rid of her as soon as possible.[3]

The final aspect of this distancing, and the one that has disturbed interpreters of the work the longest, is the displacement of Wilhelm from the center of the novel and the virtual disappearance of Natalie. This is a twofold process—first the sections dealing with him yield the center of attention to the novellas; second, within the "Wilhelm-material" Felix becomes more and more the center of attention, until in the final scene Felix, with his brown locks (Wilhelm's attribute in the *Lehrjahre*) supplants his father as the promising youth that Wilhelm was in the *Lehrjahre*. In the same way, Natalie, who appears as the addressee of the opening sections of the *Wanderjahre*, is supplanted by the younger Hersilie. This shift is clearly deliberate, for Goethe deleted a scene about Natalie from the center of the first version (ch. 13, PA XXXIV, 116 f.). Furthermore, he deliberately calls attention to the fact that she does not appear at the end to say farewell to Makarie with the rest (436).

When, in III, 16, a letter is mentioned addressed to "Wilhelm genannt Meister" (455), the reader suddenly realizes that this novel, too, has been dealing

---

[2] Max Wundt points out the parallelism between the two families and contrasts the uncles, but does not interpret the relationships between the two, in *Goethes Wilhelm Meister*, p. 378.

[3] G. Röder in *Glück und glückliches Ende im deutschen Bildungsroman* (Munich, 1968), pp. 191–94, suggests that Book II, chapter 11 in the *Wanderjahre* functions as a reinterpretation of the *Lehrjahre*.

with Wilhelm's education, which has at long last been completed. But this expression is not without ambivalence. While on the one hand it emphasizes the meaning of the last name, it also calls into question its validity: if Wilhelm is only *named* Meister, perhaps he is not really even now a master. The same disparity as this one between Wilhelm and his name appears repeatedly in the use of mythological references in the novel, for example, in the discussion of the major's dangerously appropriate comparison of the widow to Arachne.[4] Wilhelm's name was of course already ironic in the *Lehrjahre*, but it is surely significant that Goethe deliberately calls attention to the irony once again at the end of the second novel, where he has shifted the focus of the novel away from the title figure.

2. BASEDOW AND CAMPE: THE PEDAGOGIC PROVINCE

I would like to turn now to sections of the novel that refer to works other than Goethe's own. The pedagogic province is unique among them in that it is not literary parody, and therefore will be treated first.

The chapters on the pedagogic province are frequently read as the heart of Goethe's message on education and religion in the *Wanderjahre*; but it is hard to believe Goethe really was any more solemn about all of this than about Makarie. It has, for example, been pointed out that the section on teaching art in the province (II, 8) immediately follows the Lago Maggiore chapter, which presents a diametrically opposed view on teaching art;[5] thus the two perspectives qualify one another. The rejection of drama in the same chapter (II, 8) is patently absurd. Wilhelm feebly tries to defend his old hobby, but is mercilessly reproached. Under this pressure, in a passage of ironic distancing from the *Lehrjahre*, he blesses the pious men who would protect other innocents from his mistakes (257). The narrator then comments that while Wilhelm may have rejected the theater himself, it still irritates him to hear others malign his former love (258). And for those who have still missed the point, Goethe adds: "Mag doch der Redakteur dieser Bogen hier selbst gestehen: daß er mit einigem Unwillen diese wunderliche Stelle durchgehen läßt. Hat er nicht auch in vielfachem Sinn mehr Leben und Kräfte als billig dem Theater zugewendet? und könnte man ihn wohl überzeugen, daß dies ein unverzeihlicher Irrtum, eine fruchtlose Bemühung gewesen?" (258). The answer, of course, is a resounding "no." Indeed, in the same year as this passage was written (1820), in one of the morphological essays, "Verstäubung, Verdunstung, Vertropfung," Goethe refers to himself as a dramatist in a very

---

[4] See above, p. 62. E. Bahr points out the irony of these parallels in *Die Ironie im Spätwerk Goethes: "...diese sehr ernsten Scherze..." Studien zum West-östlichen Divan, zu den Wanderjahren und zu Faust II* (Berlin, 1972), p. 114.

[5] Gidion, H., *Zur Darstellungsweise von "Wilhelm Meisters Wanderjahren,"* (Göttingen, 1969), p. 30.

positive context—"Überhaupt sollte man sich in Wissenschaften gewöhnen wie ein anderer denken zu können; mir als dramatischem Dichter konnte dies nicht schwer werden, für einen jeden Dogmatiker freilich ist es eine harte Aufgabe."[6]

It is hard to take the religious system of the province seriously. The curious gestures, the secrecy and mystifying titles ("die Obern," "die Dreie") suggest the same kind of masonic hocus-pocus as in the "Märchen" and in the Makarie chapters. Furthermore, it is improbable that the inconsistencies noted by many interpreters in the three levels of reverence and their associations with the three religions and the three parts of the Creed (156 ff.) are mere carelessness. Similarly, the view that the crucifixion is too dreadful to be shown to the pupils until their graduation and must be sealed off in the "Heiligtum des Schmerzes" seems excessive. First, it leads to the strange situation that after viewing the first two series of pictures in the religious loggia, one proceeds then not to a higher level of revelation (the crucifixion), but only back to the starting point. Second, the necessity for this prohibition is exaggerated after the two preceding crucifixions in the novel. The first one is the picture Wilhelm sees in Joseph's home, which is mentioned as an especially beautiful picture. It shows the child Jesus peacefully asleep on two pieces of wood that accidentally form a cross while his parents watch with adoration (15). The other crucifixion is the ivory crucifix whose arms came to the old collector many years after the rest. Both of these crucifixions are pleasant, beautiful objects worthy of particular notice. In this context it is then especially ironic that the crucifixion in the pedagogic province is not only sealed off, but never appears at all, even though Wilhelm has been promised it will be shown him on his next visit.

The educational psychology demonstrates the same faults as the religious system. Indeed, the reluctance to display Christ's passion is related to the attempt of the province to ban the passions and uncontrolled behavior. (At the home of the old collector Goethe has already made the association between Christ's passion, symbolized by the ivory crucifix, and passion in the ordinary meaning, symbolized by the mysterious box, which is the center of the growing passion between Felix and Hersilie, p. 147). In the province, music, for example, is a social, ordering art rather than a lyric, expressive one; indeed, all art in the province represents a communal achievement. The ritual gestures, too, with their attendant peaceful smiles, express harmony with the environment, but not passionate involvement. It once more undermines the significance of the pedagogic province, then, when Felix emerges from it a passionate, hot-blooded youth. He applies his new skills, writing and riding, to furthering his private affair with Hersilie;[7] he is eventually rescued not by what he has learned in the province (just as he is not rescued by Makarie), but by Wilhelm.

---

[6] WA II, 6, 189.

[7] Horses represent passion; compare above p. 70.

Karl Schütz, in some seventy-five pages of vituperations on the province, takes exception to precisely the points just mentioned.[8] He complains that its education is too one-sided, he objects violently to the exclusion of the drama, he finds the religious and moral system fragmentary and presented in an unsystematic, enigmatic style; he considers the doctrine of the three kinds of reverence nonsensical and paradoxical, the gestures absurd. The whole thing, he says quite correctly, is "Gaukelei" (86). At one point he relates the discussion of reverence to pedagogic theory of the 1780's, when he says in a footnote to the gestures:

> Die noch überdies zu den längst *veralteten* zwecklosen, ja verderblichen pädagogischen Spielereien einer Zeit gehört, wo man von dem läppischen Grundsatz ausging, der Jugend das Wissen spielend beibringen zu müssen, und welche jetzt, wo Schiller's gewichtiges Wort: *"Ernst ist der Anblick der Nothwendigkeit"* von unsern aufgeklärtesten Schulmännern auch auf unsere Erziehungs- und Unterrichtskunst, so recht und würdig angewendet wird, Gottlob *hinter* uns liegt. Aber selbst *Basedow's* gebackenes ABC von Pfefferkuchenteig, durch dessen Verspeisen er den Kindern das Lesenlernen zu appliciren pflegte, ist als ein Gedächtnißmittel, was sich doch wenigstens auf den guten Geschmack und einen so soliden Grund und Boden, als der Magen ist, gründet, noch ungleich zweckmäßiger als diese *Götheschen* Ehrfurchtsparaden.[9]

Schütz, in spite of his hostility, almost perceived what one of his more gifted contemporaries recognized, that Goethe's treatment of the pedagogic province deliberately exaggerated Basedow's fantastic schemes, because it was intended as parody of Basedow. Apart from Schütz, only Joseph von Eichendorff, so far as I know, has pointed out the connection with Basedow. In his memoirs, Eichendorff concludes his description of the educational revolution begun by Rousseau with:

> Diese Emanzipation der Jugend vom alten Schulzwange hatte zunächst Basedow in die derbe Faust genommen, von dessen Dessauer Philanthropie [Basedow's experimental school] Herder sagte: "Mir kommt alles schrecklich vor; man erzählte mir neulich von einer Methode, Eichwälder in zehn Jahre zu machen; wenn man den jungen Eichen unter der Erde die Herzwurzeln nähme, so schieße alles über die Erde in Stamm und Äste. Das ganze Arkanum Basedows liegt, glaub ich, darin, und ihm möchte ich keine Kälber zu erziehen geben, geschweige Menschen." — Basedow war ein revolutionärer Renommist, sein Nachfolger Campe ein zahmer Philister; jener hat diesen Realismus aufgebracht, Campe hat ihn für die Gebildeten zurecht gemacht und Goethe das ganze Treiben in seinen "Wanderjahren" köstlich parodiert.[10]

---

[8] Schütz. *Göthe und Pustkuchen*, pp. 47 ff.
[9] Schütz, pp. 85 f. footnote.
[10] J. von Eichendorff, "Erlebtes," *Werke*, ed. W. Rasch (Munich, 1966), p. 1508.

As Eichendorff's description suggests, Johann Bernhard Basedow (1723–1790) was not easy to get along with. He was always fighting with someone, be it the religious authorities of Hamburg, where his works were banned in the 1760's, or his colleagues at Dessau, where his school provided a model of radical pedagogy for many decades. Basedow was trained in philosophy and achieved some notoriety in the theological controversies raging in Hamburg in the middle of the century (he had studied with Lessing's friend Reimarus). But the real contribution was in pedagogy, where he enthusiastically tried to turn the principles of Rousseau's *Emile* into a generally applicable system of education. His first work proposing a general reform of the educational system in accordance with Rousseau's ideas was the *Vorstellung an Menschenfreunde und vermögende Männer über Schulen, Studien und ihren Einfluß in die öffentliche Wohlfahrt, mit einem Plane eines Elementarbuchs der menschlichen Erkenntnis* in 1768. In addition to its proposals for reform, the work solicited subscriptions for an *Elementarbuch*, a universal pedagogic encyclopedia that was to include materials both for parents and children. The response was overwhelming—Basedow received some fifteen thousand talers in subscriptions, in part from very distinguished contributors, including the Empress of Russia. In 1770 he published the *Methodenbuch*, a theoretical outline of his principles as a basis for use of the *Elementarbuch*, which also appeared the same year. The *Elementarbuch*, originally in three volumes but expanded to four in 1774, is, in fact, a curriculum for the enlightened parent or educator. It was accompanied by a portfolio of a hundred plates to be used as teaching materials. In 1771 Basedow accepted an invitation from the prince to start a model school at Dessau, which finally opened in 1774. He attracted considerable attention by a public demonstration of his results in 1776, but the school never had more than about fifty students. Basedow left the school in 1778, due to his inability to get along with his colleagues; the school continued to exist until 1793, but ceased to be an important educational center after Basedow left. His great reforms were in technique—learning languages by using them, emphasis on manual labor and crafts as well as on studies, educational games and gimmicks —of which Schütz's cookies are an example.

Joachim Heinrich Campe (1746–1818), the other figure whom Eichendorff mentions, was also an extremely influential, though less colorful figure. From September 1776 until September 1777 he worked with Basedow at Dessau, but left because he could not get along with Basedow. He wrote on pedagogic techniques, much in the spirit of Basedow; furthermore he edited the *Allgemeine Revision des gesammten Schul- und Erziehungswesens von einer Gesellschaft praktischer Erzieher* (1785–1791). The *Revisionswerk*, as it is called, is a sixteen volume blueprint of the theory of pedagogy. It attempts a complete systematization of education—the outline of the theoretical part takes up twenty pages in itself, and it includes essays on topics ranging from the purpose and history of education to the proper diet for expectant mothers, and a detailed diary of the first year of a child's life, from gymnastics to particular childhood vices like masturbation, from methods of teaching various subjects to the education of the different social classes and the role of the state in education. The theoretical part concludes with translations and commentary of Locke on education and Rousseau's *Emile*. But Campe is best known not for this heroic labor, but for his *Robinson der jüngere* (1799), adapted from Defoe, which had gone through fifty editions by the middle of the nineteenth century and was still used as a German text in this country at the beginning of the twentieth. The frame in which the novel unfolds is an experimental school quite similar to Basedow's, and the pupils are taught partly through discussions of Robinson's story. Robinson's adventures are significant because he learns to survive by his own wits and Divine Providence alone; when he finally returns to Europe, he masters a craft and supports himself by it.

Before discussing Goethe's treatment of the "Philanthropists," as Basedow and Campe were universally called, I must point out that Philipp Emanuel von Fellenberg and Heinrich Pestalozzi are generally considered the sources for the pedagogic province. Fellenberg ran a famous experimental school at Hofwil in the first decades of the nineteenth century. He was to a large extent influenced by his more famous countryman Pestalozzi, and in 1804 the two planned to work together. But they soon discovered they could not work together; in practice there were basic differences in their educational philosophies. Pestalozzi, it seems to me, is totally irrelevant to the *Wanderjahre*; Fellenberg, although he was probably a source for various details, is irrelevant to understanding the significance of the province for the novel.

It is frankly very difficult to see what Pestalozzi has to do with Goethe's province. Music, which is so important in Goethe's pattern of instruction, is a matter of total indifference to Pestalozzi.[11] Furthermore, Pestalozzi's basic concern was for elementary education, not for the higher levels of education and specialized preparation shown in the pedagogic province. In addition, Pestalozzi directed his reform of education toward the common people: his first school was for beggar-children, his real concern was to raise the level of education of the peasants. Social class is of no concern in Goethe's province. Pestalozzi's concern to develop the technical capacities of the individual to the complete exclusion of the traditional bases of his culture was extremely distasteful to Goethe, as we know from an acerbic comment to Boisserée.[12] The real difficulty in Pestalozzi's thought is that in his attempt to apply Rousseau, he fails to perceive the essential dichoto-

---

[11] See "Wie Gertrud ihre Kinder lehrt," Pestalozzi's main theoretical statement, in *Werke*, ed. P. Baumgartner, VI (Erlenbach-Zurich, 1941), 258.

[12] K. Muthesius in *Goethe ein Kinderfreund* (Berlin, 1910), pp. 136 f., quotes a violent statement to Boisserée about Pestalozzi's system as too individualistic and empty because of the failure to respect even the existence of tradition. Also in Biedermann, *Goethes Gespräche*, II (Leipzig, 1909), 318.

my between the state of nature and the state of society. The following sentence from "Wie Gertrud ihre Kinder lehrt" may serve as an example:

> Die empirischen Versuche, die ich hierüber angestellt habe, zeigten mir vorzüglich, daß unser Mönchsunterricht durch seine Vernachlässigung aller Psychologie uns nicht nur in allen Fächern von diesem letzten Ziel des Unterrichts entfernt, sondern sogar noch bestimmt dahin würkt, uns die Mittel, die uns die Natur selber auch ohne Beihülfe der Kunst zur Verdeutlichung unserer Begriffe anbietet, zu rauben und uns die Benutzung dieser Mittel durch unser inneres Verderben unmöglich zu machen.[13]

Pestalozzi apparently failed to realize that his statement implicitly rejects the need for any education at all, and virtually suggests that the best thing would be to allow Nature to take her course unimpeded. Rousseau, by contrast, never forgets in *Emile* that at best education can only achieve a sort of mediation between nature and society. It is on this point that Pestalozzi and Fellenberg differ definitively,[14] and Goethe's province clearly agrees with Fellenberg's philosophy that education serves to bring the individual into society, and as a result necessarily concerns itself with tradition.

There is substantial direct evidence that Goethe was familiar with Fellenberg's school near Bern; among other things, Goethe recommended that the duke send his two illegitimate sons there.[15] But after discussing Fellenberg as a source, Trunz correctly points out: "Vergleicht man die Berichte über Fellenbergs Landschulheim mit Goethes dichterischer Darstellung, so sieht man zwar, daß einzelne Anregungen dorther stammen können, aber das Ganze ist durchaus anders" (663). Since Goethe seems to have been impressed with Fellenberg's school, it is difficult to know what to make of the apparent critique noted above; surely Kohlmeyer's suggestion that Goethe leaves out the "Heiligtum des Schmerzes" only because it was not present in the description he had of Fellenberg's school is too simple.[16] Furthermore, Fellenberg's ideas clearly derived in large part from Basedow's—for instance the use of pictures in instruction, especially in language instruction, and the insistence that students do some kind of manual labor—so that Goethe might easily use details from Fellenberg and yet ultimately be concerned with Basedow's principles. Right near Hofwil, it may be noted, was another experimental school, the "Armenschule der kleinen Robinsons," in Maybirch—where the pupils re-enacted Campe's novel by building their own shelters and supporting themselves.[17]

---

[13] *Werke*, VI, 320.

[14] See K. Jungmann, "Die pädagogische Provinz," *Euphorion*, 14 (1907), 281. However Jungmann misunderstands the role of Rousseau when he equates him with Pestalozzi.

[15] Trunz, HA VIII, 663.

[16] O. Kohlmeyer, *Die pädagogische Provinz in "Wilhelm Meisters Wanderjahren"* (Langensalza, 1923), p. 70.

[17] Kohlmeyer, p. 56.

What evidence is there from Goethe himself that Basedow and Campe are behind the pedagogic province? Goethe's retrospective opinion (1813) of Basedow appears in Book Fourteen of *Dichtung und Wahrheit*: the portrait he gives there explains, I think, the two major inconsistencies of the province—the religious system and Felix's contrary behavior.[18] In this part of *Dichtung und Wahrheit* Goethe describes a junket down the Rhine in 1774 in the company of Lavater and Basedow, who was trying to raise funds for his school, which was to open that fall. He clearly made a very negative impression on Goethe, who repeatedly contrasts him with the beautiful, gentle, spiritual Lavater. Basedow was neither attractive nor pleasant nor particularly comprehensible. Even so, Goethe does seem to have enjoyed his enormous energy and playfulness; he describes, for example, how they tried to outdo one another in rudeness. His summary judgment is important, considering the extent to which Basedow's ideas appear in the structure of the pedagogic province:

> Mit seinen Planen konnte ich mich nicht befreunden, ja mir nicht einmal seine Absichten deutlich machen. Daß er allen Unterricht lebendig und naturgemäß verlangte, konnte mir wohl gefallen; daß die alten Sprachen an der Gegenwart geübt werden sollten, schien mir lobenswürdig, und gern erkannte ich an, was in seinem Vorhaben zu Beförderung der Tätigkeit und einer frischeren Weltanschauung lag: allein mir mißfiel, daß die Zeichnungen seines "Elementarwerks" noch mehr als die Gegenstände selbst zerstreuten ... Jenes "Elementarwerk" ... zersplittert sie ganz und gar, indem das, was in der Weltanschauung keineswegs zusammentrifft, um der Verwandtschaft der Begriffe willen neben einander steht; weswegen es auch jener sinnlich-methodischen Vorzüge ermangelt, die wir ähnlichen Arbeiten des Amos Comenius zuerkennen müssen. (HA X, 25)

Goethe naturally agrees with Basedow in principle, since both are Rousseau enthusiasts, but he accuses him of organizing all of the life out of his ideas by over-systematizing according to abstract principles. One is reminded of the systematic fragmentation of the pedagogic province into separate districts (parallel to the painful insistence on one-sidedness throughout the novel), as well as of the deliberately confusing but highly systematic religious system of the pedagogues.

Goethe seems to remember most Basedow's ferociously anti-trinitarian viewpoint, which caused him constantly to insult the people whom he was trying to interest in his school.

> Auf eine harte und unverantwortliche Weise erklärte er sich vor jedermann als den abgesagtesten Feind der Dreieinigkeit, und konnte gar nicht fertig werden,

---

[18] Although the pedagogic province was not written until 1820, it is not unreasonable to refer to this material, since the story of the boy drowned while fishing for crabs (II, 11) in the second version also derives from the trip described in this section of *Dichtung und Wahrheit*. See *Goethes Rheinreise mit Lavater und Basedow im Sommer 1774*, ed. A. Bach (Zurich, 1923), p. 11.

gegen dies allgemein zugestandene Geheimnis zu argumentieren. Auch ich hatte im Privatgespräch sehr viel zu leiden, und mußte mir die Hypostasis und Ousia, sowie das Prosopon immer wieder vorführen lassen. Dagegen griff ich zu den Waffen der Parodoxie, überflügelte seine Meinungen und wagte das Verwegne mit Verwegnerem zu bekämpfen. (HA X, 26)[19]

Typically, Goethe enters playfully into the peculiarities of the other and combats him by exaggerating and parodying; he describes later how he wouldn't let Basedow stop for a beer, although he was very thirsty, because the signboard of the inn had triangles on it, which he claimed would be too distressing for such an enemy of the number three. The elaborate and inconsistent theology of threes in the province, then—three levels of reverence, three world religions, the three parts of the Creed, the title "die Dreie" for the overseers—is exactly the kind of parodox Goethe must have used in his disputes with Basedow.

Another of Basedow's peculiarities was his intense dislike of music.[20] Goethe describes how Basedow sat in his smoke-filled room at Ems all night long dictating to his secretary while the others danced. Fellenberg did not share Basedow's dislike of music, which was one of the required subjects in his school, but still, the exaggerated prominence given to music in the pedagogic province is clearly an element of the parody which Goethe directs against Basedow. Consider the explanation Wilhelm receives of its importance:

> bei uns ist der Gesang die erste Stufe der Bildung, alles andere schließt sich daran und wird dadurch vermittelt. Der einfachste Genuß sowie die einfachste Lehre werden bei uns durch Gesang belebt und eingeprägt, ja selbst was wir überliefern von Glaubens- und Sittenbekenntnis, wird auf dem Wege des Gesanges mitgeteilt; andere Vorteile zu selbsttätigen Zwecken verschwistern sich sogleich: denn indem wir die Kinder üben, Töne, welche sie hervorbringen, mit Zeichen auf die Tafel schreiben zu lernen und nach Anlaß dieser Zeichen sodann in ihrer Kehle wiederzufinden, ferner den Text darunterzufügen, so üben sie zugleich Hand, Ohr und Auge und gelangen schneller zum Recht- und Schönschreiben, als man denkt, und da dieses alles zuletzt nach reinen Maßen, nach genau bestimmten Zahlen ausgeübt und nachgebildet werden muß, so fassen sie den hohen Wert der Meß- und Rechenkunst viel geschwinder als auf jede andere Weise. (151 f.)

The usefulness of music in teaching arithmetic and penmanship—not to speak of spelling—is questionable at best, and even were it practical would be distinctly

---

[19] This dislike spilled into the pedagogical writings, e.g. in the forward to the second edition of the *Elementarwerk* there is a footnote stating his opposition to "symbolic theology"—*Das Basedowische Elementarwerk* 2. Auflage (Leipzig, 1785) I, iv.

[20] Bach, *Goethes Rheinreise*, p. 7.

secondary in comparison to its use in imparting moral and religious teaching. Thus the very structure of the paragraph, from possibly significant to clearly trivial, parodies the whole notion of education as a progress from lower to higher. The irony is, in fact, two-edged, for in addition to Basedow's dislike of music, Goethe is also alluding to his elaborate games for teaching spelling, vocabulary and foreign languages, which utilized structures equally irrelevant to their content. The parodistic intent of the passage is clearer in light of Rousecau's statements on music in *Emile*. Although Rousseau himself was highly musical, music occupies a very humble spot in his educational scheme; it is useful for developing the full capacities of the voice and for relaxation, but for little else. Rousseau states firmly that the young pupil should *not* be taught to read music— "On pense bien qu'étant si peu pressé de lui apprendre à lire l'écriture, je ne le serai pas non plus de lui apprendre à lire la musique."[21] There is not a hint that it might be used as a vehicle for other arts or morals, indeed, the passage ends with a strict warning to keep it in its place: "Mais c'en est trop sur la musique: enseignez-la comme vous voudrez, pourvu qu'elle ne soit jamais qu'un amusement."[22] Goethe's treatment thus suggests to the aware reader Basedow's oversystematization and trivialization of Rouseeau, illustrated with an example particularly appropriate by reason of Basedow's strong dislike of music.

A similar process is at work in the emphasis on reverence in the province. In the *Methodenbuch* Basedow suggests that children can be taught things about religion even if they do not understand them by exploiting their confidence in adults (VII. Hauptstück, §12). Such a suggestion is directly contrary to the whole idea of *Emile*, which is that children should be taught only what they can understand well enough to formulate by themselves. Goethe's ideas on teaching are clearly much closer to Rousseau than to Basedow, at least as exemplified in the overall conduct of the *Wanderjahre*, where the didactic author does not impose views, but only makes material available for the reader to form them. Thus the doctrine of reverence would seem, at least on one level, to run counter to Goethe's real feeling about pedagogy, and once more to be almost a burlesque of Basedow's overenthusiastic spirit.

This tendency to over-systematize and to feed a child as much information as possible, especially (though by no means only) about religion and morals is thoroughly typical of Basedow (compare Herder's criticism quoted by Eichendorff above). Campe also displays the same tendency: he, too, devotes essays to games for teaching Latin and to model conversations for parents to use in teaching little children about God; *Robinson der jüngere* is anxiously didactic in matters pertaining to religion. Rousseau, of course, hates nothing more than rigid systems, his ideal tutor would have but one pupil for his whole life-time. The sort

---

[21] *Emile ou de l' éducation*, ed. F. and P. Richard (Paris, 1964), p. 162.
[22] *Emile*, p. 164.

of *laissez-faire* education Wilhelm suffered at the hands of the *Turmgesellschaft* seems much closer to Rousseau than the well-meaning officiousness of the eighteenth-century pedagogues who proposed to make Rousseau widely applicable. By systematizing him they destroyed him; their systems are not for the natural, untrammeled spirit. Hence Felix, who is, after all, another Euphorion-figure, bursts free from the pedagogic province.[23] Instead of becoming a well-adjusted member contributing to the smooth running of a group, he remains an unregenerate individual. He applies what he has learned to his private ends, and surrenders himself to his passions—first with Hersilie, then symbolically with his fall into the river. Wilhelm, the real pedagogue in the novel, comes to the rescue. This, then, is the ultimate sense of the fusion of the doctor and teacher: the great teacher, like Rousseau's teacher, does not feed material to the pupil, but is there at the critical moment to provide help and support as needed. When Faust meets Chiron in the "Klassische Walpurgisnacht," he begins to rhapsodize on Chiron's reputation as a pedagogue, but the gruff centaur replies: "Selbst Pallas kommt als Mentor nicht zu Ehren;/ Am Ende treiben sie's nach ihrer Weise fort,/ Als wenn sie nicht erzogen wären (ll. 7342 ff.). So in the *Wanderjahre*, too, the pedagogues, the systematizers, are supplanted by the healer who acts in response to a particular stimulus. Thus Felix's implicit rejection of the pedagogic province should be read once more as a parody, or literary correction, of the over-zealousness of Rousseau's earliest German disciples.

Goethe clearly had great respect for Basedow, in spite of his criticisms. At the end of Book Fourteen of *Dichtung und Wahrheit* he summarizes his thoughts on both Lavater and Basedow. In both he sees high ideals forced to compromise with, and ultimately destroyed by, the world:

> Indem ich nun beide beobachtete ..., so wurde der Gedanke rege, daß freilich der vorzügliche Mensch das Göttliche, was in ihm ist, auch außer sich verbreiten möchte. Dann aber trifft er auf die rohe Welt, und um auf sie zu wirken, muß er sich ihr gleichstellen; hierdurch aber vergibt er jenen hohen Vorzügen gar sehr, und am Ende begibt er sich ihrer gänzlich. Das Himmlische, Ewige wird in den Körper irdischer Absichten eingesenkt und zu vergänglichen Schicksalen mit fortgerissen. (HA X, 39)

Goethe planned a drama on this theme—*Mahomet*; the drama was never completed, but instead, his tribute to Basedow eventually found much different form in the *Wanderjahre*.

For the current readers of the *Wanderjahre*, who are scarcely even aware of Rousseau, much less Basedow and Campe, these chapters are elusive indeed. But, as in the rest of the novel, the irony was elusive enough even for Goethe's contemporaries. I must emphasize at this point, that the level of parody discovered here

---

[23] Compare "Euphorion" = "high spirits" to "Felix" = "happy."

should by no means interfere with serious interpretations of ideas advanced in the pedagogic province, any more than it did for Makarie or the Mignon material. Like Makarie, it is one of Goethe's fairy-tales—for which the Abbé's "Märchen" was the prototype. The real and the fantastic, the serious and the ironic are so interwoven with one another, that they are no longer to be separated.

3. PRIOR AND PERCY: "DAS NUSSBRAUNE MÄDCHEN"

To turn to the novellas now, exactly the same kinds of parodistic reference can be observed—sometimes more friendly, as with the *Lehrjahre*, sometimes less, as with the pedagogic province. I have already discussed two cases of such reference: the pictures in "Sankt Joseph der Zweite" and the awareness in the frame that "Die pilgernde Törin" is a translation. "Das nußbraune Mädchen," "Der Mann von funfzig Jahren," "Die gefährliche Wette," and "Die neue Melusine" also have sources, and awareness of them is equally important in interpreting the novellas. Their sources are all minor literary figures of the eighteenth century—Matthew Prior, Bishop Percy, August von Kotzebue and J. K. A. Musäus. In this context I will also discuss Book Two, chapter eleven, and the references to Laurence Sterne that dot the second half of the novel.

The title "Das nußbraune Mädchen" comes from the fifteenth-century English "Ballad of the Not-browne Mayde." While the source of the title has long been recognized, the importance of the theme for Goethe has been ignored.[24] Matthew Prior brought the ballad to the attention of the eighteenth century when he printed it along with "Henry and Emma," his own pastoralizing heroic-couplet version of the same motif. Thence it found its way into Percy's *Reliques*, and from there into Herder's *Volkslieder*, where it appears in a particularly lovely, impressively condensed version, presumably by Herder.[25] In a footnote to the ballad, Herder writes: "Ein bekanntes und beliebtes Lied, das der feine und zärtliche Prior in seinen 'Heinrich und Emma' umgebildet hat."[26] References to its location in Prior and Percy follow. Thus Herder attests to the general popularity of the ballad, as well as to his knowledge of Prior's version. Goethe, too, was doubtless familiar with both English versions, for the discrepancy in rank between the nut-brown maid and her "lover" Lenardo (mentioned tangentially by Wilhelm[27]) is not an issue in Herder's translation, but is in the two English versions.

[24] Trunz, for example, explains it as a "geflügeltes Wort" in Hersilie's circle, 647.

[25] T. Percy, *Reliques of ancient English Poetry*, II (London, 1765), 20 ff.; J. G. Herder, *Stimmen der Völker in Liedern*, Book III, no. 11.

[26] *Werke*, ed. H. Düntzer, V (Berlin, n.d.), 150.

[27] 144. Both Hersilie and Makarie have long since been aware that Lenardo confused the poor girl with the more acceptable daughter of the uncle's bailiff, but have deliberately left him in this error, apparently to forestall any further involvements.

The English ballad is a dialogue in which A and B take the parts of the lover and nut-brown maid respectively in order to prove that women are not so fickle and faithless as men would ordinarily like to assume. The young man comes to the nut-brown maid one night to say farewell forever; he has been outlawed for murder and must flee to the forest. The girl insists she will go with him: he lists all the discomforts and dangers, she answers each by saying it will be insignificant in the face of her love for him. He tells her she will be fickle like all other women, to which she replies she has already proved her faith by loving him though he is but a squire and she a baron's daughter. He finally admits that he has another, better-loved woman waiting for him in the forest; she answers that she will follow and be their uncomplaining servant. At this the young man explains in delight that he was only testing her faith; he is neither outlawed nor even a squire, but son of the Earl of Westmoreland, and she shall shortly be his wife.

Prior refines the rambling, rather charming ballad into an even more rambling rococo idyll addressed to "Bright Chloe, object of my constant vow."[28] Instead of the didactic prologue and epilogue of the ballad a long introduction describes the development of their love affair, and it ends with a picturesque closing tableau complete with putti, Roman deities and patriotic prosopopeia. Emma, who was nicknamed "nut-brown maid" as a child for no particular reason, is a delicate English beauty, with an "ambrosial plenty"[29] of shining hair and tiny waist. She herself speaks of her "little heart"[30] and "This little red and white of Emma's face."[31] She is, of course, the most beautiful, most virtuous, and most charming lady of the land. The poem is, as Herder said of Prior, thoroughly "fein und zärtlich."

Goethe uses the ballad as the basis for his story, but with curious changes. To begin with, he turns the central motif of the ballad inside out. The man and girl exchange roles—the girl, Nachodine-Susanne, is now really of low degree, a cottager's daughter, and the man does not disguise his high standing. No longer does the man test the girl's faith by pretended exile, but Nachodine must in fact go into exile, while Lenardo discovers only through her absence that he loves none but her. The ballad aims at preventing a breach of faith; Goethe's story begins with Lenardo's failure to fulfill his promise to Nachodine. The issue at stake, finally, is not the renunciation of comforts and social station for the sake of love, but the renunciation of love itself for moral and social reasons. Thus all the elements of the ballad are present, but in altered form.

Goethe adds to the beginning Lenardo's peculiar confusion of the nut-brown maid with another girl of his acquaintance, Valerine, and has Lenardo visit the

---

[28] M. Prior, *Literary Works*, ed. H. B. Wright and M. K. Spears, I (Oxford, 1959), 278.
[29] Prior, 290.
[30] Prior, 292.
[31] Prior, 292.

other girl first by mistake (I, 11)—an episode with no apparent significance or consequences in the rest of the novel. If the episode has no particular consequences in the novel, then it must have some significance in itself—for it is by now sufficiently clear, I trust, that the *Wanderjahre* is a well thought out, if unorthodox assemblage of material. The problem is best approached through consideration of the two girls. Lenardo evidently confuses the two because their names are so similar—Nachodine, Valerine—since otherwise they are completely different.[32] In Hersilie's formulation: "Wie er [Lenardo] sich der blonden Schönheit so genau erinnern und mit der Tochter des liederlichen Pachters, einer wilden Hummel von Brünette, verwechseln kann, die Nachodine hieß und die wer weiß wohin geraten ist, bleibt mir völlig unbegreiflich" (76). Blond beautiful Valerine is the daughter of the uncle's bailiff. As might be expected from her great beauty and charm, as well as the good qualities of her father, she has made an excellent match, and is happily married to a wealthy landed gentleman. Her straightforward neo-classical name seems to be derived from the Latin "valeo," to be well or strong, to be worth something.[33] Nachodine, by contrast, is wild and strange; her dark coloring earns her the nickname "nut-brown maid." The daughter of an inefficient, but very pious cottager who is evicted in order to pay for Lenardo's grand tour, she is too young to help him, although she promises to develop into a strong, efficient woman. Her name is Bohemian in origin (Náchod is a city north-east of Prague), suggesting a certain strangeness. To judge from a very late fragment entitled "Amazonen in Böhmen" (1829), the choice also implies— at least for Goethe personally—strength of character, since he explains there a Bohemian literary tradition of strong-minded women, with reference to the legend of Libussa, a queen whose subjects forced her to marry in an (unsuccessful) attempt to lessen her too effectively wielded power.[34]

Who are these two women really? I would suggest they are the heroines of the parallel English sources: Valerine is another Emma, perfect and successful; Nachodine is the intense, strong-minded "not-browne mayde" of the ballad. Thus Valerine is adored in a perfectly manicured, modern, civilized world, while Nachodine is thrust out into a threatening life of poverty, and ends up not in a forest, but at least in the mountains in a rather old-fashioned religious community. Prior's sugary refinement is implicitly rejected, then, in Valerine, in favor of the power and naturalness of the ballad; thus the episode represents a snatch of historical-literary criticism camouflaged in novelistic form. Goethe must have delighted in such an elaborately misleading motif that looks like an innocent part of the plot, yet functions completely separately.

---

[32] Suggested by Hersilie's comment that he remembers the "Inen" and the "Trinen" but has forgotten the "Etten" and the "Ilien" (77).
[33] "Valer" is a common name for positive figures in Lessing's early comedies.
[34] WA I, 42^2, 93 f.

The rest of the story can also be understood as a reversal of the ballad. What is the result of this reversal? For one thing, Goethe presents a much more realistic plot: going into exile does not imply a Robin Hood-existence in the Forest, but a peaceful, busy life in a mountain village, neither blissful nor idyllic, but scarcely total misery. In fact, Nachodine rises in the world through her exile, for she becomes head of a small cottage industry. She is no longer called by her nickname or even by her former name, but "die Schöne-Gute" or Susanne, a more peaceful Biblical name. The story is sufficiently realistic as to admit the long technical passages on weaving, copied virtually word for word from Meyer's descriptions, which fill so much of Lenardo's diary in Book Three.[35] Goethe has written a "correction" of the ballad. While he preferred its naturalness over Prior, it is still too sentimental and somehow unreal: the important kind of renunciation is not of one's physical comforts, and one does not escape society by running off into the forest; rather renunciation of the loved one, of love itself, is the important thing, and the romantic forest must yield to the real world, which consists of communities of people, supporting and depending on one another. Thus the story would appear to be a rejection of romance, and it is in this sense that Lenardo's remark might be understood when he begins to tell his story, that it is "eigentlich keine Geschichte" (129). The remark is surely significant since the chapter, which only begins on the preceding page, does carry the title "Das nußbraune Mädchen," which would certainly have reminded Goethe's readers of the ballad and Prior's little romance. Yet the relationship of the story to the ballad is not so simple, for the cold, hard facts of renunciation do not really prevail. Lenardo represents the forces for renunciation in the story; his family and Wilhelm do everything in their power to make him forget the nut-brown maid. He himself tries not to promise her anything and to remain disengaged. Nachodine, the figure carried over from the ballad, is a warm, impetuous spirit—*she* throws herself at Lenardo's feet and presses a burning kiss on his hand. Lenardo emphasizes their moral and spiritual opposition when he says: "Ihre Gründe ruhten auf Individualität und Neigung, die meinigen auf Pflicht und Verstand, und ich leugne nicht, daß sie mir am Ende selbst zu hart vorkamen," and "sie sprach lebhaft, mit Bewegung, und indem ich immer noch Kälte und Gelassenheit heuchelte, kehrte sie ihr ganzes Gemüt nach außen" (131). Not only does Lenardo recognize the opposition, but he puts himself in the wrong. And, in fact, Nachodine's warm spirit finally prevails: Lenardo is irresistably drawn to her and their eventual union is promised at the end (448). Thus while the more romantic elements of the ballad are corrected, the central theme of Lenardo's part of the novel—renunciation of individual concerns for the benefit of one's society—is also corrected and tempered by the "nut-brown maid." Once more

---

[35] WA I, 25², 262–71.

then we observe the same ambivalence toward the source that appeared in the discussion of the *Lehrjahre* parallels and the pedagogic province.

4. KOTZEBUE: "DER MANN VON FUNFZIG JAHREN" AND "DIE GEFÄHRLICHE WETTE"

Whereas the Prior "parody" involves mutual correction of the source and novel, Goethe's treatment of Kotzebue involves mainly correction of the source. Two of the novellas in the *Wanderjahre* owe at least their titles to works of Kotzbue—"Die gefährliche Wette" to a novella of the same title, "Der Mann von funfzig Jahren" to Kotzbue's one-act comedy "Der Mann von vierzig Jahren"—and, in the case of the latter, the central motif of the plot is also from Kotzebue.

Without doubt August Friedrich Ferdinand von Kotzebue (1761–1819) was the most popular German writer of his times. He grew up in Weimar, but spent most of his adult life in Russia, where he was a civil servant and, on the side, the author of more than two hundred plays, as well as novellas. His name was a household word all over Europe, and the plays were translated into all the European languages, including modern Greek and low German; as one witness to his great popularity, a contemporary literary lexicon devotes some forty-five pages to him and only twenty-five to Goethe.[36] Kotzebue was the declared enemy of the new literary trends in Germany, and Goethe was his main target. But in spite of this, Goethe recognized his appeal: six hundred thirty-eight of the four thousand one hundred thirty-six performances of the Weimar theater under Goethe's directorship were of Kotzebue plays. The correspondence with Schiller shows that, in spite of his animosity toward Kotzebue, Goethe did try to evaluate his plays fairly.[37]

In spite of his popularity and great dramatic facility, Kotzebue was insignificant in the long run because of his superficiality. "Der Mann von vierzig Jahren" illustrates this very clearly. As the play opens, Kammerjunker von Baarkopf, a foppish young dandy, and his father, who is interested in nothing but his distinguished ancestry, come to request seventeen-year-old Julie's hand for the Kammerjunker. The latter has convinced himself on the basis of copious evidence to the contrary that Julie indeed loves him. Julie, however, is in love with her guardian, the virtuous von Wiesen, whose only fault is that he is forty years old and therefore too old for the marriage game. Strangely enough von Wiesen loves Julie, as well; both, however, are too embarrassed to admit anything for fear of

---

[36] K. H. Jördens, *Lexicon deutscher Dichter und Prosaisten*, 6 vols. (Leipzig, 1806–1811).

[37] See, for example, the letter from Schiller of 10 December 1799 and Goethe's reply on 11 December, GSB, 778 f.

being rebuffed. The play proceeds on a series of misunderstandings by the three men—first that Julie indeed loves the Kammerjunker, then that she loves the only slightly less ridiculous father. In desperation von Wiesen throws himself at her feet, and "in order not to turn down a third suitor," Julie accepts him.

"Der Mann von funfzig Jahren" is clearly an adaptation of Kotzebue's play.[38] The rivalry in love between father and son, as well as the love of a young girl for an older man still form the basis of the plot. But Goethe has considerably unified Kotzebue's loose plot by fusing the girl's guardian and the father of the young suitor into the single figure of the major—whose age is a compromise between von Wiesen's forty years and von Baarkopf's sixty-five. He has also changed these characters from simple eighteenth-century humour characters to fully developed human beings—Flavio, for example, shows no traces of foppishness. A subtle reference to von Baarkopf's humorous preoccupation with his noble blood remains in the scene between the major and Hilarie before the family tree, where the motif is used to introduce a parody of the final scene of Kotzebue's play. In Kotzebue, von Wiesen goes on his knees before Julie, who teases him a little before she accepts his hand. Von Wiesen cries out, "Sie machen mich unaussprechlich glücklich!" and the curtain falls shortly thereafter on the tableau of the two hand in hand, von Wiesen still on his knees. Goethe has Hilarie accept the major with both of them standing up. After she tells him she loves him, he cries, "Du machst mich zum glücklichsten Menschen unter der Sonne!" Then he throws himself at her feet and formally asks for her hand—to which Hilarie responds, "um Gottes Willen, stehen Sie auf! Ich bin dein auf ewig" (180). The sentimental posturing in Kotzebue is a real embarrassment to Goethe's heroine, who cannot bear to see her lover on his knees, much less to tease him at such a moment. Hilarie is not simply the virtuous, well-brought-up stage heroine, but a complex character—somewhat confused as it turns out—whom the narrator treats with considerable ambivalence. Goethe adds the baroness, the young widow, the major's older brother, and Makarie to the schematic cast of Kotzebue's situation comedy, and sets the story in the context of the major's attempts to consolidate and improve the family fortunes. Indeed, Goethe's story really just begins where Kotzebue's ends, for Kotzebue's final pairing of young and old turns out to be quite unsuitable and must be adjusted.

These changes make Kotzebue's basic situation more serious, more interesting, and more significant. The characters become complex beings emerging from a real background (Kotzebue's play takes place entirely in a conventional garden-house). The shift from forty to fifty years may perhaps have been a personal one, for Goethe himself was forty when he settled down with Christiane

---

[38] It is thus significant that Goethe began to rewrite the novella as a play in 1823. See PA XXXVI, 196 f.

Vulpius, his common-law wife of twenty-three. In any case, a man of forty is in his prime. There can be no question in Kotzebue's play that von Wiesen is preferable to the self-centered young dandy on the one hand, or to the silly old man on the other—the supposed difficulty turns out to be no difficulty at all. By making the major fifty and Flavio, the son, a real person, Goethe turns Kotzebue's apparent problem into a real one. Hilarie must choose between two real options— the promise, beauty and warmth of the youth and the dignity and solid achievement of the father. The real problem enables Goethe to have a real plot, rather than the mechanical procession of misunderstandings which constitute the action of Kotzebue's play: he has turned a completely insignificant parlor comedy into a serious treatment of ethical problems. While the novella thus moves far beyond the play in correcting its insignificance, the ironic "happy end" of the novella, with the pairs happily sorted out, parodistically recalls the end of Kotzebue's comedy.

The relationship between Goethe's "Die gefährliche Wette" and Kotzebue's short novel of the same title depends mainly on the similarity in title, but is interesting nevertheless. Kotzebue describes his story as "ein muthwilliger Scherz."[39] While it is difficult to see the story as anything more than a high-spirited joke, the phrase in fact is intended to describe the playful genesis of the story—a friend dictated to Kotzebue twelve words, which Kotzebue was then to use as chapter titles for a twelve-chapter novel. In the forward to "Die Geschichte meines Vaters," another story written in the same manner, he comments, "so viel scheint mir indessen gewiß, daß diese Beschäftigung des Witzes jungen, angehenden Schriftstellern sehr nützlich werden könnte, denn sie lehrt Ideen an einander knüpfen, Verbindungen von Wahrscheinlichkeiten erschaffen, und Dinge zusammenfügen, die beim ersten Anblick durch Berge und Thäler von einander getrennt schienen."[40] It is thus a story with no pretensions, and the brusque introduction Kotzebue gives it is entirely in place: "Ein muthwilliger Scherz, welcher auf die nämliche Art entstanden ist, wie die *Geschichte meines Vaters* im Anfang dieses Bandes. Die Worte lieferte mir mein Freund Friedrich von Ungern Sternberg, und das ist Alles, was ich davon zu sagen weiß."[41] Over and above the obvious differences, Goethe's equally brusque introduction to his "Gefährliche Wette" resembles Kotzebue's in its playful indifference to the story about to follow. It reads:

> Unter den Papieren, die uns zur Redaktion vorliegen, finden wir einen Schwank, den wir ohne weitere Vorbereitung hier einschalten, weil unsere Angelegenheiten immer ernsthafter werden und wir für dergleichen Unregelmäßigkeiten fernerhin keine Stelle finden möchten.

[39] *Ausgewählte prosaische Schriften*, VIII (Vienna, 1842), 165.
[40] Kotzebue, *Schriften*, VIII, 8.
[41] Kotzebue, *Schriften*, VIII, 165.

> Im ganzen möchte diese Erzählung dem Leser nicht unangenehm sein, wie sie St. Christoph am heitern Abend einem Kreise versammelter lustiger Gesellen vortrug. (378)

There is the same lack of pretension—the story is also just a joke ("Schwank"), indeed, an "Unregelmäßigkeit." The narrator offers no introduction or explanation for its presence, other than that he found it among his papers.

Kotzebue's story is no more interesting than its introduction. Three attractive young women are caught in a shoemaker's shop by a thunderstorm and get into an argument over whose husband is most loving and most faithful. The shoemaker suggests a wager to settle the problem. Each of the ladies shows a trinket which she is to give her husband that evening. Then each one is assigned the husband of one of the others as her prey. In four weeks they are to return to the shoemaker's shop, where they will prove that they have seduced their assigned prey by showing his wife's trinket. The shoemaker bets each one a new pair of shoes that they will all have exchanged trinkets. The story then describes the wily traps they set, and sure enough, four weeks later each one returns with the other's trinket. The shoemaker has won the bet and, in the interest of their reputations, they remain his faithful customers ever after. Of course the young ladies have enjoyed every moment of it, although they cannot admit it. The story ends with a spurious moral: "Aus dieser wahrhaften Geschichte mögen meine schönen Leserinnen die Lehre ziehen, *daß Eitelkeit oft eben so weit und irre führt, als Liebe, und daß eine Frau die Macht ihrer Reize nie ungestraft zum Gegenstande einer Wette machen darf.*"[42] Neither the wanderings nor the punishment for their vanity have been particularly painful to the ladies or anyone else—indeed, quite the contrary. Were the story not so frivolous, this would have been a suitable moral. As it is, it can only be called persiflage.

What made Goethe use Kotzebue's title for his story about St. Christoph's wild practical joke for the entertainment of a band of vacationing students? Goethe's plot is simple, economical, and has nothing to do with love. St. Christoph bets his friends that he can tweak the nose of a particularly dignified man who comes to their inn, and not only get away with it, but be thanked as well. He succeeds by offering the gentleman his services as a barber. Since the students cannot keep the joke to themselves, it soon comes to the man's ears. The students and St. Christoph scarcely escape his wrath, the man later dies from the distress the affair causes him, his son fights a duel over it with Raufbold, one of the students, and both suffer unpleasant consequences. The similarity between the two stories lies in the moral. Goethe's story begins: "Es ist bekannt, daß die Menschen, sobald es ihnen einigermaßen wohl und nach ihrem Sinne geht, alsobald nicht wissen, was sie vor Übermut anfangen sollen" (378). The sentence

---

[42] Kotzebue, *Schriften*, VIII, 235.

describes perfectly the motivations of the three young women in Kotzebue's story. If their respective marriages are not as happy as they would like the rest of the world to believe, still they are all independent and well provided for. They agree to the shoemaker's wager with such alacrity not in order to prove their own husbands' virtue so much as to amuse themselves in the exercise of their own charms. Kotzebue himself points out in his moral that vanity (parallel here to Goethe's "Übermut") is his heroines' real motivation.

The important difference, of course, is that Kotzebue's story remains frivolous, while Goethe's becomes deadly serious at the end. Indeed, except for "Nicht zu weit," it is the most serious and frightening story in the novel; the student Raufbold suggests the demonic figure of the same name in the equally pessimistic fourth act of *Faust II*. The similarity is deliberate, because the name was added to the story in the revision for publication in 1829.[43] For Goethe Kotzebue's novella is highly immoral; it is what the Abbé in the *Unterhaltungen* rejected as "lüstern." He says, it will be remembered, that these "stellen uns etwas Gemeines, etwas, das der Rede und Aufmerksamkeit nicht wert ist, als etwas Besonderes, als etwas Reizendes vor und erregen eine falsche Begierde" (HA VI, 143 f.). Kotzebue's heroines trifle with their marriage bonds, and such behavior, in Goethe's terms, is asocial, and therefore immoral in the extreme. St. Christoph's behavior is also asocial and immoral: he has a skill (barbering) that could make him a useful member of society, but instead of using it constructively, he uses it to play a not very funny joke on an innocent traveler. Unlike Kotzebue, Goethe treats this asocial behavior not as a wonderful joke, but as something criminal. His revisions of the story emphasize this aspect.[44] In the original version the narrator is not St. Christoph, but another figure, presumably the barber who tells "Die neue Melusine." St. Christoph only figures in the last scene (suppressed in the final version), where he bangs heads together in a successful attempt to cover his friends' retreat. The affair is not related to the old man's death, the outcome of the duel is unknown to the narrator. The narrator concludes that he journeyed happily on until he had spent all the money he won from his bet. But in the published version, the terrible consequences are presented with no attempt to mitigate their harshness. At the same time, St. Christoph avoids telling details of his escape, which might place his actions in a more favorable light, and thus obscure the moral thrust of his tale. The money he wins is forgotten. The opening of the story, quoted above, implicitly condemns his behavior; the inspiration for the prank is a "böser Geist" (379). The "dangerous bet," then, in both Kotzebue and Goethe, involves asocial behavior, in the one case condoned, in the other condemned.

---

[43] See WA I, 25², 164 f. Previously the character was called simply "der Baron."
[44] The first manuscript is from 1807, but the story did not appear in the 1821 version of the novel, and was first published in 1829.

It is hardly surprising, considering the extent to which the *Wanderjahre* deals with the place of the individual in society, that Goethe would write an answer to Kotzebue's story. He does not work here with the normal tools of parody, there are no direct references to Kotzebue beyond the title; yet the story just as clearly functions as a correction of Kotzebue's treatment of the theme as does "Der Mann von funfzig Jahren."

5. MUSÄUS: BOOK III, CHAPTER 1; "DIE NEUE MELUSINE"; "DIE GEFÄHRLICHE WETTE"

To say that "Die gefährliche Wette" functions as a correction of Kotzebue by no means exhausts the implications of the story, for it does not even touch on the story's material, its curious narrator the gigantic St. Christoph, or its relationship to "Die neue Melusine," which immediately precedes it. These questions may all be answered by consideration of the literary basis for the beginning of Book Three, a fairy-tale called "Stumme Liebe" by Johann Karl August Musäus (1735-1787). Although Musäus, like Kotzebue, is quite unfamiliar today—at least to American readers—he was extremely popular among Goethe's contemporaries. Material borrowed from and referring to him runs all through the first chapter of Book Three, "Die neue Melusine" and "Die gefährliche Wette"; it represents some of Goethe's most playful late writing, and certainly forms the most delightful reading in the *Wanderjahre*.

Musäus is an unjustly forgotten figure. He was not only a great satirist, but was, like Lichtenberg, a beloved personality as well. The major source of information about his personality is a eulogy written by his nephew Kotzebue, unfortunately composed in typically exaggerated sentimental style—it ends, for example, "O Geist meines theuern Musäus! meines Freundes! meines Lehrers! schwebe hernieder und hauche sanft die Thräne von meiner Wange, in welcher die Buchstaben zittern, die mein Herz meiner Feder vorsagte!"[45] But in spite of the style, Musäus emerges from the essay as an unassuming, gentle, good-humored man of great common-sense. Originally he had studied theology with the intention of entering the clergy; but when his first congregation refused him because he had once been seen dancing at a country wedding, he turned to writing and teaching instead. His first major work, a satire of Richardson called *Grandison der Zweite*, appeared in 1760; in 1763 he became court-tutor in Weimar, in 1769 professor at the Weimar gymnasium. Until Wieland came to Weimar in 1772, Musäus was the court's leading literary light, providing operettas and poems on request, as well as reviews for Nicolai's *Allgemeine deutsche Bibliothek*. The arrivals of Wieland and Goethe somewhat eclipsed his local glory, although he

---

[45] Kotzebue, *Schriften*, VIII, 159.

was not so totally neglected as Kotzebue tries to suggest in his eulogy. He participated actively in the informal dramatic activities Goethe was always organizing, and there were rehearsals held in his home. In the *Campagne in Frankreich* Goethe mentions him as a major literary figure in Weimar around 1776 (HA X, 329). The *Physiognomische Reisen*, a satire on Lavater published in 1778, was highly successful, but by far his most influential work was the collection *Volksmärchen der Deutschen*. Although the *Arabian Nights* gained in popularity and influence all through the eighteenth century, Musäus was the first to present literary versions of more or less indigenous fairy-tale material successfully (according to Kotzebue he would invite little old ladies off the street to tell him stories). Unlike its nineteenth-century successors such as Grimm's *Märchen*, Musäus's collection does not strive to reproduce a genuine "folk" atmosphere; instead, they are satirical and urbane, full of topical references, and self-consciously ambivalent about the truth of the supernatural happenings they recount. The second edition appeared in 1787, and Jördens lists ten imitations by 1800.[46] The collection retained its popularity throughout the nineteenth century.

Musäus saw himself as a critic of the popular sentimentality of his time; even the *Volksmärchen* reflect his satirical attitude, to the great distress of his nineteenth-century critics, who felt that the satire mars the pure folk-tale atmosphere. In the preface to the collection he argues that the public is understandably bored with the sentimental drivel that passes for literature, and it is time for a change: "Hieraus wird Ihnen nun wohl, werter Freund, klar einleuchten, daß die Spiele der Phantasie, welche man Märchen nennt, zur Unterhaltung der Geister allerdings sehr bequem sind und daß das hochlöbliche Publikum bei dem Tausche, statt des empfindsamen Gewinsels sich mit Volksmärchen amüsieren zu lassen, nichts einbüßen werde."[47] The stories are full of literary and political references, as well as footnotes parodying the pedantry of contemporaries by means of inappropriate classical references or spurious sources and derivations. Two examples should suffice. An impoverished lady serves her neighbor rice-pudding as a special treat; Musäus writes a long footnote on the social significance of rice-pudding in the Middle Ages, ending with "Ohne Reisbrei wurde selbst kein kurfürstliches Beilager vollzogen, wie die archivarischen Urkunden aufbewahrter alter Küchenzettel besagen."[48] At another point he remarks, with reference to his hero's boredom:

> Die Lektüre war damals noch kein Zeitbedürfnis, man verstand sich nicht auf die Kunst, mit den hirnlosen Spielen der Phantasie, die gewöhnlich in den seichtesten Köpfen der Nation spuken, die Zeit zu töten. Es gab keine empfindsamen, pädagogischen, psychologischen, komischen, Volks- und Hexenromane; keine

[46] Jördens, *Lexicon*, III, 764.
[47] J. K. A. Musäus, *Volksmärchen der Deutschen*, I (Berlin, 1909), xii.
[48] *Volksmärchen*, IV, 27.

Robinsonaden, keine Familien- noch Klostergeschichten, keine Plimplampaskos, keine Kackenlaks, und die ganze fade Rosenthalsche Sippschaft hatte ihren Höckenweibermund noch nicht aufgetan, die Geduld des ehrsamen Publikums mit ihren Armseligkeiten zu ermüden.[49]

Musäus seems a very congenial figure for the later Goethe. The *Wanderjahre* is also playfully topical, though frequently more subtly; Goethe treats the pedantic and sentimental excesses and the superficiality of popular figures of the late eighteenth century—like Basedow and Kotzebue—with similar irony. It is therefore not surprising that material from Musäus is utilized. The choice of "Stumme Liebe," in particular, is readily explained. First of all, it was one of the more popular stories in the collection—Kotzebue even made a dramatic adaptation of it. More important, one of its central characters is the ghost of a barber: and barbering is, of course, the profession ordinarily associated with surgery, Wilhelm's chosen profession. Indeed, the barber in the *Wanderjahre* is a surgeon as well. Goethe thus cuts himself down to size: if, on the one hand, surgery seems an almost holy profession for Wilhelm (as in II, 11), another view of it appears in the ghost of an irresponsible barber in a fairy-tale, as the reader is satirically reminded in Book Three, chapter one.

Since Goethe uses so many details from "Stumme Liebe" in such oblique ways, I will begin by outlining the plot. Franz, son of a wealthy merchant, rapidly feasts his way through his patrimony, so that a few years after his father's death he must sell everything and move into the narrowest, darkest corner of Bremen. There he falls in love with Meta, who lives across the street; but Meta's mother, who has also seen better times, wants her beautiful daughter to marry well and guards her closely. Inspired by his love for Meta, Franz begins to use his head for the first time in his life; finally he manages to communicate with her by playing his lute, but their speechless relationship has scarcely begun when a rich brewer asks for her hand. The latter has promised his patron saint, St. Christopher, a mammoth candle if his wooing ends successfully, and the day he first sees Meta, the saint appears to him in a vision, to which Musäus remarks in a footnote: "Sankt Christoph erscheint seinen Schutzbefohlenen nie in einem einsamen Kämmerlein wie die übrigen Heiligen, mit Himmelslicht umflossen: Für seine gigantische Natur ist jedes Zimmer zu niedrig, daher tut der heilige Enakssohn alle Geschäfte mit seinen Pfleglingen nur vor dem Fenster ab."[50] But Meta, apparently, is not the girl St. Christopher intends for his devotee: for she rejects the brewer out of hand, to her mother's distress and Franz's delight. Franz realizes that his only hope lies in recovering his fortune, so he sets off for Antwerp to collect some old debts due his father. The Antwerp merchants are too clever for

[49] *Volksmärchen*, IV, 9.
[50] *Volksmärchen*, IV, 37.

the young man, however, and have him thrown into debtor's prison for back debts his father supposedly owed them. After his release he decides in desperation to try his fortune in America; accordingly he heads for the seacoast.

On the way he stops for the night in the little town of Rummelsburg, where the innkeeper, after one look at Franz's sorry person, tells him that the inn is full. Franz mutters a few imprecations under his breath which so incense the innkeeper that he decides to revenge himself. So, as a "special favor" he offers him a room in a nearby empty palace of which he is the custodian. He even offers a free supper, wine and candles. The reason for such unwonted generosity, it develops, is that there is supposed to be a ghost in the castle, in which, naturally, the innkeeper claims not to believe. He leaves Franz in the castle, assuring him repeatedly that everyone across the street will be ready to rush to his assistance, should the ghost really come; shortly thereafter, Franz sees the inn locked up tight. After a good supper he locks himself into a comfortable bedroom and goes to sleep. At midnight he awakens suddenly, and with dreadful noises, the ghost, a barber in a scarlet cloak, duly appears. Without a single word he shaves Franz's head absolutely bald. This strange act completed, he seems unwilling to leave and makes a strange gesture, which Franz correctly interprets to mean that he, too, would like to be shaved. Franz shaves him, and in so doing breaks the curse that forbids the barber to speak. He explains that three hundred years before he had been the barber of a wicked count who once inhabited the castle. As a bad joke he had shaved the hair off everyone who requested a night's shelter at the castle, and for that had been cursed to haunt the palace, continuing his old tricks until someone should do the same to him. Now that Franz has fulfilled the curse his soul can go to rest; as a reward he tells Franz to wait on a certain bridge in Bremen at the fall equinox, when he will meet someone who will make his fortune. Franz does as he is told, but no one comes. In the evening he finally enters into conversation with an old beggar who has been watching him all day. The beggar describes a dream he had years before of where he should find buried treasure. Although the beggar lends no credence to the dream, Franz recognizes the site described as a garden that had once belonged to his father. He finds the treasure, establishes himself once more, rewards the beggar, marries Meta and lives a happy virtuous life ever after.

In chapter one of Book Three Goethe re-creates the central adventure with the ghost, casting Wilhelm in the role of the good-hearted adventurer Franz. Like Franz, Wilhelm arrives in a little town, where he is told the inn is full. At first the innkeeper wants to send him on, but then decides to get special permission for him to stay there. Although the innkeeper in the *Wanderjahre* does not offer Wilhelm lodging out of malice, still he imposes special conditions on him. As in Musäus's story, the guest will have free room and board, but he must stay three days, participate in all activities, and ask no questions. In "Stumme Liebe" Franz can ask no questions at the crucial point, since the barber cannot talk; similarly, he has no choice about submitting to the shaving ritual. Furthermore, he indeed stays more than one night; for he remains there at the innkeeper's expense until his hair grows back. As Wilhelm sits in the common-room of the inn, who should appear, but a gigantic figure named St. Christoph, who is almost too big for the building to contain him (when he sits down on a bench it begins to crack). Like Musäus's saint, he is referred to as "Enakskind" (313). After supper Wilhelm goes to bed, but at first he cannot sleep—because he is seeing ghosts! "Die Geister aller lieben Freunde zogen bei ihm vorüber, besonders aber war ihm Lenardos Bild so lebendig, daß er ihn unmittelbar vor sich zu sehen glaubte" (314). The pun on "Geister" is clearly intentional, since the vision of Lenardo is prophetic (Lenardo appears the following day). Moments later Wilhelm is terrified by a strange, unidentifiable noise, just as Franz was in the haunted castle; but the ghosts have already appeared, in the prosaic manner of the *Wanderjahre* Wilhelm simply accepts the noise and goes to sleep.[51]

The silent barber, who ought to have materialized after all the noise, actually appears in the morning. Silently he shaves Wilhelm, then prepares to leave. After fruitless attempts to get a word out of him, Wilhelm cries, "Wahrlich! Ihr seid jener Rotmantel, wo nicht selbst, doch wenigstens gewiß ein Abkömmling; es ist Euer Glück, daß Ihr den Gegendiest von mir nicht verlangen wollt, Ihr würdet Euch dabei schlecht befunden haben" (315). As in the Lago Maggiore chapter, the literary references build up, and only become explicit at the end, where Goethe's figures and their referents are already beginning to part company.

What could possibly be the point of introducing this supernatural incident into the frame of the novel? There is no evidence that the episode functions as a commentary or as distancing from Musäus, as the Lago Maggiore chapter did. The reason lies, I think, in the similarity of functions between the two incidents. Franz and Wilhelm are, strangely enough, parallel figures. Both are inspired by love for an ideal woman to undertake a long series of adventures which are to make them worthy of Meta and Natalie. The important final result is not marrying the loved one, but becoming a useful member of society. In the course of "Stumme Liebe" Franz learns to use his wits to get what his money would have gotten him otherwise (Meta), but he also learns to live wisely and temperately, and to help other people. The adventure with the ghost, the final adventure in the sequence, serves as an initiation into a new way of life more sensible than his previous one. It is the place where he wins the most for himself by using his wits, and at the same time performs an unselfish action which promises no reward. The shaving of the head is a typical initiation ritual (as, for example, in the Catholic priesthood); the result, that Franz can return to Bremen and take up a better way of life, shows that the process was indeed an initiation. Similarly, the visit to the

---

[51] In the first version of the novel, the noise turned out to be St. Christoph snoring; by dropping the explanation Goethe forces the reader to recognize that it has relevance only as a literary reference.

inn is a sort of initiation for Wilhelm. Having learned his craft and practiced renunciation, he at long last returns to his own society, here represented by Friedrich and Lenardo—appropriately, one figure from the *Lehrjahre* and one from the *Wanderjahre*. But he is now on a completely different footing with them: Wilhelm puts Friedrich in his place when the latter tries to make fun of him as he used to do in the *Lehrjahre* (331), Lenardo will never send him off on errands for him again. He is ironically tested by being forbidden to ask the significance of what he sees—ironically, because the stricture is totally arbitrary, and because everything is explained without any questions being asked. Finally, he is playfully submitted to the same ritual as Franz was in earnest. It is only after Wilhelm has undergone this playful initiation that he is shown practicing his profession to rescue Felix. There is thus a charming contrast between the serious significance of Wilhelm's initiation and the playful manner and source of its execution. As was the case with the *Lehrjahre* parodies, there is a certain ambivalence between the charm of Musäus's story and the very prosaic workday world of the last book of the *Wanderjahre*, to which I will return later.

The references to Musäus continue in the motifs and techniques of "Die neue Melusine." First, the story is told by the barber from Musäus, the "Rotmantel" who shaves Wilhelm. Then, although the basic outline of the plot comes from the chapbook "Die schöne Melusine," the use of chapbook material is entirely in the spirit of Musäus.[52] Not only do they differ little from fairy-tales, but in addition, Musäus contrasts chapbooks very favorably with contemporary sentimental drivel.[53] Goethe reverses the motif of the lute in the love relationship between Franz and Meta, where music brings together the separated lovers. Instead of opening a path of communication between two separated lovers the lute playing drives a wedge between two who are together, the dwarf-princess and the narrator. This reversal is important, because in the novel proper, both in the pedagogic province and in the scenes at the inn with Lenardo's band of workers, music is the way for people to join together in harmony. Thus Goethe takes Musäus seriously: his characters appear in the frame, and when one of his motifs appears in a story, it is reversed. Kotzebue's characters, by contrast, appear sealed off in the stories.

Most important of all, "Die neue Melusine" plays on the discrepancy between the fairy-tale and real elements of the story. This tension is basic to Musäus's fairy-tale technique: consider, for example, Franz's recovery of the treasure at the end of "Stumme Liebe." If his father had only had time to tell him about it before he died, Franz would have been spared the long detour for it via

---

[52] Düntzer points out that the introduction to "Die neue Melusine" as it first appeared in the *Taschenbuch für Damen auf das Jahr 1817* is based on a scene in another Musäus story, "Der Schatzgräber." H. Düntzer, *Erläuterungen zu den deutschen Klassikern*, 1. Abtheilung, IV (Leipzig, 1876), 20.

[53] *Volksmärchen*, IV, 9.

Antwerp and Rummelsburg and all the concomitant adventures, but as it is, Musäus comments, "es waren beinahe so viel glückliche Konkurrenzen erforderlich, ehe das verscharrte Patrimonium an den rechten Erben kam, als wenn es durch die Hand der Gerechtigkeit an die Behörde wäre befördert worden."[54] It would be a mistake to consider such a comment strictly political satire: it is also persiflage of the author's own use of supernatural motifs. Goethe handles his introduction of the heroine's dwarf ancestry with subtler, rather Goldsmithian irony. It begins when the dwarf-princess tells her lover that the more recent descendants of the mighty dwarf-king Eckwald no longer forge great weapons and invisible chains as in days of yore, but to keep pace with the times have diversified into fashionable luxury items (367). It continues in the incongruity between her belief in the preeminence of the dwarves—God created the dragons, giants and knights all because of the dwarves—and the fact that her baby brother was so small that he got lost from his swaddling-clothes and was never found again (369). The same tension comes to light in the narrator's embarrassment that the princess set out to marry a knight and came up with him: "daß sie mich anstatt eines Ritters ergriffen hatte, das machte mir einiges Mißtrauen, indem ich mich denn doch zu wohl kannte, als daß ich hätte glauben sollen, meine Vorfahren seien von Gott unmittelbar erschaffen worden" (368). His unwillingness to believe his ancestors were directly created by God emphasizes the nature of the gap between the two of them—she belongs to a world of fantasy, while his is a more mundane existence.

It is precisely in his vacillation between these two worlds introduced from Musäus—the supernatural and the ordinary—that the significance of the story for the *Wanderjahre* rests. The narrator in "Die neue Melusine" is unable to make a commitment to either of the two worlds. Before he meets the mysterious beauty he is an irresponsible wanderer with no commitments to anything. When he falls in love with the dwarf-princess she expects him to commit himself fully to her. She gives him all the money he needs to travel in comfort; in return she asks only that he take proper care of her little chest. This chest has the same significance as Felix and Hersilie's chest—it symbolizes the mysterious basis of human love and may not be tampered with.[55] The warnings that she gives him about gambling, drinking, other women and his temper show that the real issue in guarding the chest is his faithfulness, his commitment to her. Eugen Wolff points out in his introduction to the novellas that there is a folk-saying about five things for the young man to guard against: "Würfel, Wein, Weiber, Wut, Wanderschaft."[56] All of these apply to the hero in this case, and sum up his inability to

---

[54] *Volksmärchen*, IV, 124.

[55] That he later sees her living in this chest is a delightful concretization of the trite idea that he has her locked up in his heart. However, from the point at which he sees her in it, the chest loses its symbolic significance, and remains simply a curious piece of craftsmanship.

[56] *Wilhelm Meisters Wanderjahre: Ein Novellenkranz nach dem ursprünglichen Plan*, ed. E. Wolff (Frankfurt am Main, 1916), p. 30.

settle down to anything, even to the most beautiful woman he has ever seen. At the same time, he is equally unable to give her up entirely; whenever she tries to end their relationship permanently he begs for another chance and swears to do whatever he is told. In order to stay with her he must renounce first his earlier habits, then his earlier stature. He is unable to do any of these things for very long, but he cannot renounce her either. Thus at the end of the story, when he regains his normal size, he appears to himself "um vieles dümmer und unbehülflicher" (376). He has indeed failed to succeed at anything in the course of the story.

I disagree here with most earlier interpretations of the story, which argue that he was wrong to give up his proper size for the sake of a woman, and had no choice but to return to his original size, which represents an ideal.[57] But since returning to normal size is seen as moral regression, it is hard to agree. Goethe shows the narrator as an entirely unprincipled man, with no ideals either before or after his transformation (he is only interested in the monetary value of the chest, which he takes with him). If he is right to flee the dwarves, it is only in the sense that it finally leads him to renunciation and to Lenardo's band. Similarly Trunz and Henkel affirm his correctness in escaping, because they overlook Musäus and see the dwarf-princess as a dangerous demonic power.[58] In Musäus the supernatural is but a higher order of nature in which morals and ethics work better than in the human realm, not a subterranean world from which great disruptive power issues, as in the rest of Goethe.[59] The only threat in "Die neue Melusine" comes from within the hero, the princess does everything she can to help him dispel it. The chest in the story does not share the threatening properties of its counterpart in the frame, at least not after he sees her in it. Thus an understanding of the importance of Musäus for the story is crucial to its interpretation.

The narrator ends his story, then, no wiser than he began. Only later, when after a long detour he meets Lenardo, does he learn the error of his ways. At any rate, the virtually totalitarian structure of Lenardo's band provides ample means to help the narrator restrain himself. The importance of this structure is made clear when Lenardo tells Wilhelm that the barber tells his stories when Lenardo allows it—"wenn ihm die Zunge durch mich gelöst wird" (353). This severe image suggests that the barber is strictly bound most of the time. Thus like "Die pilgernde Törin," "Wer ist der Verräter?" and "Die gefährliche Wette," this story deals with a case where renunciation does not take place. The barber who tells the story is very different from the man in the story. The narrator is Musäus's

[57] See, for example, G. Küntzel, " 'Wilhelm Meisters Wanderjahre' in der ersten Fassung 1821," *Goethe*, 3 (1938), 25. This is otherwise an extremely good essay.

[58] See HA VIII, 694 f. For a recent interpretation basically in agreement with mine see A. Klingenberg, *Goethes Roman Wilhelm Meisters Wanderjahre*, pp. 131 ff.

[59] This is true not only in "Stumme Liebe," but in all of the *Volksmärchen*. There are no *wicked* witches or *destructive* magic talismans; powerful magicians are men with an especially deep understanding of nature, like Albertus Magnus in "Richilde." Nature spirits are guardian spirits, as in "Nymphe des Bronnens." If they seem impish, like "Rübezahl," it is because they are misunderstood.

barber, who, if he has not renounced, has at least done a long penance; the hero of the story is no wiser at the end than when he began.

In several respects "Die gefährliche Wette" is a parallel piece to "Die neue Melusine." Not only does it follow immediately after it with only a letter from Hersilie in between, but it, too, is told by a character from Musäus, St. Christoph. In the original version, in fact, it was to have been told by the barber. To make things interesting Goethe has reversed the relationships between the narrator and the story. "Die neue Melusine" (about a love affair) is told by the barber; in Musäus, St. Christoph appears in connection with the brewer's love affair. "Die gefährliche Wette" is told by the putative saint about an irresponsible joke (in which, incidentally, he figures as a barber); in Musäus the barber played irresponsible jokes. Goethe underlines the essential parallel, the immoral position of the hero, by making them both left-handed, the traditional emblem of villainy. Both heroes have the problem that they do not control themselves, so they give themselves up to improper, sometimes harmful, activities. Like the barber, St. Christoph finds the solution in submission to the structure of Lenardo's tightly organized group. But why have the only two supernatural figures in Musäus's story become such exemplary figures in the comparatively realistic frame of the novel? The introduction to "Die neue Melusine" offers some clues. The barber, we learn, has renounced the ordinary chattiness of his trade in order to concentrate his energies on his gift of story-telling. Like the barber in "Stumme Liebe" his silence is imposed from the outside (by Lenardo), but not as a curse, or a limitation. Instead it is seen as renunciation to a good purpose. In the introduction to "Die neue Melusine" Lenardo says:

> Sein [the barber's] Leben ist reich an wunderlichen Erfahrungen, die er sonst zu ungelegener Zeit schwätzend zersplitterte, nun aber, durch Schweigen genötigt, im stillen Sinne wiederholt und ordnet. Hiermit verbindet sich denn die Einbildungskraft und verleiht dem Geschehenen Leben und Bewegung. Mit besonderer Kunst und Geschicklichkeit weiß er wahrhafte Märchen und märchenhafte Geschichten zu erzählen ... (353)

His renunciation of ordinary speech thus enables him to raise his narratives to a high level of significance—"wahrhafte Märchen," like the Abbé's "Märchen" in the *Unterhaltungen*. There is no irony in the fact that Lenardo makes this statement about a character taken from Musäus; for the *Volksmärchen*, like Goethe's "Melusine," hover on the dividing line between the fantastic fairy-tale and the novella with its complex emotional involvements. Musäus was unashamedly, though gracefully, didactic; aside from the satiric thrust of the stories, there is a positive moral significance as well. "Stumme Liebe," for example, shows the conversion of a dissolute libertine into a happy model citizen through the power of love. This didactic message can hardly be confused with the kind of significance Goethe managed to give his fairy-tales, yet Musäus's didacticism gives his work a certain solidity that one so sadly misses in Kotzebue. And it is this moral weight, I think, that makes Goethe admit into the frame of the *Wanderjahre* the two not only fictional, but supernatural characters from "Stumme Liebe," whose origin he clearly points to as fictional. As shown for the early novellas in the novel, here too there is an ironic relationship between the reality of the frame and the fictionality of the novellas.

Although Goethe makes figures from Musäus into spokesmen, he nevertheless corrects him as well. The correction is that the discrepancy between the supernatural and real worlds discussed above is not so easily mediated as Musäus's easy-going tone suggests. The chest in the "Melusine" that initially symbolizes the relationship between the two figures is revealed first as a comfortably furnished miniature living room, then is opened at the end to finance the hero's further travels. But the mysterious chest in the frame cannot be so easily flattened into reality. Hersilie's letter about the return of the chest to her immediately follows the story, and her agitation contrasts markedly to the barber's smugness. As it develops in chapter eighteen, this chest can *not* be opened with impunity. Instead, it remains a dangerous, inexplicable, mysterious phenomenon.

In spite of this correction, the section deriving from Musäus is the most playful one in the novel. It functions, finally, very much like the references to the *Lehrjahre*: only in the broadest sense is it parody, but in its friendly reference it draws the referent, too, into the circle of the *Wanderjahre* as another of its multifarious perspectives.

6. STERNE AND GOLDSMITH: BOOK II, CHAPTER 11

The last novella that I want to discuss is ordinarily not considered a novella at all, and often treated only in passing. It is Wilhelm's letter to Natalie at the end of Book Two and includes the story of the drowned boy, the most beautiful single passage in the novel.[60] Although the story has no literary source, it nonetheless refers outside of itself in ways that are very suggestive for a final understanding of the novel.

After a rambling introduction to the chapter Wilhelm begins to tell Natalie about an incident from his childhood, his first visit to the country. Wilhelm sees the trip as his first entry into nature. He begins with a description of the many enclosures surrounding them—"Wir in einer alten, ernsten Stadt erzogenen Kinder hatten die Begriffe von Straßen, Plätzen, von Mauern gefaßt, sodann auch

---

[60] The central importance of the chapter has been pointed out by H. M. Waidson in "Death by Water: or, The Childhood of Wilhlem Meister," *Modern Language Review*, 56 (1961), 44–53; but Waidson presents neither an interpretation nor a particularly convincing view of the function of the chapter in the novel. G. Röder's discussion (*Glück und glückliches Ende*, pp. 191–94) is much more interesting, but it, too, lacks an interpretation of the story.

von Wällen, dem Glacis und benachbarten ummauerten Gärten" (269). The world of nature beyond the city is referred to as "das Freie" (270). When they finally go, he says: "bald hatten wir alles Beschränkende der Straßen, Tore, Brücken und Stadtgräben hinter uns gelassen, eine freie, weitausgebreitete Welt tat sich vor den Unerfahrenen auf" (270). First they visit a country pastor where Wilhelm experiences both the beauty of country life, and the wonders of nature at the stream. Afterwards they visit the bailiff, whose daughter shows Wilhelm the riches of the garden. Wilhelm summarizes the experience:

> Und wenn ich hier noch eine Betrachtung anknüpfe, so darf ich wohl bekennen: daß im Laufe des Lebens mir jenes erste Aufblühen der Außenwelt als die eigentliche Originalnatur vorkam, gegen die alles übrige, was uns nachher zu den Sinnen kommt, nur Kopien zu sein scheinen, die bei aller Annäherung an jenes doch des eigentlich ursprünglichen Geistes und Sinnes ermangeln. (273)

The episode thus represents to Wilhelm his most significant contact with nature, an experience of the essence of nature that is reserved for the naive spirit as yet untouched by the claims of involvement with other people. The statement is made immediately prior to the announcement that Wilhelm's new friend, the fisherman's son, has drowned. He spends the rest of the day in desperation, and awakens the next morning in a strange and confused condition (276). The first thing he hears in the morning is his aunt wrangling for the crabs which the drowned boy had caught—she wants to use these curious products of nature for her own devious purposes; they do not fill her with wonder, as they did Wilhelm the day before. Thus Wilhelm's first experience with nature was also his purest.

But this experience of nature is inextricably woven with Wilhelm's first real social relationships as well: his first experience of friendship, for the fisherman's son, and of love, for the blond daughter of the bailiff. When the boy goes swimming and invites Wilhelm to follow, Wilhelm becomes very confused. "Mir war ganz wunderlich zumute geworden. Grashupfer tanzten um mich her, Ameisen krabbelten heran, bunte Käfer hingen an den Zweigen, und goldschimmernde Sonnenjungfern, wie er sie genannt hatte, schwebten und schwankten geisterartig zu meinen Füßen, eben als jener [the boy] einen großen Krebs zwischen Wurzeln hervorholend, ihn lustig aufzeigte" (271 f.). The intense erotic atmosphere—"schweben und schwanken" of course recalls the mood associated with Hilarie in the iceskating and Lago Maggiore passages—is aroused both by the natural setting and the boy. As the two boys dry off after their swim each is overwhelmed by the beauty of the other's naked body, and they swear eternal friendship. The passage directly foreshadows the final scene of the novel, where Wilhelm and Felix embrace in a comparable setting.

Similarly, Wilhelm's first stirrings of love for the little girl are inextricably wound up with his discovery of the beauty of nature. They wander hand in hand through the garden among flowers emblematic of the course of love. First they pass the earliest spring flowers—tulips, jonquils and narcissi; the last suggests Wilhelm's state before this day of freedom, before he had been outside of himself. Then they pass hyacinths that have already bloomed. The hyacinth takes its name from Apollo's beloved who died at the height of his youth; here the flower suggests the stage of friendship, in particular Wilhelm's new friend who is about to die. Lilies and roses, purity and love, "wisely" alternating with one another are about to bloom next, suggesting that Wilhelm and his companion are approaching the threshold of young love. The promise of more mature and lasting relationships appears in the jasmine and various shady shrubs that will bloom all summer; and the well-cared for anemones and carnations that will not bloom until autumn suggest hope for love even in old age. Wilhelm interprets this catalogue himself in the following paragraph, when he says that the first feelings friendship and love seized him on the same day.

Indeed, Wilhelm matures very rapidly on this one day, for he not only discovers the whole outside world—nature and other people—but he also learns the suffering that necessarily accompanies human involvement. His new friend drowns and Wilhelm is inconsolable, he tries everything he can think of to warm the dead body, even passionate prayer, as if, he says, he could perform wonders. But all is in vain; still crying, he is dragged back to the city and the intrigues of society, personified in his aunt. Wilhelm's father decides that it would be too unpleasant for the family to eat the crabs caught by the dead boy, but his aunt is only too happy to take them, for she can use them to extend her control over a highly placed official whom she feeds well in order to use his influence in her interests. She loves neither nature nor other people; instead she uses both. The contrast between Wilhelm's incipient passions and his aunt's social machinations is mediated at the end by the description of the father, who is interested in public health, and maintains that the boy could have been saved had someone let his blood. The father's position falls in the middle between Wilhelm and the aunt: "Er sah die bürgerliche Gesellschaft, welcher Staatsform sie auch untergeordnet wäre, als einen Naturzustand an, der sein Gutes und sein Böses habe" (278).

This triangle, too, reappears in the development of Felix's fate. Felix, given over entirely to his passionate love for Hersilie, cannot fit into the social patterns prescribed by the pedagogic province. Wilhelm, himself now in the role of father, mediates between the two by bringing Felix back to life (in II, 11 there is potential mediation—the boy could have been saved by the better medical treatment which Felix receives). Like his father, Wilhelm sees life as a natural alternation of bad and good, death and renewal, when he says, "Wirst du doch immer aufs neue hervorgebracht, herrlich Ebenbild Gottes! und wirst sogleich wieder beschädigt, verletzt von innen oder von außen" (460).

It is only natural that the story should foreshadow the conclusion of the novel, for ostensibly it explains to Natalie why Wilhelm has become a surgeon. The anecdote he tells at the very beginning of the chapter hints at the long process by which he chose his profession. By chance one day a boy finds an oarlock on the beach. It arouses his interest enough to make him get an oar, but since that is no use, he gets a boat to go with it. Eventually he becomes a great ship-owner. The element of chance in the story is very typical of Wilhelm, especially as he appears in the *Lehrjahre*; in fact, this little anecdote is a clear parallel to Friedrich's simile at the end of the *Lehrjahre*, when he tells Wilhelm: "Du kommst mir vor wie Saul, der Sohn Kis, der ausging, seines Vaters Eselinnen zu suchen, und ein Königreich fand" (HA VII, 610). In both cases intention plays no role (at least at first), Wilhelm finds his destiny by chance. But the difference here is more significant than the similarity—no one accidentally finds kingdoms in the mundane world of the *Wanderjahre*. Instead, only steady purpose and discipline eventually bring Wilhelm to his rather more modest goal. There are many references to the *Lehrjahre* at the end of the chapter, both to Wilhelm's interest in the theater and to the surgery equipment. Interestingly enough, the theater, and, thus, implicitly, the world of the *Lehrjahre*, is associated with Wilhelm's need for friendship and love, with the need for individual fulfillment: "Das Bedürfnis nach Freundschaft und Liebe war aufgeregt, überall schaut' ich mich um, es zu befriedigen. Indessen ward Sinnlichkeit, Einbildungskraft und Geist durch das Theater übermäßig beschäftigt" (279). His feelings for the dead boy, and his feelings of love for Natalie (as he suggests on pp. 280 f.) finally lead him to become a surgeon. Thus once again, his profession mediates between the extreme demands of individual and society, for he combines the social necessity for a useful profession with the personal need. It must be emphasized that Wilhelm chooses his profession not because of a special talent, as the *Wanderjahre* seems to preach, in the pedagogic province for example, but because he associates it with people he has loved personally. Thus in choosing his profession, Wilhelm mediates between the world of the *Wanderjahre*, which insists on a socially useful profession, and the *Lehrjahre*, which insists on fulfillment of the individual.

The chapter treats, then, the most important themes of the *Wanderjahre*—the relation of the individual to nature and society, the mode of his participation in society. Its position at the end of the second book as the last section of narrative before Wilhelm is shown in his period of fulfillment, as well as its summarizing nature, also indicate its centrality to the novel. This chapter replaces Natalie's sole appearance in the first version. There, also between the last visit to the pedagogic province and the meeting with Lenardo's band of wanderers at the inn, there is a dream-like scene in which Wilhelm sees Natalie through a telescope on the far side of a broad deep chasm. She, too, has a telescope and both wave. In his excitement to reach the adored being, Wilhelm almost falls over the edge, except that a helpful hand catches him. He has been saved from great danger, but also from great happiness. The scene is an allegory of renunciation, as it is understood in the first version. Wilhelm's love would consume him if his vow of renunciation did not hold him back—he would fall into the chasm, just as the fisherman's son and Felix fall into the water. The scene reminds one more of one of Jean Paul's dreams than of mature Goethe. The final version is no longer an allegory, but a myth, it is a much richer treatment of a far more complex theme. In the shift from holding back to healing, the emphasis has changed from renunciation to rebirth.

So far I have discussed only the content of the chapter, but its technique is also central to the novel: its fragmented, rambling, reflective structure, always trying to approach its subject from a different perspective, is precisely the technique of the novel as a whole. It is especially significant, then, that in this chapter Wilhelm comments on its structure, for in this context it may be taken as a comment on the structure of the entire novel. Wilhelm says:

> Wenn es dem Humoristen erlaubt ist, das Hundertste ins Tausendste durcheinander zu werfen, wenn er kecklich seinem Leser überläßt, das, was allenfalls daraus zu nehmen sei, in halber Bedeutung endlich aufzufinden, sollte es dem Verständigen, dem Vernünftigen nicht zustehen, auf eine seltsam scheinende Weise ringsumher nach vielen Punkten hinzuwirken, damit man sie in *einem* Brennpunkte zuletzt abgespiegelt und zusammengefaßt erkenne. (279 f.)

Clearly this statement describes the multi-perspectivity, and the same relationship between the reader and the novel that I discussed in Chapter Two. And Wilhelm's reference to the "humorist" who is the source of the technique is at least equally enlightening.

The humorist he refers to is, of course, Laurence Sterne, who otherwise figures prominently in the last book of the *Wanderjahre*. Indeed, the novel ends with a virtual eulogy to Sterne in the final pages of "Aus Makariens Archiv." The eulogy begins with aphorism 126: "Yorik-Sterne war der schönste Geist, der je gewirkt hat; wer ihn liest, fühlt sich sogleich frei und schön; sein Humor ist unnachahmlich, und nicht jeder Humor befreit die Seele" (480). This is a very positive statement indeed, for it is the highest praise possible in the period of aesthetic idealism, that a work of art should put the viewer in harmony with himself. It is all the more striking because it comes from an artistic theory concerned with problems of classical form—such rhetoric seems more appropriate applied to Schiller or Hölderlin, than to Sterne. The following seventeen aphorisms (127–143) are all borrowed from a collection of aphorisms called *The Koran*, which at the time was attributed to Sterne, although it was in fact by Richard Griffith. The next aphorism (144) is another strongly appreciative comment about Sterne. After a few aphorisms on German literature and on the theme of limitation, Goethe returns to Sterne. Aphorisms 157–174 describe him at length, emphasizing his sense of humor but at the same time also his high moral seriousness. Goethe concludes then with another series (175–181), some of which are taken directly from the *Koran*, some of which are parallels to material in that collection.[61] Like the Musäus references, this kind of borrowing serves to widen

---

[61] References for borrowings and parallels are in W. R. R. Pinger, *Laurence Sterne and Goethe* (Berkeley, 1920), pp. 33–39.

the circle of the *Wanderjahre* by association: indeed, the concluding eulogy makes Sterne's presence in the novel loom very large.

Thus Goethe points to two ways in which Sterne is important for the technique of the novel. "Aus Makariens Archiv" emphasizes his sense of humor; Book Two, chapter eleven his structure. If Goethe's humor in the *Wanderjahre* remains more within the bounds of propriety than Sterne's, it still uses many of the same devices. Both authors treat their characters, their readers, and the structure of their novels with considerable irony. Sterne repeatedly points out the disorganization of *Tristram Shandy*, includes blind motifs, or promises chapters which he only much later writes—or does not write—and when he does finally write one, he points out gleefully how long the reader has been waiting for it. Such a one is the chapter on button-holes which he promises any number of times; finally in Book Five, chapter eight, with elaborate politeness, he requests the reader to absolve him from writing any such chapter. Similarly in the *Wanderjahre* Goethe playfully wishes he could end the volume at the "Zwischenrede" in Book Two (244): the wish is of course ironic since it falls in the middle of the book. The unexplained noise in III, 1 is a typical blind motif, while the ironic, brusque introductions to "Der Mann von funfzig Jahren" and "Die gefährliche Wette," which suggest that their position in the novel is quite arbitrary, also reflect the same kind of humor.

Goethe borrows structural techniques from Sterne, rather than verbal humor, and it is not surprising to find that Goethe applies some of these structural techniques seriously. One such example is the unfinished story. It is funny in *Tristam Shandy* when Trim does not manage to finish his story of the "King of Bohemia and his seven Castles," but Goethe uses the technique to impressive serious effect in "Nicht zu weit." Goethe is also much less playful when he presents a story in pieces scattered through the narrative: contrast "Das nußbraune Mädchen" with Uncle Toby's courtship in Sterne. He also uses Sterne's basic structuring principle in a less self-consciously humorous way than Sterne, although he uses it for the same purpose. That is, the *Wanderjahre*, like *Tristram Shandy* or the *Sentimental Journey*, has a loose schematic plot: it concerns Wilhelm's travels (like Tristram's biography or Yorick's travels). But the major substance of all three novels comes in the materials tangential to the plot, the novellas in Goethe, the digressions in Sterne. The structure of their novels is not linear, but, as Wilhelm describes it, reflective and multifarious. Sterne is thus not only the subject of final tribute in the *Wanderjahre*, but the inspiration of its structure as well.

But Sterne's organized formlessness does not really correspond fully to Wilhelm's letter to Natalie, much less to the novel as a whole, for the effect of its central episode, as well as of the other novellas, depends on a coherence totally foreign to Sterne. The choice of material, too, the visit to the country, is so unlike Sterne, that one is forced to ask how it came to form the center of a chapter avowedly patterned on him. Two of Goethe's very late remarks on Sterne will clarify this problem. Eckermann reports for 16 December 1828 the following remark: "Ich verdanke den Griechen und Franzosen viel, ich bin Shakespeare, Sterne und Goldsmith unendliches schuldig geworden."[62] The high estimate of Shakespeare seems obvious, that of Sterne is clear after the above discussion, but can he really be serious about Oliver Goldsmith, author of the *Vicar of Wakefield?* If so, why? Fortunately Goethe elaborates on the point at some length in a letter to Zelter on Christmas 1829:

> Es wäre nicht nachzukommen, was Goldsmith und Sterne gerade im Hauptpuncte der Entwicklung auf mich gewirkt haben. Diese hohe wohlwollende Ironie, diese Billigkeit bey aller Übersicht, diese Sanftmut bey aller Widerwärtigkeit, diese Gleichheit bey allem Wechsel und wie alle verwandten Tugenden heißen mögen, erzogen mich aufs Löblichste, und am Ende sind es denn doch diese Gesinnungen die uns von allen Irrschritten des Lebens endlich wieder zurückführen. Merkwürdig ist noch hiebey daß Yorik sich mehr in das Formlose neigt und Goldsmith ganz *Form ist, der ich mich denn auch ergab, indessen die werthen Deutschen sich überzeugt hatten die Eigenschaft des wahren Humors sey das Formlose.*[63]

Goethe not only sees in Goldsmith the same narrative pose as in Sterne, but above and beyond philosophical or ethical considerations, he appreciates Goldsmith's sense of form. After such a strong statement, it is possible to see the relevance of *The Vicar of Wakefield* to the *Wanderjahre*.

Indeed, Goethe's statement to Zelter points out clearly the elements of Goldsmith's novel that were important to him. Goldsmith's consistently benevolent irony is, like Goethe's, frequently easy to miss. The vicar's "Sanftmut bey aller Widerwärtigkeit, ... Gleichheit bey allem Wechsel" are a form of renunciation. In Goldsmith's novel the Primrose family must renounce first its fortune, its pretensions to elegance, and eventually, through the seduction of the elder daughter, its unstained social honor. Through all these trials the vicar encourages them to submit cheerfully to the blows of fate in order to live their lives as fully as they can, regardless of shifting external circumstances. Even in debtors' prison he persistently preaches this point of view; there his faith in humanity and life transforms the social chaos he finds into a highly organized, moral polity, which even imposes fines for swearing. This is exactly the same process the Abbé performs in the *Unterhaltungen;* it is also what Lenardo does in the *Wanderjahre,* where the barber and St. Christoph submit themselves to his authority in order to help, rather than disrupt society.

[62] Goethe's remarks on Sterne are catalogued by W. R. R. Pinger, *Sterne and Goethe*, pp. 12–45. This one is §78.
[63] WA IV, 46, 193–94; Pinger §143. The statement is inspired by Goethe's recent rereading of *The Vicar of Wakefield.*

Goethe has two earlier treatments of Goldsmith material that are important for understanding the *Wanderjahre*. The first of these is *Werther*. Werther has a great deal in common with Goldsmith's hero Burchell: both young men live in their setting with no real attachment to it. As a gentleman without fortune Burchell wanders from family to family, wherever he is welcome, but seems to lack any real reason to be in the neighborhood; Werther comes and settles more or less as a visitor. Both quickly form friendships and are generally well-liked; both are objects of sympathy; both are particularly good with small children. Werther has, of course, read *The Vicar of Wakefield*, and when Lotte talks about it in passing, Werther loses control of himself and talks about it impulsively (HA VI, 23). Shortly thereafter he accompanies Lotte on a visit to an elderly pastor in the country. They find the old man sitting in the yard playing with his youngest son. He and his family, which consists also of a wife and daughter named Friederike, recall the idyllic family life of Goldsmith's novel. The resemblance is heightened when Werther delivers a sermon on cheerfulness, a favorite theme of the vicar, to Friederike's surly lover. Following as it does so closely upon Werther's expression of enthusiasm for Goldsmith's novel, the scene must be read as a deliberate reference to it.

The second reference to Goldsmith is the description of the affair with Friederike Brion in Book Ten of *Dichtung und Wahrheit*. The use of the name Friederike for the pastor's daughter in *Werther* already suggests the relationship of the two passages to one another. As Goethe is about to begin the episode, he interrupts himself: "Mir sei jedoch, ehe ich meine Freunde zu ihrer ländlichen Wohnung führe, vergönnt, eines Umstandes zu erwähnen, der sehr viel beitrug, meine Neigung und die Zufriedenheit, welche sie mir gewährte, zu beleben und erhöhen" (HA IX, 426). This "circumstance" is none other than Goethe's first acquaintance with *The Vicar of Wakefield*, which Herder read aloud to him in Strassburg. After a discussion of the artistry and irony of the novel, Goethe proceeds to describe his first meeting with Friederike's family, which turns out to be the exact parallel to the family in Goldsmith's novel. Indeed, the whole experience is stylized in terms of *The Vicar of Wakefield* by the extended comparisons to it (HA IX, 434 f., 436, 462, 467). Friederike's father is a country pastor, her brother and sister are called by the names of their counterparts in Goldsmith, and Goethe himself appears in a role exactly parallel to Goldsmith's Burchell—like the latter he is even introduced to the family at first in disguise.

The parody in *Dichtung und Wahrheit* is particularly illuminating in connection with the *Wanderjahre*, because Goethe reports there that he first told "Die neue Melusine" in Sesenheim (HA IX, 446 f.). The story was already written down when Goethe wrote about it in *Dichtung und Wahrheit*, but he was saving it for the *Wanderjahre*, where it was thematically more appropriate. When he says, therefore, "Ich würde es hier einrücken, wenn ich nicht der ländlichen Wirklichkeit und Einfalt, die uns hier gefällig umgibt, durch wunderliche Spiele der

Phantasie zu schaden fürchtete" (HA IX, 446), he is referring more to the content than the tone, for there is something idyllic about the happy-go-lucky world in which the hero painlessly escapes all dangers and involvements. The narrative tone of the novella, too, is very much in the spirit of Goldsmith: the narrator, like Goldsmith's vicar, officially takes cognizance of his faults, yet still unconsciously betrays considerable self-satisfaction. Even in prison, Goldsmith's vicar is anxious to let his fellow prisoners know he is a scholar; comparable passages in "Die neue Melusine" would be the narrator's "ideal" view of himself as a tall man while among the dwarves, or the dwarf-princess's excessively dwarf-centered world-view.

If there are hints at Goldsmith's world in "Die neue Melusine," there are even stronger ones in Book Two, chapter eleven. The background for the events in that chapter is a visit to a country pastor, and then to a local official. Since the pastor plays no particular role in the story—certainly none concerned directly with his profession—the only reason for the choice can be a literary one. And the literary significance of the country pastor, as just seen in *Werther* and *Dichtung und Wahrheit*, is a deliberate reference to Goldsmith.[64] The other figure in the setting, the bailiff, recalls Lotte's father in *Werther*, a figure once again within the circle of Goldsmith references, though not directly borrowed from him. More specific detail finds its way into the *Wanderjahre* from Goldsmith as well. The hero Burchell, Sir William Thornhill in disguise, turns out at the end to have studied medicine and, though a gentleman, to be a competent physician. While the motif is too well-developed by Goethe to be merely a literary reference, Thornhill is an important predecessor for Wilhelm's combination of medical skill with more general capabilities for the humane improvement of his fellows. Indeed, the Goldsmith passage in *Dichtung und Wahrheit*, the Friederike episode, is interrupted by a page on Goethe's medical studies in Strassburg (HA IX, 451). Thus the association of medicine with the Goldsmith material is not simply fortuitous in the *Wanderjahre*.

It will be remembered that above all Goethe admired Goldsmith's feeling for form, as opposed to Sterne's formlessness. This statement contains the key to the curious structure of chapter eleven, and, indeed, of the whole novel. While the reflective, rambling structure may be related to Sterne, the tight coherence, the closed form of most of the novellas, even of those that flow into the frame, is most untypical of Sterne, whose anecdotes are as incoherent as the rest of his novel. But this closed, well-rounded form is precisely what Goethe admired in

---

[64] It is by no means unreasonable for Goethe to have expected the attentive reader to perceive such a reference, for *The Vicar of Wakefield* was a favorite work in Germany at the time. F. Schlegel refers to it as almost the greatest English novel in the "Brief über den Roman" (*Kritische Schriften*, ed. W. Rasch [Munich, 1964], p. 517), and Goethe says in *Dichtung und Wahrheit* that he can assume his readers are familiar with it (HA IX, 428).

Goldsmith. It is very tempting to see the structure of the chapter as a balance between the two: the rambling frame explicitly refers to Sterne as its source, the tightly formed center implicitly—by its content—refers to Goldsmith. Thus the form of the whole novel may be seen as a fusion of Goethe's most admired eighteenth-century predecessors.

7. THE *WANDERJAHRE* AND THE EIGHTEENTH CENTURY

It remains now to find some explanation for Goethe's choice of models for the *Wanderjahre*. At first sight they are a strange and varied collection—Goethe's own *Unterhaltungen* and *Lehrjahre*, a French novella ("Die pilgernde Törin"), Basedow and Campe, Prior and Percy via Herder, Kotzebue, Musäus, Sterne and Goldsmith. These figures have neither the historical significance nor the vast historical range of the parodies in *Faust II*, which sweeps through the entire history of western literature, from the Greeks to Byron. Instead they are all late eighteenth-century figures, many virtually forgotten today. But what the authors do have in common is that they were enormously popular in Germany in their own time—namely in the last decades of the eighteenth century and the very beginning of the nineteenth. That being the case, it is worth examining what Goethe thought about the period and the relationship of any of these writers to it.

In Book Thirteen of *Dichtung und Wahrheit*, Goethe describes the mood from which *Werther* arose. This description is particularly interesting here, because it is not couched in social, but in literary-historical terms. He talks about the feelings that led people to commit suicide, but immediately qualifies his discussion by saying:

> Solche düstere Betrachtungen jedoch, welche denjenigen, der sich ihnen überläßt, ins Unendliche führen, hätten sich in den Gemütern deutscher Jünglinge nicht so entschieden entwickeln können, hätte sie nicht eine äußere Veranlassung zu diesem traurigen Geschäft angeregt und gefördert. Es geschah dieses durch die englische Literatur, besonders durch die poetische. (HA IX, 579 f.)

English poets, according to Goethe, are all misanthropes; partly this is due to the importance in England of political satire, which always tries to make the rest of the world look as bad as possible, but largely it is just native melancholy, which pervades all English poetry—"Selbst ihre zärtlichen Gedichte beschäftigen sich mit traurigen Gegenständen. Hier stirbt ein verlassenes Mädchen, dort ertrinkt ein getreuer Liebhaber, oder wird, ehe er voreilig schwimmend seine Geliebte erreicht, von einem Haifische gefressen" (HA IX, 581). Young's "Night Thoughts," Gray's "Elegy" are cited as typical examples, but even Milton's "L'Allegro" and Goldsmith's "Deserted Village" do not escape criticism. Indeed, "unser Vater und Lehrer" Shakespeare himself is guilty in Goethe's eyes of seducing German youth into melancholy—"Hamlet und seine Monologen blieben Gespenster, die durch alle jungen Gemüter ihren Spuk trieben" (HA IX, 582). *Ossian* represents, of course, the Ultima Thule, as Goethe says, of this movement. He emphasizes that he is not speaking of the tragic hero who commits suicide: "Wir haben es hier mit solchen zu tun, denen eigentlich aus Mangel von Taten, in dem friedlichsten Zustande von der Welt, durch übertriebene Forderungen an sich selbst das Leben verleidet" (HA IX, 583). After conquering his own suicidal tendencies, he says, he wrote *Werther* to help others escape from this oppressive mood of the early seventies.

The *Campagne in Frankreich* comes back to this period, but from a rather different and interesting point of view:

"Werther," bei seinem Erscheinen in Deutschland, hatte keineswegs, wie man ihm vorwarf, eine Krankheit, ein Fieber erregt, sondern nur das Übel aufgedeckt, das in jungen Gemütern verborgen lag. Während eines langen und glücklichen Friedens hatte sich eine literarisch-ästhetische Ausbildung auf deutschem Grund und Boden, innerhalb der Nationalsprache, auf das schönste entwickelt; doch gesellte sich bald, weil der Bezug nur aufs Innere ging, eine gewisse Sentimentalität hinzu, bei deren Ursprung und Fortgang man den Einfluß von Yorick-Sterne nicht verkennen darf; wenn auch sein Geist nicht über den Deutschen schwebte, so teilte sich sein Gefühl um desto lebhafter mit. Es entstand eine Art zärtlich-leidenschaftlicher Asketik, welche, da uns die humoristische Ironie des Briten nicht gegeben war, in eine leidige Selbstquälerei ausarten mußte. (HA X, 321 f.)

Here, for the first time, one of the works important for the *Wanderjahre* is implicated—but really, only because he was misunderstood by the Germans; furthermore, they ignored precisely that aspect of Sterne that is most important for the *Wanderjahre*, his ironic humor. In this context Goethe criticizes Lavater's physiognomic studies for emphasizing the individual to the point that people took pride even in their faults. But both these tendencies—Sterne's sentimentality and Lavater's individualism appear here as the seed of something much more productive, the age of humanity in Germany. Goethe continues: "Was aber zugleich nach jener Epoche folgerecht auffallend hervorging, war die Achtung der Individuen untereinander" (HA X, 323). And from this, he proceeds:

"Menschenkenntnis und Menschenliebe" waren uns bei diesem Verfahren versprochen, wechselseitige Teilnahme hatte sich entwickelt, wechselseitiges Kennen und Erkennen aber wollte sich so schnell nicht entfalten; zu beiden Zwecken war jedoch die Tätigkeit sehr groß... Vielleicht sahen die Kotyledonen jener Saat etwas wunderlich aus; der Ernte jedoch, woran das Vaterland und die Außenwelt ihren Anteil freudig dahinnahm, wird in den spätesten Zeiten noch immer ein dankbares Andenken nicht ermangeln. (HA X, 323 f.)

While the first manifestations may have seemed rather peculiar, the age of sensibility in Germany led to the great blossoming of humanism, in German classicism or aesthetic idealism, during the last two decades of the eighteenth century.

All of this literary background is then followed by a specific illustration of what Goethe means. As the author of *Werther* he received numerous letters asking for friendship and advice from *Werther* enthusiasts who fancied Goethe a kindred soul. Goethe describes one such writer, a young man named Plessing in Wernigerode, as a typical sufferer of the egocentric sentimentality described above. Goethe did not answer his letter, but on a trip through Wernigerode visited Plessing in the disguise of a young painter. He describes how he tried to show Plessing that he had overcome his own *Werther* stage by turning toward activity in the real world, and how he tried to encourage Plessing to do the same. The contrast between Goethe as he portrays himself and Plessing is the temporal contrast he tries to develop in the above passage: Plessing is still caught up in himself and wallowing in sensibility, Goethe is already on his way to great heights of constructive achievement, because he has acquired the necessary distance from himself. This distance is shown concretely here by the fact that he visits Plessing in disguise and discusses himself in the third person.

In this context it is easy to see where the authors in the *Wanderjahre* fit in: they belong to the literary high-point following the age of sensibility, by virtue of their ironic distance from sentimentality. In this period the emphasis is on humanity; the individual achieves his fullest development in activity directed outward toward the real world. Goethe's letter to Zelter (quoted above on p. 121) summarizes the essential qualities of this humanity—"Diese hohe wohlwollende Ironie, diese Billigkeit bey aller Übersicht, diese Sanftmuth bey aller Widerwärtigkeit, diese Gleichheit bey allem Wechsel . . ." It also emphasizes their permanent importance: "und am Ende sind es doch diese Gesinnungen die uns von allen Irrschritten des Lebens endlich wieder zurückführen." Goethe made this statement about Sterne and Goldsmith, but it applies equally well to the figure of the Abbé in the *Unterhaltungen*, and also to Musäus, who wrote such friendly satires of the excesses of Lavater and Richardson, and who, in the *Volksmärchen*, like Sterne created his personal alternative to the dominant mode of the time. The "Ballad of the Not-browne Mayde" finds its place as a counter-example to the overwhelming negativity of English poetry that Goethe criticizes in *Dichtung und Wahrheit*. The great tragedy of the poem, that the lover must flee as an outlaw, turns out not to be true, and instead, the ballad ends as a happy, positive affirmation of human bonds. Similarly, Basedow and Campe were strong exponents of positive activity: while Goethe calls the English of the eighteenth century "misanthropes," Basedow and Campe were generally known as the "Philanthropists," and Basedow's school was called the "Philanthropinum." Kotzebue is, of course, the counter-example to all these. As Goethe's most popular rival he indulged in all the excesses of sentimentality known to the age.

The most important representative work of this period for Goethe is, understandably enough, the *Lehrjahre*, which sees the fulfillment of the individual as the basis of society. It is certainly important that Wilhelm has the same name as Werther's confidant, who, although exposed to Werther's excessive individualism, yet is not destroyed by it, as Werther is. Like the typical young man around 1770, Wilhelm is haunted by *Hamlet*, but he gets him out of his system, and leaves the theater for the real world. Yet Wilhelm does not regret the time he devoted to the theater, for he realizes that he developed his capacities there; it is only as a result of that experience that he can now look forward to a useful and happy place in the society of Natalie and the *Turmgesellschaft*. The symbol of self-fulfillment in the *Lehrjahre* is the love relationship: Wilhelm moves from one woman to another (as does Lothario), each book is dominated by one woman who educates him in some way, until finally at the end he stands at the side of Natalie, who represents the highest kind of woman possible.

The *Wanderjahre* takes quite a different view of society from these earlier works: the society rests not upon the fulfilled or fully developed individual. Rather, the individual must develop himself in a particular direction to fit into society. Renunciation in terms of the social picture in the novel is renunciation of full individual development to fit into a larger group. In the comparison of the *Wanderjahre* to its various sources in this chapter, I have repeatedly emphasized the great ambivalence in the ironic distancing of the novel from them; frequently Goethe's sympathy seems to lie more with the sources than with the world shown in the novel. The last book of the *Wanderjahre*—the plans to emigrate to America, the threatened future of the cottage industries in the mountains—presents a bleak, though by no means mistaken vision of the coming century. The most distressing aspect of Goethe's vision, however, is not the industrial revolution, but the decreasing significance of the individual in the face of society. Lenardo's band of wanderers is not only a utopian attempt to preserve certain values important to Goethe; at the same time it is a vision of the coming relationship of the individual to society—where the individual is a small part contributing to, but dependent upon, the whole. Each member of the *Turmgesellschaft* in the *Lehrjahre* was to go off on his own, or with one other; in the *Wanderjahre* all must work together in one place. In such a world there is no room for the warmth and freedom that characterized individual development in the *Lehrjahre*. Instead, love relationships are ironically sealed off into the novellas; for those in the frame the consummation is promised rather than shown. Felix's love for Hersilie puts him in direct conflict with everything he is supposed to have learned in the pedagogic province. Goethe comments drily on this stifling tendency when Wilhelm first learns of the organization of Lenardo's rather totalitarian group. Wilhelm is invited to dinner by the head of the group, who is referred to as "das Band." Goethe comments: "Als der Freund sich allein befand, dachte er über die wunderliche Person erst nach, die ihn hatte einladen lassen, und wußte nicht recht, was er daraus machen sollte. Einen oder mehrere Vorgesetzten durch ein Neutrum anzukündigen, kam ihm allzu bedenklich vor" (315). "Das Band," who is Lenardo, loses a little dignity with the appellation "wunderliche Person," but the real critique is in Wilhelm's reservation that a neuter term for the head is somehow threatening. The reason is that a neuter noun eliminates the human element, it is too impersonal to take proper account of the individual.

The plans and measures for the American "utopia" present a particularly dismal and rigid prospect, as they appear in the summary of Friedrich's presentation in III, 11. The same totalitarian spirit that holds Lenardo's band together prevails here—necessary perhaps, but distressing nonetheless. The discussion begins with religion. All religions ought to be equally suitable, for the group has agreed, "daß der Mensch ins Unvermeidliche sich füge, darauf dringen alle Religionen, jede sucht auf ihre Weise mit dieser Aufgabe fertig zu werden" (404). The settlement will have its own version of Christianity, which will emphasize its ethical beauties, and only at the very end of a child's education will he learn about Christ himself. The summary continues: "In diesem Sinne, den man vielleicht pedantisch nennen mag, aber doch als folgerecht erkennen muß, dulden wir keinen Juden unter uns" (405). The stricture may seem necessary for the cohesion of the new society, but it is also characterized as pedantic rigidity, in strong contrast to the tolerance of the eighteenth century.[65] The same rigidity characterizes all of the plans. Everywhere in the new settlement there will be clocks striking every quarter hour to remind everyone to make the best use of every minute. Even the telegraph will be used to mark the passage of time, as well as to communicate messages. This business demands a thoroughly pragmatic outlook. There will be no time for consideration of higher moral questions, only enforcement of practical regulations: "So denken wir nicht an Justiz, aber wohl an Polizei" (406). And, indeed, each district will have three police chiefs who will relieve one another in eight hour shifts—the law will never sleep. In summary, the disadvantages of culture will be left behind—"Branntweinschenken und Lesebibliotheken werden bei uns nicht geduldet; wie wir uns aber gegen Flaschen und Bücher verhalten, will ich lieber nicht eröffnen: dergleichen Dinge wollen getan sein, wenn man sie beurteilen soll" (408). A utopia in which books are of questionable value at best contrasts gloomily with the optimism of the aesthetic idealists for a great renewal of German culture—an optimism so beautifully expressed in Goethe's own "Märchen."

The ambivalent references to the *Lehrjahre* and its contemporaries are not only corrective; they are also—indeed, more importantly—nostalgic. The

---

[65] The classic example, of course, is *Nathan der Weise*, but Musäus, too, affords some charming ones. "Richilde" ends with a paragraph showing that the step-mother's wicked Jewish doctor was in fact not very wicked at all, that his soul was saved for his good deeds, and that he had perfectly respectable descendants still serving as prime-ministers to the king of Morocco.

elegaic tone of the re-evocation of Mignon in the Lago Maggiore chapter is extremely nostalgic, while the story of the drowned boy is even more purely so, since there is no ironic undertone. The nostalgia is not to be overlooked in the implicit comparison of Hersilie's family to Natalie's far more beautiful and more charming one, or in the flattening of Musäus's delightful ghost scene into the real world where a real barber shaves Wilhelm the ordinary way at the ordinary hour. In a novel dealing with the rapidly changing society of the nineteenth century, Goethe once more directs his readers toward the highest achievements of the eighteenth: in "Aus Makariens Archiv" he says, "Auch jetzt im Augenblick sollte jeder Gebildete Sternes Werke wieder zur Hand nehmen, damit auch das neunzehnte Jahrhundert erführe, was wir ihm schuldig sind, und einsähe, was wir ihm schuldig werden können" (AMA 144, p. 484). And what is this debt to Sterne and his age? Nothing less than the belief in the dignity of the individual and the possibility of his harmonious relationship to society, precisely what is portrayed in the final scene of the novel, where the emphasis is on rebirth, not renunciation.[66] Felix asserts his individuality by pursuing his love affair with Hersilie to the extreme; he is hurt, but rescued. As he rests, the others dry his clothes to allow him a properly dignified return to society when he is ready—"um ihn beim Erwachen sogleich wieder in den gesellig anständigsten Zustand zu versetzen" (460).

[66] See also Wundt's interpretation of "Aus Makariens Archiv" in *Goethes Wilhelm Meister*. He interprets this aphorism as a reminder not to lose the educational values gained in the eighteenth century, on p. 468, and as a recognition that to some extent these values must be renounced, p. 476.

EPILOGUE

The nostalgic view of an earlier, more optimistic relationship of the individual to society reflects not only the social changes that had come about in the early decades of the nineteenth century, but also a change in Goethe's views. The characters in the *Wanderjahre* do not live in a closed-off, microcosmic society, but participate in the changing society around them. It is important that the *hortus conclusus* of the *Unterhaltungen* is rejected twice in the *Wanderjahre*, and that Goethe took over Meyer's factual description of contemporary textile manufacturing in Switzerland virtually unchanged. Goethe no longer uses the device of "society in a test tube" to let his characters develop their humanity to the fullest despite the surrounding tumult of historical circumstances; instead, he allows them to enter the stream of history, and preserve their humanity as best they can, by renouncing most of the claims of their individuality.

This acceptance of history in Goethe's latest work is most dramatically illustrated by *Faust II*. The first and fourth acts of the play deal with the political struggles of the empire, the second act takes place on an ancient battlefield, and even the Helena episode can reach its climax only after Faust and Helena have fled the approaching army of Menelaus; but the vast breadth of the "Klassische Walpurgisnacht" develops this idea most clearly. When Chiron brings Faust to Manto's eternal temple, which stands at the entrance to the underworld, Manto tells them, "Ich harre, mich umkreist die Zeit" (l. 7481). At the center of time, she is the only figure in the act at peace; her mode of being contrasts strongly with Chiron's restless motion, as well as with Faust's tumultuous course, of which Chiron says, "Die verrufene Nacht/ Hat strudelnd ihn hierher gebracht" (ll. 7482 f.). The wildness of the night all around corresponds to its setting: Manto's temple stands on the site of the battle of Pydna, where the republican Romans defeated the Macedonians and their king in 168 B.C., and Chiron identifies the spot as such:

> Hier trotzten Rom und Griechenland im Streite,
> Peneios rechts, links den Olymp zur Seite,
> Das größte Reich, das sich im Sand verliert;
> Der König flieht, der Bürger triumphiert. (ll. 7465–68)

The rest of the "Klassische Walpurgisnacht" takes place on another battlefield, the fields of Pharsalus, where Caesar defeated Pompey in 48 B.C.; its significance is pointed out by Erichtho, the witch consulted by Pompey before that battle, in the prologue:

> Wie oft schon wiederholt' sich's! wird sich immerfort
> Ins Ewige wiederholen . . . Keiner gönnt das Reich
> Dem andern; dem gönnt's keiner, der's mit Kraft erwarb
> Und kräftig herrscht. (ll. 7012–15)

The element of time, then, in which Faust swirls around Manto is nothing other than human history seen as a series of political and social struggles. Not only does one power-seeker succeed another, but one class may succeed another (in Chiron's quote) in the flux. Goethe offers two alternatives for the individual to deal with the great rush of history—Faust's asocial alternative, to struggle with the flood at the expense of all social bonds, or the social alternative, to renounce individual claims for the security of participation in a larger group, the alternative of Wilhelm Meister.

In the first chapter I discussed the importance of renunciation for the preservation of the society in the *Unterhaltungen*. Why is it that the effects are so different in the *Wanderjahre*? The answer, I think, is that the treatment of renunciation in the *Unterhaltungen* is considerably more optimistic than in the *Wanderjahre*. The characters in the *Unterhaltungen* have to renounce not what is nearest and dearest to them, but, as it turns out, only their bad habits, only the exaggerated concerns that make them, as well as others, unhappy. Luise, for example, annoys herself as much as the others by worrying constantly about her fiancé. Furthermore, the highest achievement of the individual in the *Unterhaltungen* is sociability—the baroness and the Abbé, the characters best able to cope with a social situation, are also the best developed personalities, with the widest interests and most at peace with themselves. There is no real divergence between individual and social needs in the *Unterhaltungen*, while in the *Wanderjahre*, as we have seen, the development of the individual runs counter to the demands of society.

Renunciation appears quite different in the *Unterhaltungen*, because at that time Goethe's views of society were based on a society about to be transformed. The "Märchen" is the finest illustration of this hope for transformation: there Goethe shows step by step how the new society may be brought about, through the good will of the will-o'-the-wisps, the leadership of the man with the lamp, the sacrifice of the serpent, the cooperative help of all the members. The result is a completely harmonious world, where each may pursue his own constructive activities and where anything that might cause others to suffer, like the disruptive giant, is forcibly restrained at some useful task.

Utopia seemed a real possibility to German poets at the end of the eighteenth century. The ideal society would imminently be realized, a society in which the individual would be at harmony with himself, with nature, and with those about him. In the "Ästhetische Briefe" Schiller proposes a utopian state which will offer this kind of harmony; the last paragraph of the manuscript, which Schiller struck before publication, suggests at least the temporary fervor of his belief in the possibility of this society by announcing the future publication of its constitution in the *Horen*.¹ In his ironic way even Friedrich Schlegel sees a new age of wider understanding about to dawn—"Die neue Zeit kündigt sich an als eine schnellfüßige, sohlenbeflügelte; die Morgenröte hat Siebenmeilenstiefel angezogen ... Dann nimmt das neunzehnte Jahrhundert in der Tat seinen Anfang, und dann wird auch jenes kleine Rätsel von der Unverständlichkeit des Athenäums gelöst sein. Welche Katastrophe! Dann wird es Leser geben, die lesen können."² Even Goethe's *Lehrjahre* projects a society at the end, whose members, working together for common ideals in various countries will be in a position to relieve one another from the pressures of the unreformed remainder of the world.

Of all the optimistic works of the 1790's, the *Lehrjahre* is the most complex in admitting a tragic element, the figures of Mignon and the harpist, who stand in sharp contrast to the goals of the *Turmgesellschaft*. Their tragedy, however, arises from their complete inability to live in harmony with the most basic requirements of society. The harpist, Augustin, has violated the incest prohibition; as far as he is concerned he has violated no law of nature, but his family forces him to face the fact that he has broken an arbitrary social law: "Er sollte überlegen, daß er nicht in der freien Welt seiner Gedanken und Vorstellungen, sondern in einer Verfassung lebe, deren Gesetze und Verhältnisse die Unbezwinglichkeit eines Naturgesetzes angenommen habe" (HA VII, 584). Similarly, Mignon cannot even accept the simplest social conventions imposed by differences of sex. She insists on dressing like a boy; when she finally consents to wear a white gown, it is because it represents the robes of an angel, and angels are above such distinctions, as she says in the third stanza of "So laßt mich scheinen": "Und jene himmlischen Gestalten/ Sie fragen nicht nach Mann und Weib" (HA VII, 516). At the end of the novel the two figures are sealed off into the past—Mignon is enshrined in the "Saal der Vergangenheit." The tragic inability to participate in society belongs then to Mignon, an other-wordly being; the social personalities in the *Lehrjahre*, including Wilhelm, can only observe her tragedy with sympathy, but limited comprehension. The novel ends in the hopeful future of the constructive plans of the *Turmgesellschaft* and Wilhelm's engagement to Natalie.

In the *Wanderjahre* the hope for this harmonious society, in which tragedy is a thing of the past, has completely evaporated. The American settlement certainly will not fulfill the optimistic expectations of the earlier period. Rather,

---

¹ Friedrich Schiller, *Sämtliche Werke*, ed. G. Fricke and H. Göpfert (Munich, 1962), V, 1148.

² Friedrich Schlegel, "Über die Unverständlichkeit," *Kritische Schriften*, ed. Wolfdietrich Rasch (Munich, 1964), p. 539.

the strong emphasis on measures for maintaining order suggests the impossibility of a society in which all are always happy; and indeed, the settlers will all belong to the "Orden der Entsagenden." Renunciation has become necessary to make the continuance of society even possible, as the cases of the barber and St. Christoph show; these two, the only speaking representatives of Lenardo's band, must restrain themselves continually to remain socially acceptable. Unlike the "Märchen," where the establishment of harmony was an apocalyptic happening, harmony in Lenardo's band must be reestablished daily in renewed or continued acts of renunciation.

A parallel development may be observed in the motif of the mysterious chest in the "Märchen," Pandora and the Wanderjahre. The underground temple in the "Märchen" corresponds to Felix's "Kästchen"; it begins closed up under ground and contains a precious secret power related to the love of the prince for Lilie. When it is finally brought to light through the cooperation of all the characters in the story, the secret is revealed and an age of eternal harmony established. Pandora's box, the mysterious $κυψέλη$ of the schema for the continuation of Goethe's play, is another such "Kästchen," but this time it comes from the sky instead of from underground. Further, it comes this time not through the collective efforts of a group, but somehow through the special efforts of Phileros and Epimeleia, who survive the twin ordeals of fire and water for the sake of love in the first part of the play and have become reconciled with one another. After Pandora's arrival the $κυψέλη$ opens, revealing itself to be a temple which is the home of the patron spirits of science and art. It is thus just like the temple of the "Märchen," except that its revelation is not the result of the cooperative effort of the whole group. This form of the motif is clearly parodied and rejected in "Die neue Melusine." The mysterious box there opens out not into a temple, but a frivolous summer-house; it is inhabited by no patron genius, but by a very up-to-date dwarf princess. Felix's "Kästchen" is the novel's serious treatment of the motif, but here when the mysterious box is opened, it reveals nothing at all: the top is hastily shut again, with the admonition, "an solche Geheimnisse sei nicht gut rühren" (458), The power of love to bring about a new age of harmony is denied in the Wanderjahre; the "Kästchen" does not reveal its secret, it brings not harmony, but suffering. Yet, once more, the treatment of Wilhelm's rescue of Felix affirms this suffering as the pattern of human life.

The simile of Castor and Pollux in the description of Felix's rescue, the mythical culmination of the novel, sums up the whole problem. Felix plunges into the water, is pulled out almost drowned, Wilhelm lets his blood, which mingles with the water, and Felix jumps up to embrace his father and rescuer: "So standen sie fest umschlungen, wie Kastor und Pollux, Brüder, die sich auf dem Wechselwege vom Orkus zum Licht begegnen" (459). According to the legend Goethe follows here, Pollux was prepared to sacrifice his immortality for his brother, when Castor was killed; the compromise reached was that the two were to live alternate days, taking one another's place in Orkus in turn. This simile is not only an affirmation of change as the fabric of life,[3] but it is a myth of society as well. Brotherhood—emphasized in Goethe's formulation by the appositive "Brüder"—is the metaphor for the social claims of humanity (all men are brothers, therefore they should love one another), the brotherhood of Castor and Pollux stands here for the archetypal bond among men. The prerequisite for the continued existence of this bond is the one brother's renunciation of his immortality, his acceptance of death to bring about the rebirth of the other. This renunciation is not a single act, but is repeated daily as the living brother returns to Orkus to enable the other to live. But even though Pollux makes his sacrifice so as not to lose his brother, the result is, in fact, that the two can never be together except as they pass on the way to or from Orkus—they can never enjoy the light together. The social bond established by Pollux's sacrifice thus offers no escape; rather, it is based on the suffering of separation and institutionalizes it. The passage, however, affirms this suffering, it does not reject it: the possibility of that embrace on their way past one another confirms the value and meaning of their renunciation of one another. This is a very different view from the earlier works: there is no longer any hope for a society where the individual may escape from the suffering and renunciation imposed by a disharmonious world. Society is no longer a shelter from threatening tragedy, society and tragedy are no longer opposite poles as in the *Lehrjahre*. Instead, the two opposites come together—society itself has a tragic basis. There is no longer any hope for the apocalyptic society the age of aesthetic idealism hoped for, there will be no new age, no discontinuity in time, but only the continuous tumult of struggle and strife pictured in *Faust*. In the tradition of the greatest tragedy, both *Faust* and *Wilhelm Meister* affirm the suffering of this struggle as uniquely human; they both end on a tragic, yet profoundly positive note.

[3] See G. Röder, *Glück und glückliches Ende im deutschen Bildungsroman* (Munich, 1968), p. 225.

SELECT BIBLIOGRAPHY

Editions of Goethe's Works:

Goethes Werke. Hamburger Ausgabe. 14 vols. Hamburg, 1948–1960. [Abbreviated HA.]

Goethes Sämtliche Werke. Jubiläums-Ausgabe. 40 vols. Stuttgart and Berlin, 1902–1907. [Abbreviated JA.]

Propyläen-Ausgabe von Goethes Sämtlichen Werken. 45 vols. Munich and Berlin, 1909–1931. [Abbreviated PA.]

Goethes Werke: Herausgegeben im Auftrage der Großherzogin Sophie von Sachsen. 143 vols. Weimar, 1887–1920. [Abbreviated WA.]

Goethe. *Briefwechsel mit Friedrich Schiller,* Gedenk-Ausgabe, ed. Karl Schmid. Zurich and Stuttgart, 1964. [Abbreviated GSB.]

Other Works:

Albrich, Konrad. "Goethes Märchen: Quellen und Parallelen," *Euphorion,* 22 (1915), 482–524.

Bach, Adolf, ed. *Goethes Rheinreise mit Lavater und Basedow im Sommer 1774: Dokumente.* Zurich, 1923.

Bahr, Ehrhard. *Die Ironie im Spätwerk Goethes: ". . . diese sehr ernsten Scherze . . ." Studien zum West-östlichen Divan, zu den Wanderjahren und zu Faust II.* Berlin, 1972.

Basedow, Johann Bernhard. *Ausgewählte pädagogische Schriften,* ed. A. Reble. Paderborn, 1965.

———. *Das Basedowische Elementarwerk: Ein Vorrath der besten Erkenntnisse zum Lernen, Lehren, Wiederholen und Nachdenken.* 3 vols. Leipzig, 1785.

Bastian, Hans-Jürgen. "Zum Menschenbild des späten Goethe: Eine Interpretation seiner Erzählung 'Sankt Joseph der Zweite' aus 'Wilhelm Meisters Wanderjahren,'" *Weimarer Beiträge,* 22 (1966), 471–88.

Bauer, Georg-Karl. "Makarie," *Germanisch-romanische Monatsschrift*, 25 (1937), 178–97.

Biedermann, Woldemar Freiherr von and Flodoard Freiherr von, ed. *Goethes Gespräche*. 5 vols. Leipzig, 1909–1911.

Bimler, Kurt. "Die erste und zweite Fassung von Goethes 'Wanderjahren.' " Diss. Breslau, 1907.

Böckmann, Paul. "Voraussetzungen der zyklischen Erzählform in 'Wilhelm Meisters Wanderjahren,' " *Festschrift für Detlev W. Schumann zum 70. Geburtstag*, ed. A. R. Schmitt, pp. 130–44. Munich, 1970.

Bruford, W. H. *Culture and Society in Classical Weimar*. Cambridge, 1962.

Brüggemann, Werner. *Cervantes und die Figur des Don Quijote in Kunstanschauung und Dichtung der deutschen Romantik*. Münster, 1958.

Campe, J. H., ed. *Allgemeine Revision des gesammten Schul- und Erziehungswesens von einer Gesellschaft praktischer Erzieher*. 16 vols. Hamburg, 1785–1791.

Campe, Johann Heinrich. *Robinson der jüngere. Ein Lesebuch für Kinder*. Braunschweig, 1829.

——. *Sammlung einiger Erziehungsschriften*. 2 vols. Leipzig, 1778.

Cholevius, L. "Die Bedeutung der Symbole in Goethes Märchen," *Archiv für Literaturgeschichte*, 1 (1870), 63–89.

David, Claude. "Goethes 'Wanderjahre' als symbolische Dichtung," *Sinn und Form*, 8 (1956), 113–28.

Dichler, Gustav. " 'Wilhelm Meisters Wanderjahre' im Urteil deutscher Zeitgenossen," *Archiv für das Studium der neueren Sprachen*, 162 (1932), 23–29.

Diez, Max. "Metapher und Märchengestalt," *PMLA*, 48 (1933), 74–99, 488–507, 877–94, 1203–22.

Düntzer, Heinrich. *Erläuterungen zu den deutschen Klassikern*. Abtheilung I, Band IV. Leipzig, 1876.

Dürer, Albrecht. *The Complete Woodcuts of Albrecht Dürer*, ed. Willi Kurth. New York, 1963.

Eichendorff, Joseph Freiherr von. *Werke*, ed. Wolfdietrich Rasch. Munich, 1966.

Einem, Herbert von. *Goethe und Dürer: Goethes Kunstphilosophie*. Hamburg, 1947.

Eloesser, Elise. "Goethes 'Märchen': Versuch einer Deutung," *Euphorion*, 13 (1906), 58–71.

Emrich, Wilhelm. "Das Problem der Symbolinterpretation im Hinblick auf Goethes 'Wanderjahre,' " *Deutsche Vierteljahrsschrift*, 26 (1952), 331-52.

Feilchenfeld, Walter. "Pestalozzi, Goethe, Lavater," *Deutsche Vierteljahrsschrift*, 3 (1925), 431-43.

Fischer-Hartmann, Deli. *Goethes Altersroman: Studien über die innere Einheit von "Wilhelm Meisters Wanderjahren."* Halle, 1941.

Flitner, Wilhelm. *Goethe im Spätwerk: Glaube/Weltsicht/Ethos.* Hamburg, 1947.

Franz, Erich. *Goethe als religiöser Denker.* Tübingen, 1932.

Fricke, Gerhard. "Zu Sinn und Form von Goethes 'Unterhaltungen deutscher Ausgewanderten,' " *Formenwandel: Festschrift zum 65. Geburtstag von Paul Böckmann*, ed. Walter Müller-Seidel and Wolfgang Preisendanz, pp. 273-93. Hamburg, 1964.

Garrigues, Gertrude. "Goethe's 'Das Märchen,' " *Journal of Speculative Philosophy*, 17 (1883), 383-400.

Gidion, Heidi. *Zur Darstellungsweise von Goethes "Wilhelm Meisters Wanderjahren."* Palaestra 256. Göttingen, 1969.

Gilg, André. *"Wilhelm Meisters Wanderjahre" und ihre Symbole.* Zurich, 1954.

Goldstein, Moritz. "Die Technik der zyklischen Rahmenerzählungen Deutschlands. Von Goethe bis Hoffman." Diss. Berlin, 1906.

Gräf, Hans Gerhard. *Goethe über seine Dichtungen.* 9 vols. Frankfurt am Main, 1901-1914.

Gray, Ronald Douglas. *Goethe the Alchemist.* Cambridge, 1952.

Gundolf, Friedrich. *Goethe.* Berlin, 1925.

Hederich, Benjamin. *Gründliches Lexicon Mythologicum* ... Leipzig, 1741.

Henkel, Arthur. *Entsagung. Eine Studie zu Goethes Altersroman.* Hermaea N.F. 3. Tübingen, 1964.

Herder, Johann Gottfried. *Werke*, ed. Heinrich Düntzer. 24 vols. Berlin, n.d.

Hiebel, Friedrich. "The beautiful Lily in Goethe's Märchen," *Monatshefte*, 41 (1949), 171-85.

———. "Zur Sinnbilderwelt in Goethes Märchen," *Antaios*, 3 (1961-1962), 18-28.

Hoffmeister, Johannes. "Das Märchen," *Die Heimkehr des Geistes: Studien zur Dichtung und Philosophie der Goethezeit*, pp. 94-161. Hameln, 1946.

Hohlfeld, Alexander R. "Zur Frage einer Fortsetzung von Goethes 'Wilhelm Meisters Wanderjahren,'" *PMLA*, 60 (1945), 399–420.

Jördens, Karl Heinrich. *Lexikon deutscher Dichter und Prosaisten*. 6 vols. Leipzig, 1806–1811.

Jungmann, Karl. "Die pädagogische Provinz," *Euphorion*, 14 (1907), 274–87 and 517–33.

Jürgens, Ilse. "Die Stufen der sittlichen Entwicklung in Goethes 'Unterhaltungen deutscher Ausgewanderten,'" *Wirkendes Wort*, 6 (1955–1956), 336–40.

Karnick, Manfred. *"Wilhelm Meisters Wanderjahre" oder die Kunst des Mittelbaren*. Munich, 1968.

Klingenberg, Anne-Liese. *Goethes Roman "Wilhelm Meisters Wanderjahre oder die Entsagenden": Quellen und Kompositionen*. Berlin, 1972.

Kohlmeyer, Otto. *Die pädagogische Provinz in "Wilhelm Meisters Wanderjahren": Ein Beitrag zur Pädagogik Goethes*. Langensalza, 1923.

Kotzebue, August von. *Ausgewählte Prosaische Schriften*, vol. VIII. Vienna, 1842.

———. *Theater*, vol. V. Vienna, 1840.

Krüger, Emil. "Die Novellen in 'Wilhelm Meisters Wanderjahren.'" Diss. Kiel, 1926.

Küntzel, Gerhard. "Nachwort" to *Wilhelm Meisters Wanderjahre* in *Gedenk-Ausgabe* VII, 885–955. Zurich, 1949.

———. "'Wilhelm Meisters Wanderjahre' in der ersten Fassung 1821," *Goethe. Viermonatsschrift der Goethe-Gesellschaft*, 3 (1938), 3–39.

Lange, Victor. "Zur Entstehungsgeschichte von Goethes *Wanderjahren*," *German Life and Letters*, 23 (1969), 47–54.

Lockemann, Fritz. "Die Bedeutung des Rahmens in der deutschen Novellendichtung," *Wirkendes Wort*, 6 (1955–1956), 208–17.

Loeb, Ernst. "Makarie und Faust: Eine Betrachtung zu Goethes Altersdenken," *Zeitschrift für deutsche Philologie*, 88 (1969), 583–97.

Lucerna, Camilla. *Das Märchen: Goethes Naturphilosophie als Kunstwerk*. Leipzig, 1910.

———. "Goethes Rätselmärchen: Eine Betrachtung," *Euphorion*, 53 (1959), 41–60.

———. "Wozu dichtete Goethe 'das Märchen'?" *Goethe. Neue Folge des Jahrbuchs der Goethe-Gesellschaft*, 25 (1963), 206–19.

Martens, Wolfgang. *Die Botschaft der Tugend: Die Aufklärung im Spiegel der deutschen moralischen Wochenschriften.* Stuttgart, 1968.

Mayer, Hans. "Das 'Märchen': Goethe und Gerhart Hauptmann," *Gestaltung Umgestaltung. Festschrift zum 75. Geburtstag von Hermann August Korff*, ed. Joachim Müller, pp. 92–107. Leipzig, 1957.

Meinecke, Friedrich. *Die Entstehung des Historismus.* Munich and Berlin, 1936.

Meyer von Waldeck, Friedrich. *Goethes Märchendichtungen.* Heidelberg, 1879.

Mommsen, Katharina. *Goethe und 1001 Nacht.* Berlin, 1960.

Monroy, Ernst Friedrich von. "Zur Form der Novelle in 'Wilhelm Meisters Wanderjahren,'" *Germanisch-romanische Monatsschrift*, 31 (1943), 1–19.

Morris, Max. "Herzogin Luise von Weimar in Goethes Dichtung: Das Märchen," *Goethe Studien* II, 29–73. Berlin, 1902.

Müller, Joachim. "Zur Entstehung der deutschen Novelle: Die Rahmenhandlung in Goethes *Unterhaltungen deutscher Ausgewanderten* und die Thematik der französischen Revolution," *Gestaltungsgeschichte und Gesellschaftsgeschichte. Literatur-, Kunst- und Musikwissenschaftliche Studien. Fritz Martini zum 60. Geburtstag*, ed. H. Kreuzer and K. Hamburger, pp. 152–75. Stuttgart, 1969.

Musäus, Johann Karl August. *Volksmärchen der Deutschen.* 5 vols. Berlin, 1909.

Muthesius, Karl. *Goethe ein Kinderfreund.* Berlin, 1910.

Nitschke, Otfried. "Goethes pädagogische Provinz." Diss. Heidelberg, 1937.

Ohlmer, August. *Musäus als satirischer Romanschriftsteller.* Hildesheim, 1912.

Ohly, Friedrich. "Römisches und Biblisches in Goethes 'Märchen,'" *Zeitschrift für deutsches Altertum*, 91 (1961–1962), 147–66.

Percy, Thomas. *Reliques of ancient English Poetry*, vol. II. London, 1765.

Peschken, Bernd. *Entsagung in "Wilhelm Meisters Wanderjahren."* Bonn, 1968.

Pestalozzi, Heinrich. *Werke*, ed. Paul Baumgartner, vol. VI. Erlenbach-Zurich, 1946.

Pinger, W. R. R. *Laurence Sterne and Goethe.* University of California Publications in Modern Philology, 10. Berkeley, 1920.

Pochhammer, Paul. "Goethes Märchen," *Goethe Jahrbuch*, 25 (1904), 116–27.

Pongs, Hermann. *Das Bild in der Dichtung.* 2 vols. Marburg, 1927–1939.

Popper, Hans. "Goethe's *Unterhaltungen deutscher Ausgewanderten*," *Affinities: Essays in German and English Literature*, ed. R.W. Last, pp. 206–42. London, 1971.

Prior, Matthew. *Literary Works*, ed. H. Bunker Wright and Monroe K. Spears. 2 vols. Oxford, 1959.

Pustkuchen, J. F. W. *Wilhelm Meisters Wanderjahre.* 5 vols. Quedlinburg and Leipzig, 1821–1828.

Raabe, August. "Der Begriff des Ungeheuren in den 'Unterhaltungen deutscher Ausgewanderten,'" *Goethe. Viermonatsschrift der Goethe-Gesellschaft*, 4 (1939), 23–39.

Reichard, H. A. O., ed. *Cahiers de lecture.* Gotha, 1789.

Reik, Theodor. *Fragment of a Great Confession. A Psychoanalytic Autobiography.* New York, 1949.

Reiss, H. S. "Bild und Symbol in 'Wilhelm Meisters Wanderjahren,'" *Studium Generale* 6 (1953), 340–48.

———. *Goethes Romane.* Bern and Munich, 1963.

Richli, Alfred. *J. K. A. Musäus: Volksmärchen der Deutschen.* Zurich, 1957.

Riemann, Robert. "Goethes Romantechnik." Diss. Leipzig, n.d.

Röder, Gerda. *Glück und glückliches Ende im deutschen Bildungsroman.* Munich, 1968.

Rousseau, Jean-Jacques. *Emile ou de l'éducation*, ed. F. and P. Richard. Paris, 1964.

Sarter, Eberhard. *Zur Technik von "Wilhelm Meisters Wanderjahren."* Berlin, 1914.

Schiller, Friedrich. *Sämtliche Werke*, ed. Gerhard Fricke and Herbert Göpfert. 5 vols. Munich, 1962.

Schiller, Friedrich, ed. *Die Horen: Eine Monatsschrift*, 1 (1795).

Schlechta, Karl. *Goethes Wilhelm Meister.* Frankfurt am Main, 1953.

Schlegel, Friedrich. *Kritische Schriften*, ed. Wolfdietrich Rasch. Munich, 1964.

Schneider, Hermann. *"Das Märchen" eine neu aufgeschlossene Urkunde zu Goethes Weltanschauung.* Leipzig, 1911.

Schütz, Friedrich Karl Julius. *Göthe und Pustkuchen, oder: über die beiden Wanderjahre Wilhelm Meister's und ihre Verfasser: Ein Beitrag zur Geschichte der deutschen Poesie und Poetik.* Halle, 1823.

Seidlin, Oskar. "Zur Mignon-Ballade," *Von Goethe zu Thomas Mann: Zwölf Versuche*, pp. 23–37. Göttingen, 1963.

Spranger, Eduard. "Der psychologische Perspektivismus im Roman," *Jahrbuch des freien deutschen Hochstifts* (1930), 70–90.

———. "Die sittliche Astrologie der Makarie in 'Wilhelm Meisters Wanderjahren,'" *Goethe und seine geistige Welt*, pp. 350–63. Tübingen, 1967.

Staiger, Emil. *Goethe*. 3 vols. Zurich, 1952–1959.

Steer, A. G. "The Wound and the Physician in Goethe's *Wilhelm Meister*," *Studies in German Literature of the Nineteenth and Twentieth Centuries. Festschrift for Frederic E. Coenen*, ed. Siegfried Mews, pp. 11–23. Chapel Hill, 1970.

Steiner, Rudolf. *Goethes geheime Offenbarung. Exoterisch und esoterisch*, ed. Marie Steiner. Dornach (Switzerland), 1932.

Stern, Adolf. *Beiträge zur Litteraturgeschichte des siebzehnten und achtzehnten Jahrhunderts* (pp. 128–74 on Musäus). Leipzig, 1893.

Stöcklein, Paul. *Wege zum späten Goethe*. Hamburg, 1949.

Strich, Fritz. *Goethe und die Weltliteratur*. Bern, 1957.

Thalmann, Marianne. *J. W. Goethe, "Der Mann von fünfzig Jahren."* Vienna, 1948.

Thomas, L. H. C. "Germany, German Literature and mid-nineteenth century British novelists," *Affinities: Essays in German and English Literature*, ed. R. W. Last, pp. 34–51. London, 1971.

Viëtor, Karl. *Goethe: Dichtung, Wissenschaft, Weltbild*. Bern, 1949.

Voerster, Erika. *Märchen und Novellen im klassisch-romantischen Roman*. Bonn, 1964.

Wahle, Julius. "Auslegungen des Märchens," *Goethe Jahrbuch*, 25 (1904), 37–44.

Waidson, H. M. "Death by Water: or, The Childhood of Wilhelm Meister," *Modern Language Review*, 56 (1961), 44–53.

Wolff, Eugen. *Wilhelm Meisters Wanderjahre: Ein Novellenkranz. Nach dem ursprünglichen Plan herausgegeben von Eugen Wolff.* Frankfurt am Main, 1916.

Wundt, Max. *Goethes Wilhelm Meister und die Entwicklung des modernen Lebensideals*. Berlin and Leipzig, 1913.

Wukadinović, Spiridion. "Das Märchen," *Goethe-Probleme*. Halle an der Saale, 1926. 35–65.

Ziolkowski, Theodore. "Goethe's 'Unterhaltungen deutscher Ausgewanderten': A Reappraisal," *Monatshefte*, 50 (1958), 57–74.

www.ingramcontent.com/pod-product-compliance
Lightning Source LLC
Chambersburg PA
CBHW031316150426
43191CB00005B/247